THE SHERLOCK HOLMES LETTERS

THE
SHERLOCK HOLMES
LETTERS

EDITED BY
RICHARD LANCELYN GREEN

University of Iowa Press  Iowa City

International Standard Book Number 0-87745-161-3
Library of Congress Catalog Card Number 86-50620
University of Iowa Press, Iowa City 52242
Copyright © 1986 by the University of Iowa
All rights reserved
First edition, 1986

CONTENTS

———————————◆———————————

INTRODUCTION

---◆---

Christopher Morley once said of Sherlockian criticism that never had so much been written by so many for so few, and those who have examined the massive bibliographies of "writings about the writings" might be tempted to agree with him. Certainly no single volume could now hope to encompass the wide variety of material that is available to the dedicated Sherlockian, or do justice to the scholarship of those who have turned their attention to the subject. But, as Sherlock Holmes is fast approaching the first centenary of his original appearance on the world stage, it is perhaps appropriate to give some account of the literature that has grown up around him and to provide examples of the letters and other public correspondence that have over the years dealt with his life and work.

Sherlock Holmes needs no introduction. He is familiar to everyone in a way that is not typical of other literary characters and yet that has been constant since his name was first mentioned. Some people have found fault with him and with his chronicler, but all, whether they be dedicated enthusiasts or members of the general public, have agreed that he is superior to his rivals and that he is worthy of the esteem in which he has been held. Tributes to him have come from all quarters, and some of the finest have for many years been lost in the pages of newspapers. That they are now made available to a wider readership is itself proof of Holmes's enduring legacy and, though not explicitly, it is proof also of the achievement of A. Conan Doyle, without whom Holmes would have rotted in the obscurity of his Baker Street lodgings.

Doyle was a delightful, amusing, and occasionally naïve man, an author whose other novels and stories were read and enjoyed by thousands, but who with Sherlock Holmes had an audience of millions. He had produced a figure who jumped at once from the printed page into the living consciousness. It was a formula that can be analysed but

1

not copied. Sherlock Holmes is a real character who is above reality; a person living in a distinct place and at a distinct period, yet one who is present in many places and seen by many different minds, who lives beyond life's span and who is constantly rejuvenated. He has become a part of the national heritage as well as being a citizen of the world.

As the critic tends to fall into the fancy of Holmes's existence, straight criticism is difficult, but some have attempted it. In the *Criterion*,[1] for example, T. S. Eliot spoke of the romantic and nostalgic picture that the stories provided; he praised their dramatic quality and their near-perfect form. He also made direct allusions to them in his serious work, could quote from them at length, and was adept at the "Higher Criticism". E. T. Raymond, Hesketh Pearson, Desmond MacCarthy, and Edmund Wilson are others who have delved into the mystery surrounding Sherlock Holmes. Raymond spoke of the "romance of the ultra-prosaic"[2] and suggested that the spell succeeded through the simplicity of Dr. Watson: "Not great himself," he wrote, "he is the cause of greatness in another. Faith breeds faith. Worship is catching. 'My conviction gains infinitely,' says the Sage, 'the moment another soul will believe in it.' Seeing Watson constantly on his knees, we fall on ours by mere force of suggestion."[3] Pearson believed it was the magnetism of his personality that endeared Holmes to his readers and allowed his improbabilities to become him: "We feel we know everything about him, yet we want to know much more about him. We badly want to meet him."[4] For MacCarthy, the supreme "advantage" was that Holmes had no character, only characteristics, so the interest was focussed on the surface, on appearance, foibles, behaviour, on his words and actions. The stories were distinctive, he said, and whether good or bad, each was "a story of Sherlock Holmes and of no one else".[5] But it was Edmund Wilson, writing in the *New Yorker*,[6] who paid Holmes the finest compliment. "Sherlock Holmes *is* literature," he said, "on a humble but not ignoble level." The stories had wit, style, and a vein of fantasy to commend them; they were of an ideal length and were neatly constructed; they evoked the "sinister" by a subtle use of cliché and of the commonplace, and Holmes was, he thought, the product of a genuine spell which deceived author and readers alike and which raised him far above the level of the other members of his profession.

The debt of other detective story writers to the "patron saint" is again and again evident in their books. Agatha Christie, for example, includes hundreds of references to him and but a few to his predecessors and rivals. And those who deal with real crime have often felt it necessary to defend and justify their own methods. One of the first was Sir Robert Anderson, sometime head of the C.I.D., who gave Scotland Yard's

2

attitude to Sherlock Holmes in an article for *T. P.'s Weekly* in 1903.[7] Sir Basil Thompson later did likewise, as have his successors. The view of the police tends to be that their work is harder because they need evidence to bring a prosecution, whereas Holmes had only to find the solution and had the advantage that his locks were made to fit the keys that he held.

The real detective, said George Edgar in an article in *Outlook* in 1910, lived a dull and unexciting life. He could not take drugs without suffering the side effects, nor could he fashion the crime to suit the clues. The "unromantic detective" waited for events that never happened, failed as often as he succeeded, had a wife and baby to support, and could never be expected to acquire the god-like manner or to have insight as swift and lucid as lightning:

> The ordinary detective cannot look at the mud on a man's trouser-ends and tell to a yard where he keeps his country house. He cannot look at the finger-prints on a bell-push and deduce the facts that the finger which last pressed the button belonged to a seafaring man, who was unvaccinated, had red hair, a green parrot, a wooden leg, and his name, Jack Johnson, tattooed on the left shoulder-blade. Sherlock Holmes could do all this with one hand tied behind his back.[8]

On the Continent, the reputation of Sherlock Holmes was even greater. Bertillon, for example, while admitting that the detective had on occasion confused certainty with presumption, believed he had analytical genius and that the stories provided a vision of the future of the scientific police. His students went further. Edmund Locard, of the Lyons Police Laboratory, and his assistant, H. Ashton-Wolfe, heaped praises on Conan Doyle and caused a hall at Lyons to be named after him.

Private detectives have naturally also bathed in the glamour of Sherlock Holmes. The most notable was William J. Burns of the Burns Detective Agency. He became a close and admiring friend of Conan Doyle and was to say, in 1913, that the principles outlined in the stories were indeed applicable to life. The qualities that Holmes possessed, his imagination, resourcefulness, and knowledge of human nature, were those needed by the good detective. Burns was delighted by the logic found in the stories and by the apt portrayal of the various criminal types – though those in the stories, he once said, were actually of superior intelligence to the ones to be met with in real life. (Professional pride prevented him saying the same of the detective!)

The only people who have ever attacked the stories are those who feel that Doyle did not fully acknowledge his debt to his predecessors. The charge is based on the comments Sherlock Holmes makes about Dupin and Lecoq in *A Study in Scarlet*, where he calls one "a very inferior fellow", and the other "a miserable bungler". The first to take offence was Robert Blatchford, who wrote a long article on "The Evolution of Sherlock Holmes" which he published in the *Clarion* on 24 July 1897, and in which he gave examples from Poe, Gaboriau, and Doyle to show the many similarities between them. He ended by saying that "the character, the theories, the position, and the methods, always; and the incidents and phrases often, which have made Sherlock Holmes a household word, are taken directly from Dupin and Lecoq", and that Edgar Allan Poe "had enough genius in his little finger to make a whole regiment of Conan Doyles".[9] For his part, Doyle was only too ready to admit his indebtedness and in the years that followed again and again referred to Poe as having been one of the major influences upon him. In 1912, for example, Arthur Guiterman published some verses in *Life* (and in *London Opinion*) accusing him of ingratitude. In his reply, also in verse, Doyle pointed out that Sherlock Holmes did not voice the opinions of his creator. Although the debt to Poe and Gaboriau is real enough, those who, like Henri Mutrux in his book *Sherlock Holmes: Roi des Tricheurs* of 1977, attempt to "explode the myth", find only that the argument rebounds on themselves.

THE FIRST CRITICS

The first Sherlock Holmes story, *A Study in Scarlet*, was written at Bush Villas, Southsea, early in 1886 and was published at the end of the following year as part of *Beeton's Christmas Annual*. A pre-publication announcement, which appeared in the *Publishers' Circular* on 1 November and in the *Bookseller* on 5 November 1887, contains what is perhaps the earliest reference to it in print. It was also used in a shortened form at the time of publication (as, for example, in the *Daily News* of 22 November 1887). The publisher said:

> This story will be found remarkable for the skilful presentation of a supremely ingenious detective, whose performances, while based on the most rational principles, outshine any hitherto depicted. In fact, every detective ought to read "A Study in Scarlet" as a most helpful means to his own advancement. The surprises are most cleverly and yet most naturally managed, and at each stage the reader's attention is kept fascinated and eager for the next event. The sketches of the

"Wild West" in its former trackless and barren condition, and of the terrible position of the starving traveller with his pretty charge, are most vivid and artistic. Indeed, the entire section of the story which deals with early events in the Mormon settlement is most stirring, and intense pathos is brought out of some of the scenes. The publishers have great satisfaction in assuring the Trade that no Annual for some years has equalled the one which they now offer for *naturalness, truth, skill, and exciting interest.* It is certain to be read, not once, but twice by every reader; and the person who can take it up and lay it down again unfinished must be one of those rare people who are neither impressionable nor curious. "A Study in Scarlet" should be the talk of every Christmas gathering throughout the land.[10]

Nor, perhaps, did the publisher exaggerate the merits of the story. A leading article from the *Hampshire Post* of 2 December 1887, and short reviews from the Flintshire *County Herald*, the *Glasgow Herald*, and the *Scotsman*, all of which are included in this volume, will show that the critics recognised the special quality of the story and of its central character. The reviews were so good that extracts were printed in the first book edition of 1888. Others also included there came from *Lloyd's Weekly Newspaper* of 11 December 1887, which called the story "a tale replete with stirring incidents"; from the *Weekly Times and Echo* of the same date, which said that "as a detective story it equals anything we have ever read"; and from the *Bristol Mercury* of 21 December 1887, which found it "very exciting and well told".[11]

The next story was commissioned at the end of August 1889 by J. M. Stoddart of Lippincott's. By 3 September, Doyle had decided that he would use his detective. "I shall," he said, "give Sherlock Holmes of *A Study in Scarlet* something else to unravel. I notice that everyone who has read the book wants to know more of that young man."[12] It was first published under the title *The Sign of the Four* in the February 1890 issue of the Philadelphia-based *Lippincott's Magazine*, and it was from Philadelphia that one of the earliest Sherlockian letters came. Doyle mentioned it in a letter to Stoddart on 17 March 1890:

It's a triumph ever to get a rise out of you shrewd people on the other side, but a Philadelphia tobacconist actually wrote to me under cover to you, to ask me where he could get a copy of the monograph in which Sherlock Holmes described the difference in the ashes of 140 different kinds of tobacco.[13]

Although the new story was included in the English issue of

Lippincott's and soon afterwards serialised in local newspapers, as well as being published in book form in October 1890, it was not until July 1891, when the first of the short stories appeared in the *Strand Magazine*, that the public at large became aware of Mr. Sherlock Holmes. His success was then immediate and lasting.

The enormous popularity was reflected in *Tit-Bits*, a weekly paper founded by George Newnes in 1881 which after 1891 included material relating to the *Strand Magazine*. It was here that the earliest letters about Holmes were published and here also that Newnes and his staff gave their replies to correspondence received at the offices. These "Answers to Correspondents", some of which are reprinted here, are of interest because they provide evidence of the immediate impact that Holmes made on the readers. The column was written by the editor, Galloway Fraser, with the help of Newnes himself and of other members of the staff, such as Harry How and J. L. Munro. The announcements about forthcoming stories were by Herbert Greenhough Smith, who was editor of the *Strand* and who worked in an adjacent office. Continuity was ensured as Fraser remained at his post until 1921 and Smith until 1930. The readers of *Tit-Bits* were given snippets of information that were not previously available. They were, for example, the first to learn that Sidney Paget had used his brother as the model for the drawings of Sherlock Holmes, and that the guides at the Reichenbach Falls were, in 1895, pointing out the ledge from which Holmes and Moriarty had fallen. Their questions were also often amusing. One reader asked if the detective was the son of Oliver Wendell Holmes; another recorded his outrage when he learnt of a judge who professed not to know the name of Sherlock Holmes; and there were other anecdotes in the same vein.

Tit-Bits is the earliest repository of Sherlockian writing. It reprinted *The Sign of Four* and *A Study in Scarlet*, which enabled readers to follow the saga as it unfolded while also knowing how it had started. There was an examination paper on the methods of Sherlock Holmes, a competition to find the most popular story with reasons for the choice, and there were proposals for a monument or memorial in Baker Street. There were also countless references, allusions, parodies, imitations, and sequels. The readers talked of Mr. Holmes as of a friend, they mourned him as a man whom they had known intimately, and they jealously guarded his reputation even when they made a mock of it.

Between 1891 and 1901 the interest in Sherlock Holmes manifested itself in a variety of ways that are still familiar today. There was pastiche written in imitation of the author's style and using the original name; there were parodies, burlesques, and travesties using a perversion of it; and there were comic strips, plays, and advertisements; also, because

Holmes was presumed to be dead at the end of 1893, there were posthumous stories featuring his ghost, and others again that explained how he had escaped alive. There were also imitations and sequels by other writers which were an attempt to fill the vacuum, and there were important interviews with Conan Doyle and with the Edinburgh professor, Joseph Bell, who had served as the model for Sherlock Holmes.

The earliest pastiche is thought to be "My Evening with Sherlock Holmes", which appeared in the *Speaker* on 28 November 1891 and described a visit to Baker Street. The earliest known burlesque is one by C. C. Rothwell in the *Ludgate Weekly* of 9 April 1892, which concerned Sherwood Hoakes of Quaker Street; but Robert Barr's "detective story gone wrong" in the May 1892 *Idler* is far better known. It describes how Sherlaw Kombs and Dr. Whatson unsuccessfully investigated the Pegram Mystery by an expert misreading of the available clues.

Equally good, in its way, is "An Adventure of Sheer Lecoqmes", which was published in the *Privateer*, the student magazine of University College, London, on 16 June 1892. This contains many surprisingly shrewd observations, such as those in the opening paragraphs:

My name is Boswell Chorus, and I am a doctor with no practice to speak of. Sometimes I stick a stethoscope in my hat, so that Sheer Lecoqmes may exercise his supernatural shrewdness in detecting the bump, but that is all. I find that the worship of a genius like Sheer Lecoqmes, and the celebration of his powers in the *Mand Stragazine*, take up all my time. This reminds me of an instance of his extraordinary deductive faculty. The other evening, he said to me quite suddenly, "You've got a story in this month's *Mand*." His cold steel eyes were on me. "Yes," I gasped faintly, "b-but how d-did you know?" "I saw it in the contents bill," he replied calmly. I bowed before him. He does things like this every day, and never turns a hair.

Sheer Lecoqmes lives in Baker Street. . . . On his front door, guarded always by the Baker Street army of gutter boys, is a brass-plate bearing the words "Sheer Lecoqmes. Detective to the Crowned Heads of Europe. Secrecy guaranteed for one month only. Telegraphic address: Cocaine, London." In the window are the following testimonials: –

"I prefer Sheer Lecoqmes to all others."

A. DONAN COYLE

"M. Sheer Lecoqmes a cuit mon oie."

LE SPECTRE DE GABORIAU

"I find Sheer Lecoqmes matchless for the circulation."

NEORGE GEWNES, M.P., Ltd.[14]

On 29 October 1892, the *National Observer* had the first interview with Sherlock Holmes, a discussion about the recently published volume of his adventures. The "Real Sherlock Holmes" acknowledged that some of the accounts were true, but said that others were pastiche. He would not, for example, have been outwitted by a woman, nor would he have sent an innocent man to his death. It was, however, *Tit-Bits* which set the pace. By the end of 1892, Holmes's name was being used as a synonym for the ideal detective, with, for example, "A Female Sherlock Holmes"; and shortly afterwards, a prize was offered for the best story "in the manner of Sherlock Holmes". It was awarded to a parody called "The Adventures of Shylock Oames. The Sign of Gore", which was published on 3 December 1892.

The following August, *Punch* had the first of "The Adventures of Picklock Holes" by Cunnin Toil (otherwise R. C. Lehmann) and thereby began the association between the detective and the magazine that has continued to the present. A rival paper, *Fun*, had already published a parody, and the halfpenny papers soon followed suit. Harmsworth's *Comic Cuts*, for instance, had what may be the earliest strip cartoon on 18 November 1893, "The Adventures of Chubb-Lock Homes". Also at this time, Holmes and Watson made their stage début in a revue at the Royal Court called *Under the Clock*. It was written and performed by Charles Brookfield and Seymour Hicks and is perhaps best remembered for Watson's refrain, the catchphrase: "Sherlock, you wonderful man!"

When the death of Sherlock Holmes was first announced in *Tit-Bits* on 25 November 1893, there was an outcry. Letters were sent to the proprietors of the *Strand Magazine* imploring them to use their influence to persuade Conan Doyle to revoke the sentence of death, and others went to him direct. "I never thought they would take it so much to heart," he said later. "I got letters from all over the world reproaching me on the subject. One, I remember, from a lady whom I did not know, began 'You beast'."[15] When it became clear that Doyle would not relent, obituaries and tributes to the memory of Sherlock Holmes became necessary. None did it better than the *St. James's Gazette*, which published an "Involuntary Elegy" on 16 December and also had an account (by J. M. Barrie) of Watson's arrest on a charge of murder. His complicity was self-evident and the police, said the report, had amassed evidence against him and were even contemplating the possibility of bringing over the Reichenbach Falls.

Barrie's parody was the second he had written. The first was sent privately to Conan Doyle in May 1893, soon after the disastrous opening performance of *Jane Annie*, a comic opera on which they had both collaborated. It was called "The Adventure of the Two Collaborators" and in it Holmes explained in a bathetic way why it was that the public were not rushing to see the opera: the reason being that they preferred to stay away. As Doyle included this in his autobiography it has since become one of the best known Sherlockian parodies.

The failure of *Jane Annie* had, in this, one beneficial outcome, and another of Doyle's plays might have done likewise; for at the same period, he, Barrie, Thomas Hardy, and others had all agreed to dramatise short stories for a quintuple bill. It was the idea of Charles Charrington and was first given at Terry's Theatre on 3 June 1893. Once again it was a failure, so Charrington's wife, the acress Janet Achurch, asked Doyle if he would consider writing a play about Sherlock Holmes. With hindsight, the reply is of interest. He said:

Dear Mrs. Charrington,
I would do anything I could to save the situation, but I am well convinced after much thought that Holmes is not fitted for dramatic representation. His reasonings & deductions (which are the whole point of the character) would become an intolerable bore upon the stage. I would do both him and you an ill service by dramatising him. If I can in any way be of use I am always ready to come in and meet you.

Yours very truly, A. Conan Doyle[16]

Barrie's article in the *St. James's Gazette* on "The Late Sherlock Holmes" accepted that the detective was dead. So too did E. E. Kellett (or "K") in his "Monody on the Death of Sherlock Holmes", which ends:

Let scoundrels all rejoice
  Throughout our mourning land;
For Sherlock Holmes is gone.
  Gone to a better Strand.[17]

But the death was complicated by the lack of a corpse, and this led many to swear that Holmes was still alive. Doyle, however, was not among their number. "I, for one," he told an interviewer from the *Daily Mail* in 1904, "firmly believed that he was dead. It was merely by accident that I didn't chronicle the finding of his body."[18] Though this did not prevent him from indulging in a few parodies of his own. The first, called "The Field Bazaar", was written in 1896 for the Edinburgh *Student*, and he wrote another in 1922 for the Queen's Dolls' House Library called "How Watson Learned the Trick". Nor, despite his earlier statements, did it prevent him from writing a play about Holmes.

This he did at the end of 1897 and it was the precursor of the melodrama by William Gillette.

Other writers were equally busy. The *Bohemian* followed its "Ideal Interview" with Sherlock Holmes with an account of the doings of Thinlock Bones and Dr. Whatsoname; *Phil May's Christmas Annual* for 1896 had a case involving Shylock Bones and Röntgen Rays; and other famous characters, such as Herlock Sholmes and Sheerluck Gnomes, made the first of many appearances.

A widowed Mrs. Herlock Shomes appeared as early as 1894, while Herlock Sholmes himself was mentioned in *Tit-Bits* on 26 June 1897, but the name was made famous by Maurice Leblanc in his Arsène Lupin stories. Another Shomes (or Sholmes) is found with Dr. Hotsam in the trench newspapers of the Great War, and with Dr. Whyson in a prisoner-of-war magazine; another flourished for many years in the *Greyfriars Herald* and other associated papers, and there have been countless others. "Sheerluck" was used as early as 1893 on the type-script of *Under the Clock*. Then there were two "misadventures" of Sheerluck Gnomes in the *Modern Detective* in March 1898 (also a Sherlock Gnomes in *Scraps* in 1900). And there was the amusing *Sheerluck Jones* of 1901, by E. F. Spence and Malcolm Watson, a burlesque of Gillette's play.

Stories and verses about the ghost of Sherlock Holmes were numerous. A music-hall song by Richard Morton and a poem from the *St. James's Gazette* are included here. But the most famous was *The Pursuit of the House-Boat* by John Kendrick Bangs, which was published in 1897 and described how Sherlock Holmes had assumed the leadership of the "Associated Shades". The same author also wrote other stories in the same vein, such as "The Mystery of Pinkham's Diamond Stud" in *The Dreamers*, a story in *The Enchanted Typewriter*, and some "Posthumous Memoirs" of Shylock Homes which were published in the *New York Herald* in 1903. And he in turn inspired Laurence Daniel Fogg to introduce Sherlock Holmes into *The Asbestos Society of Sinners*, which is a parody based on *The Pursuit of the House-Boat*. Two examples by other writers would be "A Visit from the Ghost of Sherlock Holmes" in the 1897 Christmas number of *Tit-Bits*, and "The Ghost of a Detective. Sherlock Holmes as an Apparition" from the *Modern Detective* of 16 March 1898. In the second of these, Holmes returns to haunt Dr. Watson only to find that his surgery has passed into other hands.

Conan Doyle did not describe the return of Sherlock Holmes until 1903, but as he then revealed that Holmes had been in London since 1894, it was not inappropriate that others should have pre-empted him. One was Frank Marshall White with "The Recrudescence of Sherlock

Holmes", which appeared in the New York *Life* in October 1894 and described how Holmes had escaped and made his way to America via China. He finds Watson in New York and – having read the newspapers – is able to say exactly what his friend has been doing. The story coincided with Conan Doyle's own lecture tour of America and it may have inspired the anecdote he told about a Boston cabman who had correctly identified him by reading the name on his luggage.

"The Reappearance of Sherlock Holmes", in *Puck* on 25 September 1895, had Holmes and Moriarty survive the fall by using parachutes, and John Kendrick Bangs put forward another theory in "Over the Plum Pudding". It purported to be an account of a Christmas book planned by Horace Wilkinson to which many famous people had contributed. Doyle, it was said, had written a story which revealed that Holmes was not dead but had lost his memory. After his rescue by a group of Swiss yodellers, he travelled around Europe under the name of "Higgins" until he discovered a diamond brooch in the gizzard of a turkey. This convinced him that he must be Sherlock Holmes. It was, Bangs felt, "one of the most keenly interesting studies of detective life that Dr. Doyle or any one else has ever given us", and its loss – caused by the dragon Fafnir, who escaped from his own story and consumed all the characters in the book – amounted "almost to a positive grief".[19]

Three other categories of Sherlockiana can also be traced to this period: the thinly disguised imitation; the story in which the detective plays a minor part; and the one in which he is the inspiration or guiding spirit. They together make up the "School of Sherlock Holmes". The adventures of Martin Hewitt, Investigator, are the classic example of the first as these were written for the *Strand Magazine* and illustrated by Sidney Paget, and were a conscious attempt by Arthur Morrison to capitalise on, if not to repeat, the success of Sherlock Holmes. Another example would be Gertrude Clay's female detective, Miss Clara Beauchamp, whose methods were so similar to those of Sherlock Holmes that *Punch*, in its review on 10 November 1894, suggested that they should get married.

The best known examples of the second category are Conan Doyle's own stories, "The Man with the Watches" and "The Lost Special", both written in 1898, which introduce a "well-known criminal investigator" and an "amateur reasoner of some celebrity". These are now considered to be "apocryphal" Sherlock Holmes stories, a notion that first gained widespread currency in the 1930s when put forward by Christopher Morley in the *Saturday Review of Literature*. An earlier example is Montgomery Carmichael's "On the Threshold of the Chamber of Horrors", which appeared in the *Illustrated Sporting and Dramatic*

News on 27 October 1894. This concerns the London Road murderer, Edward Clay, who was so inconspicuous that the police were unable to trace him. No one could have looked less like a notorious murderer:

> But as he strolled down Baker Street, his eyes happened to wander up to a window. Two men were looking down into the street, one cadaverous, clean-shaven, his keen face full of power and intelligence, the other heavy, commonplace, good-natured, with a thick moustache hiding his indolent mouth. Clay recognised in the former a celebrated detective, and started slightly. [20]

He was then forced to take refuge in Madame Tussaud's and managed to mislead his pursuers by taking the place of his own effigy. Few readers would have failed to appreciate who the pursuers were.

Tit-Bits provides some typical examples of stories that mention Holmes by name. In October 1894, there was "The Man who 'bested' Sherlock Holmes"; a few months later, "A Student of Sherlock Holmes"; in 1898, "A Disciple of Sherlock Holmes", and shortly after that, "Sherlock's Rival". The first involved a private detective who found himself investigating a case with the great detective; while the "student" was Sergeant McQuade of the Royal Irish Constabulary. He had always believed that "there was a great reason in Holmes's methods, and that, as a detective, he was a standing lesson to the police". By applying the same methods he rose to be chief inspector of a large district: "He says that his promotion was entirely owing to his having studied 'Sherlock Holmes', and he urges every man under him to go and do likewise." [21]

Also popular were stories about Holmes's relatives, short anecdotes, and advertisements. As early as 1894 there were references to the detective's widow. Two years later, *Tit-Bits* had a piece on "Sherlock in Love", and before that had described "Mrs. Dr. Sherlock Holmes". But it was "Sherlock Holmes on the Domestic Hearth", in the *Tatler* of 18 December 1901, that took the joke to its logical conclusion by describing his wife, Harriette, his son, and all his domestic staff – a maid, cook, and butler. In 1905 there were the adventures of Raffles Holmes by Kendrick Bangs, this being a son of Sherlock Holmes and a grandson of the amateur cracksman, and the same year there was "Sherlock Holmes's Daughter" in the Boston *Brown Book*. She was Miss Elsie V. Holmes and was afterwards joined by Shirley and Sheila, as well as various younger brothers, cousins, and distant relations. Watson also had his family, as did Moriarty. An illegitimate daughter, fathered by Holmes, was mentioned in *Le Matin* in 1908, and others have claimed descent from him. But William Gillette alone had the author's permission. "You may marry him, or murder him, or do anything you like with him," he had been told, and, as a result, Sherlock Holmes became engaged, night after night, to Miss Alice Faulkner.

The Sherlockian anecdote tends to be predictable, consisting of people who cannot be compared with Sherlock Holmes, or of those who can. Thus, in *Tit-Bits* on 29 April 1893, there is "Not a Sherlock Holmes", a local professor who diagnosed gout from the state of a patient's teeth only to learn that they were false; or later, "Not in it with Sherlock Holmes", about an amateur detective who believed a man to be untrustworthy because of the way he stooped, clenched his fists, and glanced sideways, while he was in truth only a cyclist. And there are countless others with headings such as "Not a Case for Sherlock Holmes" or "Sherlock Holmes Not Needed". Among those who have been compared to Sherlock Holmes, there is "A Rural Sherlock Holmes", who could tell how long a man had been married by watching him drink a glass of water; also "Sherlock Holmes at the Bar", "Sherlock Holmes Three Hundred Years Ago", and "A Burmese Sherlock Holmes".

The earliest known advertisement involving Holmes was issued in November 1893 by Beecham's. It is an account of "Sherlock Holmes and the Missing Box", and is notable for the facsimile of a telegram which had been sent by Dr. Watson:

| To | Holmes, Baker Street, W. —— Come immediately —— in great distress —— box and valuable contents missing —— no clue |
| FROM | Watson |

Holmes solved the problem by sending one of his own boxes. It was, he admitted, to their head-clearing qualities that he attributed much of his success, or what the advertisement called the "marvellous detective feats" that had "startled the entire civilised world and set them wonderingly twiddling their thumbs while discussing his extraordinary ingenuity".[22] His need for the product was again evident in January 1894 when, soon after his disappearance, Beecham's published "The Last Letter from Sherlock Holmes", which contained a request for a box to be sent out to him. A year later there was "A Sherlock Holmes Dialogue" advertising *Woman's Life*, and Holmes afterwards allowed his name to be used to advertise Doan's Backache Kidney Pills, the Wood-Milne Rubber Heel, the Autostrop Safety Razor, Ronuk Furniture Cream, Craig's Velvet Blotting Paper, and a variety of other likely and unlikely products.

Although in the early stages England provided much of the best writing about Sherlock Holmes, the Americans soon proved that their enthusiasm was equal to that found in England. They coined the word "Sherlockian" and introduced a new element of whimsical scholarship. It was first evident at the time of Holmes's death, but it really developed out of Doyle's lecture tour at the end of 1894, which inspired a series of parodies, anecdotes, and stories. It took a firm root and was sustained by some of the country's greatest writers. In November 1900, the *Saturday Evening Post* published a "Condensed Novel" by Bret Harte called "The Stolen Cigar Case", a sharp and incisive critique of the pretensions of Hemlock Jones. In 1902, *Harper's Magazine* published Mark Twain's book *A Double-Barrelled Detective Story*, which introduces Sherlock Holmes. "I wonder," says one character, "if God made him?" To which his friend replies: "Not all at one time, I reckon."[23] And there were the books by Kendrick Bangs. But these writers were not responsible for the Sherlockian movement: that was the work of the editors of the New York *Bookman* – James MacArthur, Harry Thurston Peck, and Arthur Bartlett Maurice – and of those associated with it, such as Carolyn Wells and Stanley Hopkins Adams.

James MacArthur, who founded the *Bookman* with Peck in 1895, had retired from the staff and was working for Harper's when he wrote a series of documents for the "Notes of a Bookman" column in *Harper's Weekly* about the return of Sherlock Holmes. They were published on 31 August 1901 and revealed that Holmes had been in Switzerland working as a waiter and that he had just returned to London. It remains one of the finest examples of Sherlockian writing and was so convincing that many took it as the gospel truth. Conan Doyle, said *Munsey's Magazine* shortly afterwards, "permits it to be known that Sherlock has been protesting against an inglorious career as a Swiss waiter during the last few years".[24] MacArthur also wrote the introduction for a three-volume edition of the Sherlock Holmes stories which was published by Harper's in 1904.

Harry Thurston Peck's major contribution was "A Chat about Sherlock Holmes", which was published in the *Independent* on 21 November 1901 and afterwards included in his *Studies from Several Literatures*. Peck believed that Doyle had permanently enriched English literature by creating a character whose interest went beyond the stories themselves; he considered Watson to be an equally great creation and a perfect foil to Holmes, while the idea of Mycroft Holmes was a "stroke of genius". "The Speckled Band" was a story worthy of Poe and indeed better than Poe's best, but all were cleverly constructed in such a way as to allow the solution to remain obscure until Holmes revealed it, even though the clues were given fairly and frankly. He believed that *The Hound of the Baskervilles* (of which only two parts had appeared when he wrote the article) was Doyle's masterpiece, that in it he had "attained the perfection of his method", and that it would prove to be the best of all the Sherlock Holmes stories.

Peck was a classicist by training and had a well-developed sense of fun and a sound judgement. When MacArthur retired in November 1899, Peck became the "Senior Editor" of the *Bookman*, while Arthur Bartlett Maurice, then a young man, became the "Junior Editor". They were both responsible for the "Chronicle and Comment" columns, but the majority of the pieces concerning Holmes were written by Maurice.

In 1899, interest in Shelock Holmes was limited. The October number had a letter pointing out the similarities between Dupin and Holmes and between *Treasure Island* and *The Sign of Four*, but in December Doyle was cited as an example of the "pitiful uncertainty of literary popularity"; he was not forgotten, the editors said, but "the keen edge of the appetite for his work has been dulled, and we wonder rather curiously as we recall the ardour, the zest, the enthusiasm with which we awaited each new problem for Sherlock Holmes to solve".[25] However, interest was reviving because of the play by William Gillette, and this was more evident by the Spring of the following year. Even so, the only references to Sherlock Holmes during 1900 tended to be derogatory. Lecoq was praised while Holmes was dismissed as a "builder of fancy hypotheses",[26] and Maurice, for he was without doubt the author of these comments, referred to "The Speckled Band" – which has always been the most popular of the stories – as being one of the most poorly constructed stories ever to have come from the hand of a practised novelist, and as one that had "very little of the great detective's personality, and very little of the science of deduction"![27]

The enthusiasm began to build up when it became clear that Doyle was considering the possibility of reviving Sherlock Holmes. This was revealed in an interview published on 15 December 1900 in the one thousandth number of *Tit-Bits*. In it, Doyle told "The True Story of Sherlock Holmes". He said that he had never for one moment regretted his decision to kill Holmes:

That does not mean, however, that because he is dead I should not write about him again if I wanted to, for there is no limit to the number of papers he left behind or the reminiscences in the brain of his biographer.[28]

This suggested that he might be on the point of relenting, and many of the English papers commented on it. So too did the editors of the *Bookman*, who gave a synopsis of the interview in February 1901. They said:

> If Holmes is to be taken up again simply to arouse a little additional interest for some ignoble potboiler, then we devoutly hope that he may be allowed to rest in peace. If, however, Dr. Doyle has any more real stories to tell about the science of deduction, then we think that he cannot begin too soon.[29]

A weekend at Cromer and a long discussion with Bertram Fletcher Robinson convinced Doyle that he did have a "real story" to tell, and by July 1901 the editors knew that Holmes would be revived. Taking their cue from Doyle, they mentioned what was to become a constant theme in the months and years ahead, the cases Watson had referred to but which he had not yet written. Later they gave a full list, but on the first occasion only three were mentioned, "The Adventure of the Tired Captain", "The Third Window", and "The Green Sapphire", of which only the first would have been familiar to students of the stories.

The Hound of the Baskervilles took America by storm – though Maurice complained that Holmes was different from the earlier Holmes and suggested that Fletcher Robinson was probably the author. Peck, however, was full of enthusiasm and in January 1902 the editors admitted that this was the first story they had felt compelled to read in serial form and that it had caused them to argue over its possible outcome. The readers shared these feelings and many, inspired by Edgar Allan Poe's famous article in the *Commercial Advertiser* in which he gave a summary of the plot of *Barnaby Rudge* after seeing the first part, sent in theories of their own.

The correspondence about the "houndfoot" theory formed part of the May 1902 issue, which the editors promised in advance would be a "Sherlock Holmes Number". It also contained a review of the book by Maurice, as well as other articles and a ballade on detective fiction. Although in the main laudatory, Maurice's review is best remembered for its final, curious assertion:

> As a story of mystery and horror, *The Hound of the Baskervilles* is a success; for Sherlock Holmes, the Master of the Science of Deduction, whose creator has proclaimed him the peer of Dupin and Lecoq, it is a *débâcle*.[30]

Samuel Hopkins Adams was the person responsible for the publicity for *The Hound of the Baskervilles*. Having worked for the *New York Sun*, which had close ties with S. S. McClure, he then ran McClure's newspaper syndicate, and in 1901 took over as Advertising Manager for the publishing side of the business. McClure had bought all the American rights and, after the story had run in the American issue of the *Strand*, he sold serial rights to newspapers and also published the book. The publicity was on a large scale, using not only advertisements, but also the manuscript itself. Individual pages were sent to bookshops, and many still survive with a small label that reads: "Original Manuscript Sheet / from / The Hound of the Baskervilles / By A. Conan Doyle / Published by McClure, Phillips & Co., New York." (One chapter remained intact, Chapter XI, and that, with the copy of the letter addressed to Fletcher Robinson which serves as a foreword to the book, found its way into the collection of Harry Thurston Peck.)

The first advertisements for *The Hound of the Baskervilles* described it as "The Event of the Year in Fiction" and as "The most absorbing, the most bewildering, the most brilliant mystery story in English literature", but the *New York Sun* provided an even better idea for publicity when its critic said: "The reader will take it to bed to shiver with. And he will finish it before he blows out the candle."[31] It was therefore called the book "the critics are sitting up at night to read", and Adams quoted the review from the *Sun* as saying: "The reader will take it to bed with him and he will finish it before he blows out the candle."[32] Advance orders for the book and its sale were very large, some 70,000 copies within a few weeks, but Adams decided to go further and on 3 May 1901 there appeared the first of his six "Doyley Dialogues". These were published in the *New York Sun* and described the effect the book was having on various types of people, such as a man on the subway train who was going from one end of the line to the other, or a bride and bridegroom who had missed their wedding because they become so engrossed in the book.

Later, in March 1907, the *Bookman* was to call Adams an "understudy to Sherlock Holmes" on account of the letter he had written to Stuart Edward White, with whom he collaborated on *The Mystery*. It described the deductions made about a shaving brush that White had returned to him with only a label attached to it. Adams said:

Examining it with my Sherlock Holmes patent magnifying glass, and my knitted brow, I made several discoveries. First: a red-headed, cross-eyed, knock-kneed, left-handed brakeman on the Southern Pacific shaved with it somewhere between Needles, California, and

Tucson, Arizona, using a low grade of Barren Island soap. This is shown by the small red sprinklings, intermixed with desert and a last-rose-of-summer fragrance, while the physical peculiarities of the shaver are sufficiently obvious ("My dear Holmes, you surprise me," here broke in Watson), by the irregular streaking of the bristles, though to be sure, he may only have been drunk. A little beyond Yuma, while the engine stopped for water, the mail-clerk threw the brush at a prairie dog. To the trained eye this is perfectly clear, as the marks of the outraged animal's teeth are not to be mistaken, while the location is indicated by the thorn of a cactus which grows only in that locality.

At Denver it was used for applying stove blacking, in Kansas for cleaning a pipe, at Chicago as a shoe brush, and at Buffalo as a toothbrush. Adams punctuated the letter with what he called the "asinine Antiphonies" of Dr. Watson.[33]

A number of famous suggestions which have since become a part of Sherlockian mythology had their origin in the *Bookman*. One concerned Doyle's knighthood. In August 1902, the editors said that if they were the King of England they would offer him further honours for any new Sherlock Holmes stories he might write. They, of course, never had the opportunity to put this into practice, but others did so. The Sultan of Turkey gave Doyle an honour in recognition of the Sherlock Holmes stories, and in April 1895 the Italian Government made him a Cavalier of the Order of the Crown of Italy. Doyle had mentioned the reason in a letter to his mother dated 24 January 1895:

> I had a letter from an Italian agent offering me a decoration (!) if I would allow Signor Crispi's paper to translate "The Naval Treaty" story. It is funny, is it not? I wonder what it will be. "Knight Commander of the Imperial Order of the Iron Crown of Lombardy" would do for me.[34]

Another famous suggestion, which was later developed by Christopher Morley, concerned Holmes's nationality. He was so much at home in America, said the editors in January 1903, that they were unwilling to concede the entire possession of him to "any part of the British Empire nor to the whole thereof" and, until evidence to the contrary was produced, they would "cherish the secret belief that he was born somewhere up in Maine".[35] But most of all, it was the *Bookman*'s "Sherlockian" speculation that has earned it a place in the history books. The word was first used in December 1902, when the editors admitted that one scene in Gillette's play, in which Holmes fails to check whether or not Moriarty has a second pistol concealed on him, was "un-Sherlockian"; but it was the problem of Watson's wedding present that really launched Sherlockian speculation. This had caused a crisis as neither of the editors could agree what Holmes would have given Watson, and despite their own suggestions and J. Alston Cooper's "partial solution", the matter remains unresolved.

The magazine was at its most Sherlockian in 1903. In March, there was a cryptographic puzzle for "real Sherlockians"; in April, a prospectus for "Dr. Doyle's Academy of Crime", which envisaged an art department under Professor Stapleton giving "elaborate training in the painting of spectral hounds";[36] and in June, there was not only the announcement that Sherlock Holmes was being revived, but also a list of his lesser known cases and a cartoon by John T. McCutcheon. The climax came during the summer, when Maurice visited Europe and met Conan Doyle. The readers of the *Bookman* learnt that he had had "a very serious conference with Sherlock Holmes and Dr. Watson in the rooms in Upper Baker Street" and that he had afterwards visited Paris to learn further details about "The Second Stain" and about Baron Maupertuis.[37] In fact he had urged Doyle to write "The Second Stain", and as Doyle did so, Maurice may well deserve the gratitude of posterity. Also at that time it was announced that Peck's daughter had joined the "Innermost Circle" of real Sherlockians. Her father had heard her computing the sums Doyle would earn from his new stories, for which he was being paid approximately two dollars a word. Thus: " 'My dear Holmes, you positively astonish me!' would be fourteen dollars. "Quite so, said Sherlock', another eight dollars."[38]

In December 1903 there was a critical parody, "The Resources of Mycroft Holmes", which poked gentle fun at the cryptographic methods of literary criticism. This and "The Bound of the Astorbilts", which had appeared in June 1902, were the only parodies that had as yet been published in the magazine. And, as before, there were throughout these years letters and editorial comments. One writer criticised "The Reigate Puzzle"; another implored the editors to prevent Doyle from reviving "the revered Sherlock Holmes"; another protested against the editors' Sherlockian tastes. In 1905, an observant reader noted the misprint that occurred in "The Adventure of the Golden Pince-Nez" when it was serialised in *Collier's Weekly* – the word "convex" was used instead of "concave". But perhaps the most intriguing editorial comment was one referring to Moriarty's Christian name, for it was said: "The man who patiently wove a net around Professor Robert Moriarty would have run down Raffles in twenty-four hours."[39] The odd point being that both his own name and that of his brother were given in the stories as "James".

Peck retired from the *Bookman* in February 1907 and died in 1914, but his influence has continued to be felt because Maurice collected all the material together and used it as the basis for an article on "Sherlock Holmes and His Creator" which appeared in *Collier's Weekly* on 15 August 1908 alongside the first part of "Wisteria Lodge". Maurice and the later editors of the *Bookman* remained faithful to Holmes until the demise of the magazine. It carried articles by Vincent Starrett and in one of the last numbers had Hugh Kingsmill's parody, "The Ruby of Khitmandu", featuring Holmes and Raffles.

Carolyn Wells, whose "Ballade of Baker Street" appeared with Maurice's article in the 1908 *Collier's*, was another of the *Bookman* Sherlockians. She was greatly admired by the editors as a poet and first made her name with a series of anthologies. In 1902, she contributed a "Ballade of Detection" to the "Sherlock Holmes Number" of the *Bookman*, which had the following "envoy":

> Sherlock, thy subtle powers I know,
> Spirit of search, incarnate quest,
> To thee the laurel wreath I throw –
> I like Detective Stories best.[40]

She was herself a collector of detective stories and became an authority on them. In 1913, she wrote one of the first handbooks on the subject, *The Technique of the Mystery Story*, and later became well known as a detective story writer. She also wrote a number of Sherlockian parodies which were published in the *Century Magazine*, with illustrations by Frederic Dorr Steele, and in the *New York American*. These concerned the Society of Infallible Detectives, of which Holmes was President. In the best-known, "The Adventure of the Clothes-Line", published in 1915, they attempted to solve the mystery of a lady suspended from a wire. Despite their name, none succeeded, but it transpired that she was Miss Flossy Flicker of the Flim-Flam Film Company and was engaged in making a six-reel thriller called *At the End of Her Rope!*

THE LITERATURE OF SHERLOCK HOLMES

In England, *The Hound of the Baskervilles* and *The Return of Sherlock Holmes* were enormously successful and this was reflected in *Tit-Bits*, where there were essays, stories, and anecdotes, as well as the comments made by George Newnes at the Shareholders' Meetings. Sherlock Holmes was also busy elsewhere as an assistant to other detectives, as a *doppelgänger* for Conan Doyle, and as the butt of further parodies. And by then there was a new spirit abroad in the schools and Universities, where students and teachers were examining the texts with a more critical eye.

Much of the credit for the development of Sherlockian criticism must go to Cambridge. The University had connections with many of the best humorous writers of the day through R. C. Lehmann, of *Punch*, who edited *Granta*. This was the main undergraduate magazine and provided a springboard for many writers, such as Frank Sidgwick ("Sigma Minor"), Anthony C. Deane (whose initials often caused confusion), Archibald Marshall (A.H.M.), and E. E. Kellet ("K"). It was edited at one time by Bertram Fletcher Robinson and at another by A. A. Milne, and all made important contributions to Sherlockian literature.

King's College, Cambridge, became one focal point because of the interest of two of its dons, M. R. James and J. Willis Clark. One undergraduate, Gerald Kelly, who became President of the Royal Academy, dated his own critical interest from around 1900, when he had examined the dates in "The Red-Headed League". In the story, Jabez Wilson calls on Holmes on a Saturday and tells him of the dissolution of the League, which he had read that morning on a notice dated 9 October 1890 (a Thursday!); he also produces an advertisement from the *Morning Chronicle* of 27 April 1890 (a Sunday), which he describes as being "just this day eight weeks". Kelly recalled:

> I took these discrepancies round to Monty James (a great mediaeval scholar and a writer of admirable ghost stories) and he suggested that perhaps Dr. Watson was of the realistic school of writing and was content to record Jabez Wilson's inaccuracy, but he agreed that it was surprising that Holmes had not commented upon it. He also thought that it was a pity that 9 October was not a Saturday, which would have made things a little easier.[41]

James then suggested that Watson's handwriting might have been bad and that he had mistaken a "4" for a "9", but this idea was abandoned. Unfortunately Kelly never published his findings, at least not until 1954, and by then others had pre-empted him.

A famous anecdote about James, and one he often told against himself, concerned his and Clark's enthusiasm for *The Hound of the Baskervilles*. Recalling his friendship with Clark, or "J" as he was known, James spoke of his "boyishness" when attending a detective play:

> Boyish also was his fervid interest in *The Hound of the Baskervilles* when it was coming out in tantalising monthly instalments in the *Strand*. Sir Arthur Conan Doyle should be gratified if he knew how many evenings were devoted to speculation by undergraduates and others

gathered in my rooms, and knew that the numerous false leads he laid down were eagerly followed. J. shared to the full in the excitement. Lady Day came on, when the completed story was to appear in book form, a little before the last instalment in the *Strand*. It was also the day when the University (represented by a few Heads of Houses, officials and professors) assembled by custom in the Provost's Lodge at 11.15 a.m. to partake of coffee and chocolate before proceeding to King's Chapel to hear a sermon. J. and I were both there, and I had told him that my copy of the *Hound* would be awaiting me in my rooms. We partook of chocolate, and we started from the Lodge door with the procession: but – oh, how it irks me to recall it! – when we reached the corner of the path that turns towards Chapel, J. made me a sign – I fear a preconcerted sign – by laying his wicked old finger on his lips, and we slipped out of the procession and stole up to my rooms: where J., I fancy, was a little disappointed to find that his latest anticipations about the plot were not borne out as they should have been.[42]

Both were fond of telling the story and it caused amusement among the younger men. "If one of *us* had done it, of course," said Archibald Marshall, "they would have called it cutting chapel."[43]

The most remarkable concentration of future Sherlockians was at Trinity College. They included Frank Sidgwick, A. A. Milne, Maurice Baring, Desmond MacCarthy, and Bernard Darwin. It was Sidgwick's "Open Letter" to Dr. Watson in the *Cambridge Review* of 23 January 1902 that marked the official birth of "Watsonology", or the study of the chronology of the stories, for he pointed out, while it was being serialised, that there were discrepancies in the dates given in *The Hound of the Baskervilles*.

Maurice Baring's first contribution to the subject was "Sherlock Holmes in Russia. The Story of a Skat Scoring Book" (which is collected in his *Russian Essays and Stories*). "It was," says Watson in the opening paragraph, "in November 1907 that I went to Moscow to meet Sherlock Holmes, who was returning via Kiachta by the Trans-Siberian Railway from Afghanistan, where rumour said he was connected with certain not altogether official negotiations between the British Government and the Ameer of Afghanistan."[44] Baring, of course, went to Russia at that time and Holmes was very much in evidence. Baring's masterpiece came three years later when the *Eye-Witness* published extracts "From the Diary of Sherlock Holmes", one of a number of previously lost diaries. Holmes had kept it to record a few of his less successful cases: he had, for example, made a series of deductions from a man's clothes only to learn that the client had woken that morning to find his own clothes stolen and replaced by the ones he was wearing. "This is a case," Holmes wrote, "of my reasoning being, with one partial exception, perfectly correct. Everything I had deduced would no doubt have fitted the real owner of the clothes."[45]

A. A. Milne's first piece was "The Rape of the Sherlock", which appeared in *Vanity Fair* on 15 October 1903. Then in 1922 there was his detective story, *The Red House Mystery*, which created two new words, "Sherlocky", to describe the hero, Tony Gillingham, and "Watsonish", for his companion, Bill Beverley. He also wrote two memorable reviews, one after the publication of *His Last Bow* called "The Watson Touch" and another, "Dr. Watson Speaks Out", for the *Nation & Athenæum* of 17 November 1928. In the first he pointed out how lucky Holmes often was in his deductions, while the second, a review of the collected short stories, had Watson disclose a number of the errors Holmes had committed which he had previously concealed; this out of pique at Holmes having chosen to write some of the later stories himself.

At the time of Milne's second review, Desmond MacCarthy and Bernard Darwin were also making their presence felt, but by then Sherlockian criticism had become a more detailed affair because of Ronald Knox. He was a Junior Fellow at Trinity College, Oxford, when, in 1911, he wrote the "Studies in the Literature of Sherlock Holmes". It was for the Gryphon Club and was published in the Oxford *Blue Book* in 1912. He gave it again on various occasions and in 1928 it was included in his *Essays in Satire*. It is the earliest, the best, and the wittiest of all the "Higher Criticism". But before considering it, a few of the works that preceded it should be mentioned.

In 1904, Andrew Lang wrote two important articles, a review of the "Author's Edition" of Doyle's work for the *Quarterly Review* which contained valuable criticism of Sherlock Holmes, and an article in *Longman's Magazine* which pointed out the various solecisms in "The Three Students", such as the setting of Thucydides for an unseen. Lang believed that the tutor had deceived Holmes on purpose, whereas Belsize, who was to raise exactly the same points in 1917, in Vernon Rendall's *The London Nights of Belsize*, was convinced that Dr. Watson had been behind it. Lang also twice used Sherlockian parody when reviewing books about Edwin Drood, first in *Longman's Magazine* for September 1905, and again in the *Cambridge Review* of 2 March 1911.

Another person who was amused by Sherlock Holmes was P. G. Wodehouse, who became addicted to the stories when he was a student at Dulwich College. Early in his career he wrote a number of parodies, such as "The Prodigal", which was written for *Punch* in 1903 and inspired by a newspaper report that Doyle was thinking of setting his new stories in America; or "The Adventure of the Missing Bee", which was published in *Vanity Fair* on 1 December 1904 and dealt with the first case to confront Holmes on his retirement, one that involved another great authority on bees, Maeterlinck. Wodehouse also contributed some verses to the *Reader* in 1905, "Sherlock Holmes's Lament", and made frequent allusions to the stories in his articles for such publications as *Sandow's Magazine*. His novels, too, contain references and some would say that Sherlock Holmes and Dr. Watson provided him with the idea for Jeeves and Bertie Wooster.

G. K. Chesterton was equally fond of Sherlock Holmes, as his essays on detective fiction and his articles in the *Daily News*, the *Morning Post*, and *G. K.'s Weekly* bear witness. He is, however, best remembered in Sherlockian circles for his often stated opinion that there should be a statue of Sherlock Holmes in Baker Street, and for the remarks about Holmes made in 1906 in his book on Charles Dickens. In it he said that Holmes was the one figure of the day who was known to the populace at large:

Ordinary men would understand you if you referred currently to Sherlock Holmes. Sir Arthur Conan Doyle would no doubt be justified in rearing his head to the stars, remembering that Sherlock Holmes is the only really familiar figure in modern fiction. But let him droop that head again with a gentle sadness, remembering that Sherlock Holmes is the only familiar figure in the Sherlock Holmes tales. Not many people could say offhand what was the name of the owner of Silver Blaze, or whether Mrs. Watson was dark or fair. But if Dickens had written the Sherlock Holmes stories, every character in them would have been equally arresting and memorable. A Sherlock Holmes would have cooked the dinner for Sherlock Holmes. A Sherlock Holmes would have driven his cab.[46]

Max Beerbohm is one of the more unexpected admirers. He made his interest known in an article in the *Saturday Review* on 6 May 1905. It was ostensibly a criticism of *John Chilcote, M.P.* at the St. James's Theatre, but it began as a parody and developed into a discussion of the merits of the Sherlock Holmes stories, which he felt provided the only suitable format for John Chilcote. "Evidently," he said, "I am growing old":

Sherlock Holmes is dead, and to young readers of this *Review* he is not even a dear memory. But I was at an impressionable age when he burst upon the world; and so he became a part of my life, and will never, I suppose, be utterly dislodged. I cannot pass through Baker

Street, even now, without thinking of him. Long ago I had decided exactly which were the two windows of the sitting-room where Watson spent his wondering hours; and, only the other day, I had a rather heated dispute with a coeval who had also long since "placed" that sitting-room – "placed" it, if you please, on the side of the street opposite to that where it really was (need I say that I mean the right-hand side as one goes towards Regent's Park?). My sentiment for Sherlock Holmes was never one of reverence unalloyed. Indeed, one of the secrets of his hold on me was he so often amused me.[47]

An even more remarkable enthusiast was A. C. Swinburne. When the editor of the *Strand Magazine* visited him and Theodore Watts-Dunton at The Pines, Putney, he was expecting an "Immortal", but found instead a deaf and withered "peony", one of the "very strangest of the sons of man". Greenhough Smith described the meeting and the conversation that followed, thus:

> Gliding into his seat, he poured out his bottle of beer, and just as I, remembering, was about to roar out a remark about his poems, he fixed me with his eye and broke into a rhapsody – on Sherlock Holmes!
> The adventures of that eminent detective were at his finger-ends. He would talk of nothing else; and, as he was only one shade deafer than his friend, the reader must imagine the conversation carried on by three stentorian voices, each like a skipper's with a speaking-trumpet, which made Rossetti's paintings dither on the walls.[48]

Less familiar today are the works of Frank Richardson, Harry Graham, and Bernard Capes. Richardson was a barrister whose main obsession and recreation was "the whisker question"; but he was also a brilliant satirist and in 1905 introduced Sherlock Holmes into *The Secret Kingdom*. At the start of the twelfth chapter, the hero jumps into a cab:

> "Sherlock Holmes, Baker Street."
> "Yes, sir."
> The driver stopped at an unpretentious house near Klein's the hairdresser's, on the front of which was a small circular tablet bearing the words:
>
>
>
> SHERLOCK
> HOLMES
> LIVED HERE
> 1890 –
>
>

The second date had happily not been filled in.

25

Holmes was found to be totally under the domination of Dr. Watson and was not seen to his best advantage; nor did the "whiskery sentiments" that he voiced quite become him. But the book is of interest as evidence of the growing importance of the deer-stalker in the public's mind. It is mentioned only once in the stories, and then as an "ear-flapped travelling cap", but Sidney Paget showed Holmes wearing one on various occasions and it was made popular by William Gillette. "Watson," says Holmes in *The Secret Kingdom*, "we sail tonight. My deer-stalker cap is here, and I shall require no other luggage"; or later: " 'I must put on my thinking cap,' said he, adjusting the famous deer-stalker."[49]

In the same year, 1905, Harry Graham celebrated the detective's achievements in *More Representative Men*, and in the last stanzas gave the following account of his departure from London:

> No more on Holmes shall Watson base
>   The Chronicles he proudly fabled;
> The violin and morphia-case
>   Are in the passage, packed and labelled;
> And Holmes himself is at the door,
> Departing – to return no more.
>
> He bids farewell to Baker Street,
>   Though Watson clings about his knees;
> He hastens to his country seat,
>   To spend his dotage keeping bees;
> And one of them, depend upon it,
> Shall find a haven in his bonnet!
>
> But though in grief our heads are bowed,
>   And tears upon our cheeks are shining;
> We recognise that ev'ry cloud
>   Conceals somewhere a silver lining;
> And hear with deep congratulation
> Of Watson's timely termination.[50]

But as often as Holmes retired, he was recalled. On one occasion, according to Bernard Capes in *The Great Skene Mystery* of 1907, it was at the insistence of the Italian detective, Valombroso. "I will telegraph to Mr. Holmes," says Mr. Shapter, "I cannot, of course, answer for his being disengaged at the moment." Fortunately a favourable reply was received and, though the expectations of the narrator were high, he was not disappointed when he first set eyes on the great detective:

> It is true that there was a trifle more grey in the hair, a trifle more vagueness, or shall I say less brilliancy in the eye than I had looked for; but it must be remembered that at this period Mr. Holmes was at least approaching that state of premature superannuation which his adventures, countless and diversified beyond the common human experience or endurance, had necessarily imposed upon him.

He was less impressed by Dr. Watson, who "had grown rather fat and inert, and, in suggestion, not unlike a prosperous impresario". But the account of the case was undoubtedly spurious as Holmes withdrew from it leaving a letter for Watson that could hardly have been written by the acknowledged expert on the tracing of footprints, for it read:

> MY DEAR WATSON, – I find this must be counted among my unsuccessful cases. I am under the necessity of admitting that the footmarks I have been following were my own. I traced them all the way to the "Black Dog", and so up the stairs to my bedroom, where the boots themselves lay under a chair. *En passant*, why did you never remind me, my dear Watson, that they were a pair of yours which I had borrowed, and put off for some of my own when I went out for the second time? It was that misled me. Make my apologies to our friends. I enclose the half of your third-class return ticket, and am off to Siberia by the night mail. An important political prisoner has escaped from Kara Baigarama. I believe him to be hidden under an ice-floe in the Arctic Ocean. Tell this to nobody.

Watson thereupon sank back in his chair, gasped, and swallowed the piece of bloater that was sticking out of his mouth. "I believe," he said to Mr. Shapter, "that that fall into the river gave him water on the brain."[51]

Not everybody was fortunate enough to meet Holmes himself, but many met Watson, such a J. Storer Clouston's Carrington. Asked, in *Carrington's Cases* of 1920, if he had met the great detective, he shook his head:

> "I've often wanted to, but unfortunately he was before my time. I've met Dr. Watson though."
>
> "What, *the* Dr. Watson, Holmes's pal?"
>
> Carrington nodded.
>
> "The very fellow. He came to consult me once. It was his case not mine, so I don't know whether I really ought to tell you the yarn."

Of course, he did so. It was the case of "The Truthful Lady", in which

Watson had eaten the evidence. "Is that story literally true?" asked a sceptical member of the party when Carrington had finished. "Ask Dr. Watson when you next meet him," said Carrington.[52]

As well as undertaking a number of cases of which Conan Doyle was unaware, Sherlock Holmes also followed his creator around the country and aped his activities. "It is rumoured that in the event of Mr. Chamberlain forming a Ministry, Sir Conan Doyle's political services will be rewarded by an offer of the posts of Holmes Secretary and Secretary for Scotland Yard," said *Punch* on 24 February 1904,[53] when Doyle announced that he would be standing as the Liberal-Unionist candidate in the Border Burghs. Holmes followed his example and, on 1 November 1904, the *Border Advertiser* described "How Holmes Tried Politics"; how he had been persuaded to fight the seat, and how soon after his arrival he had written to Watson:

> DEAR WATSON, – Arrived safe. This is going to be a rum affair. I have made, so to speak, my maiden speech. You never saw a purer Scotch audience. It was the greatest conglomeration ever I saw. In my professional capacity there were a few things I observed, and these may prove of much value should this election go against me. In fact, as it is, I am doing a little bit on my own. You might go over to Baker Street and get my little hand-bag, the one with the steel bottom and the double locks, and forward it here.
>
> HOLMES[54]

Neither Sherlock Holmes nor Doyle were elected, but their lives continued to cross. In March 1913, when Doyle entered for the Billiard Association Amateur Championship, the *Billiard Monthly* published "The Mystery of the Three Grey Pellets", which revealed that Holmes was also proficient at the sport. He had recognised that the initials "S.S.S." which were on the envelopes containing the pellets stood for "Spink's Self-Sticker tips". "I play my own tie to-day," he tells Watson, "and I play with the new tip, and shall win with it."[55]

"But, Holmes – *fairies*?" gasps Watson at the start of Reginald Berkeley's "Adventure of the Chuckle-Headed Doctor", occasioned by Doyle's belief in fairies and by James Douglas's articles in the *Sunday Express*. Holmes admits he is at a loss: "The voice in the trumpet I can account for; the articles in the *Sunday Express* I can explain. But how did a sober-minded and apparently abstemious doctor, last seen at midnight at the National Sporting Club, come to be found at four a.m. on the Mendip Hills, bereft of his wits and professing to have spent the night dancing with fairies?"[56] At least the detective remained unconvinced. Worse was to come when Watson revealed in the psychic newspaper, *Light*, how Holmes had dealt with critics of spiritualism. "I had no idea, Holmes, that you were so staunch a champion of Spiritualism," he says. Holmes demurs; he is interested only in the truth – the truth of spiritualism, that is![57]

The small stage at Baker Street saw many dramatic entrances, but few was stranger than the arrival of Brigadier Gerard, whose conversation with Holmes was recorded in *Tit-Bits* on 3 October 1903. The old soldier, who had taken the night train from Paris, via Dieppe, was angry that his stories had been discontinued in favour of Holmes. Another strange case was that of "The Footprints on the Ceiling", recorded by Jules Castier;[58] it was "an account of an adventure of Professor George E. Challenger, Lord John Roxton, Mr. Sherlock Holmes, Dr. Watson, M.D., and Mr. E. D. Malone". Holmes also tangled with Captain Kettle in "The Cat of the Bunkervilles"; he was unmasked by Dupin; he many times solved the mystery of Edwin Drood, and has on more than one occasion brought Raffles to justice. He has also since met Dracula, Tarzan, and Fu Manchu, and has travelled all over the world and been into Space.

The majority of Holmes's lesser known cases are in the "Donan Coyle" style, but an amusing variant was suggested by A. B. Cox in his *Jugged Journalism* when considering literary style. He suggested that if Conan Doyle were to be indisposed or if he wished to play a round of golf and had handed over the writing of a Sherlock Holmes story to P. G. Wodehouse, then it would not be done in his own style, but in the Wodehouse style, thus:

Holmes and the Dasher

It was a pretty rotten sort of day in March, I remember, that dear old Holmes and I were sitting in the ancestral halls in Baker Street, putting in a bit of quiet meditation. At least Holmes was exercising the good old grey matter over a letter that had just come, while I was relaxing gently in an arm-chair.

"What-ho, Watson, old fruit," he said at last, tossing the letter over to me. "What does that mass of alluvial deposit you call a brain make of this, what, what?"

The letter announces that Cissie Crossgarters will be rolling round to see jolly old Holmes; it is all dashed rotten and pretty thick, but when Holmes has splashed a little soda into his glass of cocaine, he heaves himself out of his chair and trickles out with her. "What ho!" says Bertie Watson when Holmes returns. Everything is top-hole and the chappie Holmes anounces that Cissie and he are engaged to be married.[59]

Before, during, and after the First World War there were a number of articles that nurtured the legends surrounding Sherlock Holmes. One was an interview in the *Daily Mail* on 8 October 1904, "The Last of Sherlock Holmes", in which Doyle spoke of Holmes's retirement. "For a long time," he said, "he has nursed the idea of a country life with its simple delights. He will take a little place and will go in for bee-keeping."[60] Then in November 1912 there was an article by A. St. John Adcock in the London *Bookman* (and later in the American *Strand*) which included some of the letters that had been sent to Holmes at the time of his retirement and described the visitors who had tried to call on him in Baker Street. Further particulars were given by Doyle in his article "Some Personalia About Mr. Sherlock Holmes" in the December 1917 *Strand*, and again in a speech to the Stoll Convention Dinner in 1921, and also in his autobiography, written a few years later.

But the great age of Sherlockian scholarship began in earnest only at the end of 1926, when Doyle was writing the last of the stories. It was heralded by John Gore, the "Old Stager" of the *Sphere*, who on 6 November "read Ichabod on the page" and criticised Holmes's creator for spoiling such a cherished character. Doyle replied at once, and the criticism led him to suggest to the editor of the *Strand Magazine* that there should be a competition to test the widely held belief that the later stories were inferior to the earlier ones. The comments introducing the competition, which later served as an introduction to *The Casebook of Sherlock Holmes*, and the reasons for Doyle's own choice, echoed and answered the points made by Gore. Doyle also made it clear that he would not write any further stories about Sherlock Holmes.

Gore's two articles in the *Sphere* were followed by a Fourth Leader in *The Times* on 10 December 1926 which paid tribute to Sherlock Holmes, Doyle, and the *Strand*, and which, perhaps, led others to consider the remarkable qualities that had so endeared Holmes to his readers. Certainly, with the publication of *The Casebook* in June, the majority of the critics looked back over the whole of Holme's career, rather than forward to other adventures yet untold. The Great Detective had ceased to be an ageing figure surrounded by a rising generation of younger detectives, and had become a man apart whose achievements deserved recognition and whose works deserved the closest study.

The naming of a locomotive was the first step. It was at a meeting of the Traffic Committee of the Metropolitan Railway on 18 March 1927 that it was decided to give names to twenty reconditioned Metropolitan-

Vickers Locomotives. They were to be those of celebrities associated with the part of London and of the suburbs served by the railway. Some of the names put forward were a cause of argument, but "Sherlock Holmes", chosen for No. 8, was never in dispute. Doyle was asked for his permission and gave it readily, admitting that he was greatly honoured. The final list was as follows:

1. John Lyon
2. Oliver Cromwell
3. Sir Ralph Verney
4. Lord Byron
5. John Hampden
6. William Penn
7. Edmund Burke
8. Sherlock Holmes
9. John Milton
10. William Ewart Gladstone
11. George Romney
12. Sarah Siddons
13. Dick Whittington
14. Benjamin Disraeli
15. Wembley 1924
16. Oliver Goldsmith
17. Florence Nightingale
18. Michael Faraday
19. John Wycliffe
20. Sir Christopher Wren

The first nameplates were installed in October 1927 and all were in position by the end of the following year. They were cast in bronze and flanked by ornamental pieces. The Sherlock Holmes ran on the line from Baker Street to Rickmansworth, and it continued to do so until September 1946, when the plates were removed and the engine, previously vermilion, was painted a wartime grey.

The loss of the plates passed unnoticed in the aftermath of war, but with the new interest aroused by the Sherlock Holmes Exhibition in 1951, many clamoured for their reinstatement. Some went further, such as G. Cullis, who in a letter to the Marylebone Public Library suggested that British Railways might be induced to name one of their newest 7,000 h.p. "Pacific Class" engines after the detective, but his main concern was to see the old plates restored.[61] His letter was passed on to the London Transport Executive. But the Public Relations Officer regretted that the plates had been removed for salvage and were not available; London Transport also felt that it had nothing of sufficient dignity and that the old locomotives were now "unsuited for the distinction of individual names".[62] However, two years later, new nameplates were supplied by the Sherlock Holmes Society of London and these were officially reinstated on 5 October 1953. The Sherlock Holmes then hauled passengers in and out of Baker Street on the Aylesbury line until 22 January 1962, when the engine was withdrawn from service. The nameplates were returned to the Society at a dinner on 14 November, and the train, which for so many years had borne Holmes's name and had travelled over a million miles, went to the breaker's yard.

"Book about Watson," wrote Doyle in a letter on 3 July 1928 to his American publisher, George H. Doran, "I fear not. To solemnly discard Holmes in public and then write a book which must indirectly be about him would never do."[63] Doran believed that a biography of Dr. Watson would provide Doyle with a legitimate vehicle for further stories. "I was full of the brilliance of my plan," he said in his autobiography when describing how he had visited Doyle at the Psychic Bookshop in Westminster, "not only for Doyle, but for some fortunate editor and for myself as publisher. I unfolded it as best I could between the interruptions of friends and purchasers. Doyle listened with a mild receptivity. The idea was good, the best he had heard for the revival of Sherlock Holmes, but really he could not take himself away from his psychic work." Doran felt however that it was just as well, for had it been written "it is almost certain that Doyle would have made Watson psychic".[64]

Interest in the details of Watson's life was then acute and it was made more so by the re-publication of Ronald Knox's "Studies in the Literature of Sherlock Holmes" in his *Essays in Satire*. "Any studies in Sherlock Holmes," he said at the start of his famous paper, "must be, first and foremost, studies in Dr. Watson." First, there was the question of the authenticity of the stories. Although Knox had learnt from Doyle himself that the use of the name "James" by Watson's wife had been an editorial slip, it had led Professor Backnecke to propose the theory of the proto- and the deutero-Watsons; the second being responsible for *A Study in Scarlet*, "The *Gloria Scott*", and the stories in *The Return*; and for other reasons, M. Piff-Pouf had dismissed "The Final Problem" as a fake. But Knox believed all were written by Watson, though the stories in *The Return* were spurious travesties of the genuine cycle. The evidence against those stories was threefold: the methods and character of Holmes were different, he was discourteous and he split infinitives; secondly, the narratives contained many impossibilities, such as the bicycle in "The Priory School" (though Doyle, in a letter to Knox, insisted that Holmes's deduction was possible); and finally, there were serious inconsistencies. The whole of the Moriarty gang was secured at the time of "The Final Problem" and yet Colonel Sebastian Moran was at large in "The Empty House"; or again, Moriarty's brother was called James in "The Empty House", while "The Final Problem" proved that it was the name of the Professor himself. Knox next considered the problem of the chronology of the stories, which was to become the main subject of debate; then he examined the construction and listed the eleven parts, some or all of which, according to Ratzegger, were to be found within them. These were the *prooimion, exegesis kata ton dikonta, ichneusis, anaskeue,* first *promenusis,* second *promenusis, exeteasis, anagnorisis,* second *exegesis, metamenusis,* and *epilogos.* Following this there was a consideration of the literary affinities with Gaboriau, Poe, Wilkie Collins, the *Dialogues* of Plato, and the Greek drama. Scotland Yard, he said, filled the role of the Sophists; Holmes was the Socratic figure, and Watson served as the chorus. Finally he dealt with Holmes's character and gave examples of the distinctive epigram that, he said, was known as the "Sherlockismus". He ended by saying:

> To write fully on this subject would need two terms' lectures at least. Some time, when leisure and enterprise allow, I hope to deliver them. Meanwhile, I have thrown out these hints, drawn these outlines of a possible mode of treatment. You know my methods, Watson: Apply them.[65]

The first to do so was S. C. Roberts in "A Note on the Watson Problem", written for the *Cambridge Review* of 25 January 1929.[66] Roberts acknowledged that the studies by Knocksius were a suitable *prolegomenon* to *das Watsoniche-chronologieproblem,* but asserted that his survey was superficial and some of his dates inaccurate. Also, as it had been written in 1911, it was in need of revision. One particular error was Knox's suggestion that the colour of Holmes's dressing-gown could be used as a "test of canonicity", in that the real garment was described in "The Man with the Twisted Lip" as being blue, while that in "The Empty House" was mouse-coloured, for, as Robert said, in "The Blue Carbuncle" it was purple! But the major point he made was the one that had not been faced either by Keibosch or by Pauvremütte, even though it was the area most in need of elucidation. This was the date of Watson's marriage. He ended by suggesting that the two final collections of stories were likely to have been the work of a deutero- or even a trito-Watson.

Another major discovery was revealed by A. G. Macdonell in the *New Statesman* on 5 October 1929; this was "The Truth about Professor Moriarty". Macdonell had been collecting statistics of the Period of Maximum Mental Activity of certain selected figures in history, of whom Holmes was one, when he realised that there was a previously unrecorded Period of Mental Stagnation. Holmes had fallen sick in 1887 and, thereafter, his powers were in decline. He disappeared in 1891 and returned in 1894. It was a period of Minimum Intellectual Activity. Suddenly, the truth struck him. Holmes had invented Moriarty to conceal the fact that he had been forced to take a rest cure! All the details given in "The Final Problem" were invented. And the proof, of course, if any were needed, was to be found in *The Valley of Fear*. "You told me once, Mr. Holmes," says the Inspector, "that you had never met Professor Moriarty." Holmes agrees. "I need hardly remind experts in the Holmes Saga," Macdonell added, "that the Valley of Fear occurred in 1895, four years after the mythical episode at the Reichenbach Falls."[67]

Desmond MacCarthy felt that it was a biographical age and therefore turned his attention to the problem of how he would write the life of "the most representative Englishman of the latter half of the nineteenth century". The result was a brilliant "Miniature Biography" of Dr. Watson, which was broadcast on 4 December 1929 and published in the *Listener* on 11 December.[68] His major contribution to the subject, he said, would be to fix the date of Watson's marriage. He had not been married in two different years and kept two establishments, as some scholars wildly surmised. The date of his wedding was the autumn of 1887. The fact that Watson seemed to imply in *The Sign of Four* that it was in the autumn of 1888 could be explained away by the emotional confusion he felt at the time (which also led him to prescribe strychnine in large doses as a sedative!) and by the existence of the six pearls belonging to his future wife, Mary Morstan; these had been sent annually since 1882. But those who preferred the 1888 date were quick to point out that one pearl might have been lost or mislaid.

MacCarthy wrote many articles about Holmes, whether as drama critic of the *New Statesmen* or as a reviewer for the *Sunday Times*; he was also the editor of *Life and Letters* and that, too, reflected his interest. In December 1928, there was "An Examination Paper on 'Sherlock Holmes'" by "one of the leading Sherlock Holmes scholars of the day", who was, in fact, R. Ivar Gunn (it was the second such examination that autumn, as *Punch* had, on 31 October 1928, published "A Final Examination-Paper on the Life and Work of Sherlock Holmes", set by Ronald Knox's brother, "Evoe"). Then in February 1930, *Life and Letters* included an essay by S. C. Roberts on Watson's early career, the "Prolegomenon to the Life of Dr. Watson", one which became widely known when it was included in the *Essays of the Year* anthology for 1929–30. It was followed by a second essay dealing with the later years of Watson's life, and Christopher Morley's brother, Frank, arranged for both to appear as one of Faber's *Criterion Miscellanies*. It was soon accepted as the "standard biography", and is best known for two theories, the first concerning Watson's middle name, which Roberts suggested may have been "Henry", after John Henry Newman; and the other concerning the identity of Watson's second wife. He thought she might have been Violet de Merville of "The Illustrious Client".

The first major books between hardcovers appeared in 1932, T. S Blakeney's *Sherlock Holmes: Fact or Fiction?*, which the publisher described as "the first really authoritative biography of this famous detective"; and H. W. Bell's *Sherlock Holmes and Dr. Watson: The Chronology of Their Adventures*, which, by listing all the cases in chronological order, led to the discovery that Watson had been married three times and that there had been three adventures of "The Second Stain". The two books, in their turn, produced a spate of reviews by other scholars. The best known was one headed "Sherlockholmitos" in *The Times Literary Supplement* on 27 October 1932. This took the textual criticism of the canon to its limits with a *Codex Maritimus A* and *B*, with the division of the "so-called" *Study in Scarlet* (it having been titled by a later hand) between the author of C.M.A. and another, an "Americaniser", A, responsible for the U section (the scenes in Utah) and derived from "D.A." (the Destroying Angels of Stevenson's *Dynamiter*); the interweaving by R (the Redactor) of the exploits of "Altamont" and "Lightfoot Jim" was also mentioned and was given as the chief cause of the textual contamination. The article was highly amusing for those who had the patience to read it, and at one point unintentionally so, as the typesetter gave the false "Holmes", not a brother, but a "highly placed butler in the Civil Service".

The "terrifyingly erudite article" in *The Times Literary Supplement* led to a Fourth Leader in *The Times* on 29 October 1932 which marvelled at the innocence of the new critics as they had no ulterior motives in their work. They had not cast ridicule on the "Higher Criticism", nor was their work satirical in intention: "It is only their fun – the single-minded fun of spiritually young Sherlockians at play." Among the reviews, there was "The Watson Problem" by S. C. Roberts, in the *Observer*, and "Sherlockismus" by Desmond MacCarthy, in the *Sunday Times*, both on 30 October; then there was "The Mathematics of Mrs. Watson" by Ronald Knox in the *New Statesman* of 12 November; a series of "Lucubrationes Watsonianae", which were published in the *Oxford Magazine* between 3 November and 1 December (and which proved that Holmes had been an alcoholic); and, on 11 November, the *Cambridge Review* had "A Plea for a More Liberal Spirit in the Criticism of the Sherlock Holmes Canon". "Looking back," said S. C. Roberts when discussing the work of Blakeney and Bell, "I am amazed at the number of columns which editors allotted to reviews of these two books."[69]

Knox ended his review in the *New Statesman* with the words of the veteran Sauwosch: "It is not to be feared that the Holmes-problem is a mine which suffers from a diminishing returns law. Watson has this genius, that, however deeply we probe his work, he has always fresh inconsistencies to reveal, which will be the basis of fresh theories."[70] And proof of this came in 1933 with the publication of Vincent Starrett's *The Private Life of Sherlock Holmes*, and in 1934 with the volume of essays edited by H. W. Bell called *Baker Street Studies*, to which many of the leading Sherlockian scholars contributed.

One of those who did so was Dorothy L. Sayers. She had been intrigued by Bell's *Chronology* and had written him a series of letters in 1932 and 1933 explaining her theories about the dates in "The Red-Headed League" and other canonical problems. He persuaded her to contribute an essay proving, as she hoped, that Holmes had been at Cambridge. Later she also set down her views on the "Red-Headed League" dates and on Watson's Christian name. The latter she thought may have been "Hamish" as that was the Scottish for "James". There was one further essay on Dr. Watson as a widower. All of these were collected in *Unpopular Opinions* in 1946, and it was in the foreword to the book that she gave her now famous description of the "game of applying the methods of the 'Higher Criticism' to the Sherlock Holmes canon": "The rule of the game is that it must be played as solemnly as a county cricket match at Lord's: the slightest touch of extravagance or burlesque ruins the atmosphere."[71] Many people have agreed with her, but doubts had also been expressed in some quarters as to whether such scholarship was not self-defeating.

"I perused this work of careful research and wild conjecture with mixed feelings: resentment, envy, uneasiness," said Desmond Mac-Carthy when reviewing *Baker Street Studies* in the *Sunday Times*.[72] Resentment because his own work had been mentioned only once; envy because of the thoroughness of the authors, which made his own conjectures appear perfunctory; and uneasiness because there were signs that public patience on the subject was nearly exhausted. His own enthusiasm remained strong and he, indeed, argued the case for Holmes having been at Trinity, but he could appreciate the arguments, put forward by Cyril Connolly in a review of Starrett's book in the *New Statesman* called "Mother Watson",[73] that such "diversions of scholarship" and escapist musings could be overdone. The same point was made by G. K. Chesterton in *G. K.'s Weekly* on 21 February 1935 in an article headed "Sherlock Holmes The God". He recalled how greatly amused he had been by Ronald Knox's satire, which was both solemn and funny:

But now we may note the appearance of new books which mark the next stage. These books are not only solemn but solid. They are, like very learned reports on purely scientific questions, almost avowedly dull. They also may be written for fun; but they are not funny. They cross-examine poor Watson about every detail of date and weather and topography and time-table, like hanging judges investigating a real murder. They refute him with tables of figures no more amusing than columns in a ledger. They may not really regard it as real history, but they take as much trouble as the greatest scholar would take about real history, unrewarded by a smile. It may be a grim joke. But I think myself it is getting beyond a joke. The hobby is hardening into a delusion. Not once is there is a glance at the human and hasty way in which the stories were written; not once even an admission that they were written. The real inference is that Sherlock Holmes really existed and that Conan Doyle never existed. If posterity only reads these latter books, it will certainly suppose them to be serious. It will imagine that Sherlock Holmes was a man. But he was not; he was only a god.[74]

Other works during the 1930s were plentiful. Dr. Maurice Campbell gave talks at Bart's and at Guy's Hospital which were published in pamphlet form in 1935 as *Sherlock Holmes and Dr. Watson; A Medical Digression*;[75] there was an article in the London *Bookman* of May 1934 by Eustace Portugal, "The Holmes–Moriarty Duel", which suggested that Moriarty had taken the place of Holmes; there was J. Alan Rannie's article in the *Railway Magazine* of May 1935 on "The Railway Journeys of Mr. Sherlock Holmes"; and on 26 December 1936, an "occasional correspondent" (G. F. McCleary) contributed a paper to the *Lancet* answering the question "Was Sherlock Holmes a Drug Addict?" (and suggesting that he was not). There were other articles in America of no less interest, some of which contained expressions that have become part of the folklore of the Sherlock Holmes "cult". The most famous of these is Vincent Starrett's statement first made in the New York *Bookman* in December 1932 in his article "The Private Life of Sherlock Holmes" (which is included in, and provided the name for, his famous book). There could be no grave for Sherlock Holmes or Dr. Watson, he said, they would forever reside at Baker Street as they had always done: "So they still live for all that love them well; in a romantic chamber of the heart, in a nostalgic country of the mind, where it is always 1895."[76] And he made the same point again at the end of his verses on "221b":

Here, though the world explode, these two survive,
And it is always eighteen ninety-five.[77]

Another famous expression that also originated in the *Bookman* is to be found in Edmund Pearson's article, "Sherlock Holmes among the Illustrators", in which he refers to Arthur I. Keller's portrayal of Dr. Watson in the frontispiece picture for the American edition of *The Valley of Fear* as that of a *boobus Britannicus* or "near-moron"![78] There were also other important studies, of which the most notable is, perhaps, Walter Klinefelter's oddly named *Ex Libris: A. Conan Doyle* of 1938, but the most significant development was the foundation in 1934 of Sherlock Holmes societies in London and in New York.

THE SHERLOCK HOLMES SOCIETY

The decision to form a Sherlock Holmes Society was taken early in 1934 and during April there were letters in the papers seeking out members. The first dinner, however, was largely by invitation and was held on Derby Day, 6 June, at Canuto's Restaurant in Baker Street. It was a great success, thanks to the presence of many eminent Sherlockians, and a full account of it, which is included in this book, was given by R. Ivar Gunn in an article for the *British Medical Journal*. The moving spirit behind the society's formation and its self-appointed Honorary Secretary was A.G. Macdonell, while the President was Canon "Dick" Sheppard.

Further dinners were held in 1935 and 1936, after which members received a laconic postcard informing them: "The Sherlock Holmes Society, like the Red-Headed League, is dissolved." Other than Gunn's article, few relics survive, but one of the later dinners was described by E. C. Bentley in his autobiography, *Those Days*:

I remember well the debate initiated by Sir Eric Maclagan, the Director of the Victoria and Albert Museum, who delivered a comprehensive attack on the reputation of Watson as a chronicler. In one place Watson had made an important point of "a dark-blue eggshell Ming saucer": whereas, said Sir Eric, there is no dark-blue Ming. Again, Holmes had spoken of the Blue Carbuncle (according to Watson) in moralising vein as follows: "There have been two murders, a vitriol-throwing, a suicide, and several robberies brought about for the sake of this forty-grain weight of crystallised charcoal.' Yet Holmes, whose knowledge of chemistry was "profound", could never (Sir Eric argued) have said this of a kind of gem which contains no carbon at all. In reply, the suggestion that Watson was to blame for this tendency to the adornment of his facts was hotly contested by Canon J. K. Mozley, who lent the weight of his immense learning to a comparison of Watson with the Venerable Bede, and included the Doctor as a historian in the school of Gibbon and Macaulay. These symposia were fine fun: joy in the magnificence of the saga underlay it all.[79]

THE BAKER STREET IRREGULARS, OF NEW YORK

Frank Morley provided a link between the English and American Sherlockians, but it was his brother, Christopher, who was the moving spirit behind the plans to create an American society dedicated to Sherlock Holmes. Christopher Morley was a columnist on the *Saturday Review of Literature*, and he had written for it a brilliant article at the time of Doyle's death, "In Memoriam: Sherlock Holmes" (which serves as the introduction to the Doubleday omnibus volume, and thus for many of the subsequent new editions). On 6 January 1934, there was a meeting at which the proposal for the Baker Street Irregulars was put forward. The date was Holmes's "birthday", or at least was to become established as the traditional date. The evidence for this belief comes from the opening of *The Valley of Fear*, where Holmes is discovered leaning on his hand with his untasted breakfast before him. It was 7 January. It implied a hangover and a hangover implied a party and a party implied a birthday. Corroborative evidence was the fact that Holmes twice quoted from *Twelfth Night* (unshakable as this evidence may seem, a few people did point out that it may have been Watson's birthday!).

The Baker Street Irregulars were first mentioned in the *Saturday Review* on 27 January 1934, and on 17 February the paper published the famous Constitution and Buy Laws drawn up by Elmer Davis. The purpose of the society was the "study of the Sacred Writings"; the officers would be called a Gasogene (President); Tantalus (Secretary), and a Commissionaire (Treasurer). The fourth buy law, which followed those about the annual meeting and the "canonical toasts", was that "All other business shall be left for the monthly meeting"; the fifth was: "There shall be no monthly meeting." There was also the threat of an examination, but it was never rigidly adhered to. Many of the most knowledgeable did, however, attempt to solve Frank Morley's fiendishly hard Sherlock Holmes crossword which appeared in the *Saturday Review* on 13 May 1934 as membership of the Society was offered as a prize for those sending in correct solutions.

The first official meeting was held on 5 June and the first annual dinner on 7 December 1934. Frederic Dorr Steele was one of the guests

39

at the dinner and, according to Alexander Woollcott, who was also present and who described the occasion for the *New Yorker* of 29 December 1934, he wept "softly into his soufflé" at the sight of the other star guest, the actor William Gillette.[80] The second dinner was on 6 January 1936 and that was the first attended by Edgar W. Smith, a Vice-President of General Motors, who was to ensure the continuing success of the Society and who in 1946 became the first editor of the irregular quarterly of Sherlockiana, the *Baker Street Journal*. He also edited a number of anthologies, of which the best known is *Profile by Gaslight* of 1944.

While Sherlockian studies flourished in America, England was being drawn into the war. The death of Canon Sheppard in 1937 had marked the end of the Sherlock Holmes Society, and Sherlockians received a further blow when A. G. Macdonell was killed in an air raid on 16 January 1941. A year earlier, during the winter of 1939, he had visited the neutral Scandinavian countries and at the suggestion of the British Council had lectured on Sherlock Holmes. "Ce n'est pas la guerre," was the opinion of the audience, who were more accustomed to German propaganda, "mais c'est magnifique."[81]

Anthony Boucher's mystery story, *The Case of the Baker Street Irregulars*, was published in 1940. It reprinted the Constitution and Buy Laws and also had a memorable dedication. "All characters portrayed or referred to in this novel are fictitious," it said, "with the exception of Sherlock Holmes, to whom this book is dedicated."[82] The following year, H. F. Heard published his story, *A Taste for Honey*, which in certain editions featured Mr. Mycroft, a thinly disguised portrait of the elderly Sherlock Holmes. But the most memorable event was the B.S.I. Dinner on 31 January 1941 at which Rex Stout made a famous speech announcing his discovery that Watson was a woman. The suggestion received widespread publicity and one of the reporters responsible was H. Allen Smith of the New York *World-Telegram*. He first asked Stout about Christopher Morley's theory that Watson was American. "That is pure bosh," replied the author. "This Watson woman was certainly not an American." With that settled, he spoke of his theory: "I have been working out this theory for years. In the daytime I do my regular work with Nero Wolfe, and at night I work on this theory. It is such a complex theory that I may ultimately publish a series of books about it – maybe a whole set of books, bigger than the set of Sherlock Holmes."[83] He had by then reached the stage at which it was becoming obvious that Lord Peter Wimsey was the son of Holmes and Watson.

There were at this period a number of other developments. Vincent Starrett edited a volume of essays, *221B: Studies in Sherlock Holmes*, which was published in 1940; and four years later Ellery Queen collected together a representative series of parodies which were published as *The Misadventures of Sherlock Holmes*. There was also a biography of Conan Doyle by Hesketh Pearson, which was published in 1943 and announced the discovery of what was thought to be an unpublished Sherlock Holmes story, "The Case of the Man who was Wanted" (it was published in America in 1948 and in England in 1949, but then shown to be by somebody else). And most significant of all were the films featuring Basil Rathbone as Sherlock Holmes and Nigel Bruce as Dr. Watson.

The Hound of the Baskervilles and *The Adventures of Sherlock Holmes* were both made by Twentieth Century-Fox and released in America in 1939. Holmes's own views on the first were somewhat mixed; he was, according to the account by Dilys Powell in the *Sunday Times* on 9 July 1939, a little worried by the vacuity of the dialogue, the cardboard moor, and the inattention to detail, but his anger was reserved for the suggestion that he might have been trapped in an empty grave. "They dare to suggest that I could be caught by so childish a trick!" he exclaimed. "I'll have them, Watson, I'll have them!"[84] He saw it again at the New Savoy cinema in Glasgow in October and was both amused and annoyed. His report in the *Glasgow Herald* on 24 October 1939 criticised the studio gothic of the moor: the mist "clung about our feet like cotton grass, and the air was full of serenading sounds from unseen Californian bullfrogs", he told Watson.[85] But whatever he thought, the public were delighted by Rathbone, and the twelve Universal films that followed between 1943 and 1946 further endeared him to them, as did a long-running series of radio broadcasts. He was for many, and because of television still is for many, the actor who most closely resembles the great detective.

THE SHERLOCK HOLMES EXHIBITION

In 1949, Michael Hall published the first number of the *London Mystery Magazine*, having chosen 221b Baker Street as its official address, and he did so with the sanction of the Abbey National Building Society, whose offices contained that number. It was a precursor to the next great age of Sherlockian enthusiasm. Further evidence of its growth was afforded by the interest shown in an article by Christopher Morley on "The Baker Street Irregulars" which appeared in the *Sunday Times*. Then came the suggestion, from James Edward Holroyd, that the St. Marylebone Public Library might stage a Sherlock Holmes exhibition as its contribution to the Festival of Britain. "The exhibition would include such things as copies of the original magazines in which the legendary figure appeared," said the report of the Public Libraries Committee of 3 October. "This proposal commends itself to us, and as such an exhibition could be staged without interfering with the normal use of the library, we have given instructions for the requisite arrangements to be made."[86]

The suggestion and proposal were put to the full Council on 26 October. No, said a Labour member, it would be more constructive to show the world how the borough had cleared away its slums; and a Conservative agreed it was a childish idea. The borough should boast about Lord's Cricket Ground, instead. "Holmes looked thoughtful," said the *Daily Graphic*, "when Dr. Watson reported this, and left 221b in a taximeter brougham."[87] The *Evening Standard*[88] pointed out that Americans were unlikely to be over-enthusiastic about a new dustcart, whereas they would travel half-way round the world to see the reality behind a phrase in a book. The *Evening News*[89] accused the councillors of being ungenerous towards the man whose spirit brooded over Baker Street in saturnine splendour; and the *News Chronicle* poured scorn on the "vaunted Cricket Club":

> If the baying of a strange hound is heard in the purlieus of Lord's or a poisoned dart from an Andaman Island blow-pipe strikes down a fast bowler, they will know that Holmes has summoned his old enemies to his cause, for they too, by implication, are included in the insult.[90]

But the most remarkable development was the effect caused by a short announcement in *The Times*: Dr. Watson wrote urging the councillors to reconsider their verdict, and letters followed from Holmes's brother, Inspector Lestrade, Mrs. Hudson, and others who had known the detective. Support was also forthcoming from many distinguished quarters. The Council was hastily reconvened on 31 October and its members, who insisted that they had never actually rejected the suggestion, then gave a firm assurance that the exhibition would go ahead.

Many people had suggested material that would be appropriate and others had offered to loan rare items, The members of Conan Doyle's family would be happy to assist; so too would the members of Sidney Paget's family and the relations of Dr. Joseph Bell. Thus the original, limited conception began to expand. One idea was to move the Junior Library elsewhere and hold the exhibition there, but by November a far better idea had been put forward. This was to hold it at Abbey House. And by the first week in December, this had been arranged. There was to be an area of 1,200 square feet on the first floor cleared for the use of the Library.

By January 1951, the details of the exhibition, the site, dates, and opening hours had been arranged, and £3,500 was set aside by the Council to pay for it. A sum of £500 was to be used for a "tableau of a portion of the sitting-room" at 221b. This was designed by Michael Weight, then well known for his work in the theatre, and was to prove the major attraction. He started working on it in February and had the drawings and a model ready by April. The equipment for the chemistry table was supplied by Dr. W. T. Williams of Bedford College, who also supplied various exhibits illustrating aspects of Holmes's scientific career. Major Hugh Pollard offered to supply a representative selection of guns. "These were collected by Holmes as souvenirs," he said of some of the more exotic examples, "but I have not any great acquaintance with the 'crimes'."[91] Scotland Yard supplied the footprint of a hound, though not as a gigantic as some would have wished; the Science Museum produced samples of the typefaces of different typewriters; there were samples of tobacco ash supplied by a leading tobacconist; and the publishers of Who's Who, A. & C. Black, set up the entry that had for so long been left out of its volumes (though the information it contained, based on one written by Kenneth MacGowan for The Misadventures of Sherlock Holmes, was unreliable). There were manuscripts, original drawings, photographs, film posters and theatre programmes, translations, Sherlockiana, and much else besides. Many items came from collectors, but others were loaned by members of the general public, whose help was sought in a series of letters to the newspapers. "I may be enabled to offer you an old and well-coloured calabash pipe," said one correspondent. "This is, as far as I can remember, the very article so often shown pendant in Holmes's teeth in the early illustrations."[92] The newspapers also offered advice. Surely, said Truth, the Admiralty would be happy to provide a new Secret Naval Treaty and "some prosperous fruit firm could perhaps be persuaded to send along five orange pips".[93] The final choice was made by Charles Tranfield ("Jack") Thorne and he was the person most responsible for the success of the exhibition.

On 21 May 1951, the Press was called to the Official Opening, at which Jean and Denis Conan Doyle replied to a lacklustre speech from the Mayor; then on 22 May the doors opened to the general public. By the time the exhibition closed on 22 September there had been 54,972 admissions. Some visitors came many times and for those who felt unable to keep away there was a season ticket at 5/-. There was also a well-printed catalogue ready at the beginning of July which sold some

5,000 copies during the exhibition, and which was later reprinted both in an ordinary and in a limited edition.

Interest in Sherlock Holmes during 1951 was unprecedented and the exhibition featured again and again in the gossip columns. There was the question of the authenticity of the music played on the barrel organ; there was a Japanese magazine that had been inadvertently opened at an advertisement for tooth-paste; there was the tobacco tin for which Michael Weight had had labels specially printed saying "Bradley's of Oxford Street, W.1", only to have it pointed out that the London district "W.1" had not existed before 1920; again, there was the problem of Watson's stethoscope, of whether crumpets were or were not in season, and there were suggestions for the reconstruction of the room to be saved by being placed in the London Museum (then at Kensington Palace). Best of all were the comments overheard and the confusion that existed in certain quarters. At the Press preview, a few of the photographers were unable to work out which of the items had actually belonged to Holmes and which had not (for some of the furniture supplied by the Times Furnishing Company was obviously modern). When local opinion was canvassed in St. Marylebone, a Mrs. A. Johnson of Balcomb Street thought she could recall a Mr. Holmes (or, possibly, a Mr. Hunter) who had an office in Baker Street, though she thought he was a fortune-teller by profession. An elderly lady told the commissionaire at Abbey House that Sherlock Holmes had extracted four of her teeth when she was a little girl, and another had been to school with him. An elderly gentleman, on the other hand, cherished the memory of a cricket match in which he and Holmes had both played for the M.C.C.

The best and fullest description of the exhibition was given by Mollie Panter-Downes in her London letter, "A Reporter at Large", in the *New Yorker* of 7 July 1951. Among other things, she learnt that Sherlock Holmes had himself visited the display and, according to the staff who had seen him, had looked well preserved and erect. She had expert guides and therefore, of course, understood the significances of the small details, such as a sign that directed visitors up "seventeen plus six" stairs. Others were less fortunate and none more so than the artist of the *Perth Daily News*,[94] who drew the exterior of 221b with seventeen stone steps leading up from the street to the front door!

Those who had offered to help with the Sherlock Holmes Exhibition were soon agreed that the time had come to revive the Sherlock Holmes Society, and after informal discussions a meeting was held at Marylebone Town Hall on 18 April 1951. Then on 17 July, the members met at the Victoria and Albert Museum, where S. C. Roberts was to give a talk on Sherlock Holmes, and he was installed as President. A number of those invited to join, such as Gerald Kelly and Maurice Campbell, had been members of the original society, while others had proved themselves eminent in the field by arranging the exhibition, by forwarding letters from Watson and Mrs. Hudson to *The Times*, or by other means; and one, at least, had actually seen the great detective. Mrs. Wynne-Jones, when applying for membership, explained that her interest dated back to her childhood when she used to stay at Eastbourne. "An elderly gentleman," she said, "attending to some hives was pointed out to me as Sherlock Holmes by my father, though how he recognised him in a bee-hat I do not know!"[95] R. Ivar Gunn, another of the original members, was Chairman and also author of the Society's constitution. Other early members included Gavin Brend and James Edward Holroyd.

The first issue of the *Sherlock Holmes Journal* appeared in May 1952, and four years later, under the editorship of the Marquis of Donegall, it became a well-printed, well-illustrated, and eminently readable magazine. The Society amuses itself with river trips in search of the Agra treasure, visits to Baker Street, Dartmoor, and other such locations; it has regular annual dinners, film evenings, lectures and discussions. It also produces its own Christmas cards and has its own tie. Its finest hour came in the Spring of 1968 when there was a pilgrimage to Switzerland during which the scenes at the Reichenbach Falls were re-enacted.

Although the Society provided the new nameplates for the Sherlock Holmes locomotive, other people were responsible for the memorial tablets that had suddenly become fashionable. In 1952, one was placed at the Reichenbach Falls. Then, the following year, one was erected outside the Criterion Bar in Piccadilly Circus – or, as it then was, Forte's Puritan Maid Cafeteria. It was to commemorate the meeting with Stamford which had led to the introduction between Watson and Sherlock Holmes. It was the idea of Richard Hughes, the "Chief Banto" of the Baritsu Chapter of the Baker Street Irregulars, a society he had founded in 1948 while serving as a foreign correspondent in occupied

Tokyo. His original plan had been to erect a plaque at Bart's to mark the spot where Holmes and Watson first met, but this had been vetoed by the authorities, so he chose the alternative site. Work started at the end of 1951 and an expensive circular bronze plaque was prepared by J. Dixon & Sons of Hatton Garden with enamel lettering stating that it commemorated "the historic meeting at this hotel on 1 January 1881". Unfortunately the exact date was not known, nor was the chosen site within a hotel, so the plaque was turned over and new words were painted on the reverse, this time commemorating "the historic meeting early in 1881 at the original Criterion long bar". Considerable publicity surrounded the unveiling on 3 January 1953, at which Fabian of the Yard was present, and it again made the news three years later following its theft on Derby Day. Its whereabouts remained a mystery until 1961, when it was discovered in an empty house in the suburbs and given to the Sherlock Holmes Society. They had custody of it until 9 January 1978, when it was returned to the Forte Group. It was then placed on an inside wall of the Quality Inn at Piccadilly Circus, where it was soon joined by a second plaque commemorating the centenary of the famous encounter. For a few years all was well, but in 1984 the restaurant was closed for restoration. When it reopened on 6 July of that year, as the Criterion Brasserie, only one plaque remained, the original one having again disappeared. Its present whereabouts remain a mystery, though a replacement has been promised.

"It was sad and shameful," said Adrian Griffith when referring to the Sherlock Holmes Exhibition in an article for the December 1951 issue of the hospital magazine, "that St. Bartholomew's Hospital did not provide a single relic."[96] Shameful, too, had been the initial refusal of the authorities to allow a plaque to be raised near the spot where Watson first met Holmes. But they were soon persuaded to change their minds and on 21 January 1954 made ample amends when Sir George Aylwen invited a group of Sherlockian experts to witness the unveiling of a handsome bronze plaque. It recalls the historic occasion on which Sherlock Holmes first greeted Dr. Watson with the words: "You have been in Afghanistan, I perceive." This, at least, may still be seen. It is above the fireplace of the caretaker's office, which is situated near the gallery entrance to the hospital's pathology musuem. The curious visitor will also be shown a Victorian lab stool which was subsequently discovered and has the name of Sherlock Holmes inscribed upon it in poker-work with the date, November 1878. Needless to say, no evidence has yet been found to suggest that it is not the work of the great detective himself.

The proliferation of Sherlockian plaques in the 1950s led J. B.

Boothroyd, writing in *Punch*, to say of the "plaqueteers": "Before very long, when the thing catches on, and equipment can be bought at mass-production prices from the Holmes & Watson Souvenir Plaque & Novelty Company (1954), Limited, there won't be a building in London unrecognised. In the world, you might say."[97] For Trincomalee, where the Atkinson brothers came from, was a promising site; somewhere in Sumatra there would be the grave of the Giant Rat awaiting its memorial; the "reigning house" of Holland would deserve one; and memories of the Trepoff case were no doubt still green in Odessa. But, in fact, though other plaques have been erected – and there is continual talk of a memorial at Maiwand – their number is less than some people would wish. The most essential, the blue plaque for the house in Baker Street where Holmes and Watson lived has never been erected. A plaque was placed in Baker Street in 1985 on the building whose number is now 221, but the argument as to the correct location has in no way abated and only a few would agree that this is the site of the famous rooms.

221B BAKER STREET

In his autobiography, Doyle said of 221b Baker Street: "Many have asked me which house it is, but that is a point which for excellent reasons I will not decide." Nor is it easy for others to do so, as the evidence found in the stories is inconclusive. But a visit to Baker Street with the intention of solving the problem has long been a national, even an international, pastime. The most famous early visitors were a group of French schoolboys whose one ambition was to see the house where Sherlock Holmes lived. Doyle mentioned them in an interview in 1912 and again on subsequent occasions, but he never disclosed whether their wish had been granted.

Another visitor, and one who was clearly disillusioned by what he found, was Karel Capek. In the section on "London Streets" in his *Letters from England* of 1925, he says:

Before I forget: of course, I went to look at Baker Street, but I came back terribly disappointed. There is not the slightest trace of Sherlock Holmes there: it is a business thoroughfare of unexampled respectability, which serves no higher purpose than to lead to Regent's Park, which, after a long endeavour, it almost manages to achieve. If we also briefly touch upon its underground station, we have exhausted everything, including our patience.[98]

Those who have high expectations are bound to be disappointed, but curiosity remains strong and many people have been asked to point out the house. Arthur Croxton, for example, in his autobiography, *Crowded Nights – and Days*, of 1931, described how he had done so:

> Only the other day, when on a motor bus passing along Baker Street, I was earnestly asked by an American tourist to point out the house in which Dr. Watson and Sherlock Holmes lived. To send him away happy I had to direct his attention to one of the few early Victorian houses left in the street. No amount of persuasion would have convinced him that Sherlock Holmes was purely a figure of fiction.[99]

Or again, in 1933, when Basil Mitchell's play, *The Holmeses of Baker Street*, focussed attention on the problem, the "Londoner's Diary" of the *Evening Standard* described the "Pilgrims of Baker Street" thus:

> I was talking to some American friends during one of the intervals of *The Holmeses of Baker Street* last night. That afternoon they had walked up and down Baker Street in an endeavour to "locate" Sherlock Holmes's rooms, for Conan Doyle gives the actual street number.
> "Many Americans make this pilgrimage," I was told, "just as they go to the inn where Sam Weller cleaned the boots and to Mr. Pickwick's bedroom in the hotel at Ipswich."[100]

Perhaps the most amusing anecdotes of all concerned the American G.I.'s during the war, whose knowledge of London was in many cases limited to the single fact that Sherlock Holmes had lived there. And there is a story of a Canadian soldier who was being shown the historic sites of Westminster. When the guide pointed out Downing Street, he is reputed to have said: "Ah, yes. I know . . . Sherlock Holmes!"

At the time of Holmes's residence, the present Baker Street was divided into three sections: Baker Street to the south, York Place in the centre, and Upper Baker Street beyond the Marylebone Road. These were each numbered separately, up the east side and down the west. Baker Street went from 1 to 43, 44 to 85; York Place, 1 to 21, 22 to 40; and Upper Baker Street from 1 to 26, 27 to 54. This remained so until July 1920, when the London County Council issued a renumbering order which took effect on 1 January 1921. York Place was abolished and new numbers were allocated to both streets, the even numbers alternating with the odd ones, thus 2 to 134 up the east side, and 5 to 133 up the west. Upper Baker Street was incorporated into Baker Street on 28 March 1930 and was also renumbered, 188 to 236 on the east, and 185 to 247 on the west. This created a real postal address at 221 Baker Street on the site of what had been 41 or 42 Upper Baker Street. The Victorian houses, however, had by then been demolished to make way for the Abbey Road Building Society's offices, which had been opened in June 1927. Further houses to the north were demolished in November 1930 to make way for Abbey House, which opened on 18 March 1932.

In the summer of 1921, just after York Place had been renamed, Dr. Gray Chandler Briggs, of St. Louis, attempted to locate the house and found to his surprise that Camden House, which is given as the name of the "Empty House", did exist. It was then, as now, 118 (formerly 13 York Place), while the house opposite was 111 (30 York Place). Briggs revealed his discovery to Frederic Dorr Steele in a letter dated 30 October 1921. He said:

> It may be of interest to you to learn that, for the sake of accuracy, I "mapped" Baker Street, checking every house on the street. In the "Adventure of the Empty House" the description of this old pile is definite. It is approached by turning into an alley or passage which is "narrow"; going through a wooden gate, through a yard, through a straight hall which extends to a front door of solid wood but having a transom of glass semi-circular and fanned or ribbed. This house Doyle refers to in this way: "We are in Camden House which stands *opposite* our own old quarters."
>
> There is only one house on the whole of Baker Street which answers this description. It has a rear entrance of wood reached by going into a blind alley. I saw the long straight hall extending clear through the house. And when I told Sir Arthur that the sign "Camden House" was over the door he was amazed.[101]

Steele quoted the letter in an article for the William Gillette Souvenir Programme of 1929 and included the map Briggs had drawn and his photograph of 111 Baker Street. He also visited the house when he was in London in May 1931. "I spent a pleasant evening following the ardent Doctor's footsteps," he wrote in an article for the *New Yorker*, "and can report that, save for a new arc light near the 'kerb', the premises remained as he described them."[102] Briggs's theory was also given in Vincent Starrett's *The Private Life of Sherlock Holmes* in 1933, with a further photograph showing Camden House.

Working from the assumption that Camden House is the "Empty House", others have preferred 109 (28 York Place), next to 111, as the house where Holmes lived. One was Ernest H. Short, the theatre critic, whose findings were published in the *Baker Street Journal* in 1949; another was James Edward Holroyd, who discussed the problem in an article for the Summer 1951 *Cornhill Magazine*. But 111 remains the best known site. During the mid 1930s the residents became accustomed to handling mail from Sherlockians who were anxious to discover if there were

49

seventeen steps up to the first floor – as there were – and other details of the interior arrangements. The claim of this stretch of the street was further enhanced following the creation of Sherlock Mews (which runs up from Paddington Street to the side of Bedford House). The suggestion was made at the end of 1936 by Alan J. D. Stonebridge of the Marylebone Public Library and it was included in the L.C.C. Town Planning and Building Regulation Committee's renaming order of January 1937, which took effect on 1 July 1937. York Mews South became Sherlock Mews, and it thus joined Watson Mews and Watson Close, which are both in the neighbourhood. It was named in honour of Sherlock Holmes, though the other two had preceded Dr. Watson by many years – the first being the name of the builder who leased the land in the 1790s and the other being that of Archdeacon John James Watson, who died in 1839.

One other address should also be mentioned. This is 19 York Place, opposite what would now be 121 Baker Street. According to a letter in the *Daily Telegraph* of 24 July 1937 from Commander Poland, this was believed to be the "Empty House". He was, however, referring to the school at Fretherne House and that is at 113 Baker Street (it was not 19, but 29 York Place). As it was almost opposite Camden House, the pupils probably felt that Holmes lived next door, rather than across the road!

By 1939, 111 Baker Street had become established as "the traditional home of Sherlock Holmes", but unfortunately during the war it was twice hit and on the second occasion almost entirely destroyed. It remained as a shell until 1955, when it was rebuilt in the original style. To-day it houses a Post Office and has business premises above. Camden House, however, remains intact and its claim may seem unshakable. The gas lamp outside, which was a little too close, may be dismissed, and the fact that the front room was on the wrong side is immaterial. Even York Place can be explained away, for Baker Street station and Upper Baker Street were both to its north and many of the residents used "Baker Street" as their address so as to avoid confusion, just as Madame Tussaud's uses it to-day even though it is now situated on the Marylebone Road.

Others, however, have disagreed. They would prefer a house in the original section of Baker Street. Their evidence again comes from "The Empty House", where Watson says that he and Holmes emerged into Blandford Street and "turned swiftly down a narrow passage". This, as H. W. Bell noted in 1932,[103] would seem to imply either Kendall Mews (now Kendall Place) to the south, or Blandford Mews (Broadstone Place) to the north. He would not commit himself, but his contemporary, T. S. Blakeney, did so. He opted for a house to the north, No. 49

(originally 63), as this was favoured by local opinion; it meant the "Empty House" was 50 or 52.[104] Gavin Brend in 1951 also chose a house to the north. Having argued in *My Dear Holmes* that it was one of three, either 59, 61, or 63, he settled for 61. "In the unlikely event of the Government of London passing into our hands," he said, "we propose to put up three plaques. That on No. 61 will commemorate Holmes, whilst those on No. 59 and 63 will be allocated respectively to Watson and Mrs. Hudson."[105] More evidence in favour of this theory came on 12 August 1951, when Peter Nelson revealed in the *Empire News* that a friend of his had been told by Conan Doyle that 61 was the house where Holmes lived. The whole of the block, which suffered severe damage during the war, was redeveloped in 1957.

Maurice Campbell, in his "Medical Digression" of 1935,[106] was one of the first to choose a house to the south of Blandford Street. He opted for 27 as this was owned by Hudson Brothers and was a storey higher than its neighbours. In 1947, James T. Hyslop, writing in the *Baker Street Journal*, suggested 19 as that was the residence of Madame Verneau (the Vernets having been Holmes's ancestors).[107] And twelve years later an analysis of the back yards of Baker Street led Bernard Davies to select 31.[108]

In 1960, Harold Morris claimed that it was 21 Baker Street. He did so in his autobiography, *Back View*, which contained an account of the various traditions handed down by his father, Malcolm Morris. He and Conan Doyle both went to Berlin at the end of 1890 to study the Koch tuberculosis cure and it was at Morris's suggestion that Doyle gave up his practice in Southsea and established himself in Upper Wimpole Street as an eye specialist. This involved a visit to Vienna, and the book that Doyle dedicated to Morris, *The Doings of Raffles Haw*, was written there. This much was known from Doyle's own account, but Harold Morris went considerably further. He had been told that his father's watch had provided the idea for the one belonging to Watson's brother, and also that 21 Baker Street, which had belonged to his great-grandfather, had been used as the original of 221b. Doyle had, he said, paid a number of visits to the house before choosing the address and had pored over plans made at the time of its sale in 1840. He described how Doyle had allocated the rooms, thus:

The dining-room on the ground floor is a large room, 23′6″ by 15′, and he turned it into a bed-sitting-room for a City gentleman, because, as my father pointed out, the good Mrs. Hudson could not possibly make a living by letting rooms to Holmes and Watson only and she must have another lodger to make it pay. Conan Doyle

51

dallied with the idea of bringing the City gentleman into one of the adventures, but no suitable occasion arose.

Mrs. Hudson's sitting-room was the room behind the dining-room. Behind that again was a smaller room which was the bedroom of Billy the page, and beyond that again were the kitchen and scullery. The sitting-room we know, and the back drawing-room leading out of it was Holmes's bedroom. Watson's bedroom was the front room on the second floor and the back room was the laboratory and workshop. On the top floor were the bedrooms of the maid and Mrs. Hudson, and a third room on that floor was the lumber room.[109]

Whatever the truth may be, and his imagination almost certainly played a part, Harold Morris provided an excellent addition to the mythology; but he got on dangerous ground by describing the "Empty House" as No. 22, for this showed that he was unaware of the renumbering. His great-grandfather's house would today have been 48, which is on the east side, where the "Empty House" should be. It cannot therefore be claimed as the site of 221b, but some of his arguments remain valid.

All the houses facing the section south of Blandford Street were demolished in the mid 1960s to make way for a new office block. This was used by the Abbey National Building Society as its temporary headquarters while Abbey House was being rebuilt, so that between 1979 and 1984 the letters to Sherlock Holmes were forwarded on from 221 to 27 Baker Street – a fact that would undoubtedly have pleased Maurice Campbell.

The third location is Upper Baker Street and this also has arguments in its favour. During the 1880s it consisted almost entirely of lodging or boarding houses of the type that would have appealed to the young Sherlock Holmes, and there is evidence that Doyle intended it as the original site, for on his manuscript notes for *A Study in Scarlet*, he put: "Lived at 221b Upper Baker Street." These notes were first reproduced in the *Strand Magazine* in 1923 and again on the dustjacket of the American edition of his autobiography and in Vincent Starrett's *The Private Life of Sherlock Holmes*. Attention was drawn to them by Frank Walker in an article, "Sherlock Doesn't Live Here Any More", which appeared in the Autumn 1935 *Abbey Road Journal*. The New York *Bookman* had provided evidence even earlier, in August 1903, when Arthur Bartlett Maurice was described as having visited Holmes and Watson in their rooms at Upper Baker Street. As 221 Baker Street, which is contained in Abbey House, was chosen as the address for the *London Mystery Magazine* and officially called 221b, and as the Abbey

National Building Society allowed the Sherlock Holmes exhibition to be held on their premises and have ever since continued to answer his mail, it has a very solid claim. Not that the arguments put forward by John Shand, the assistant editor of the *London Mystery Magazine*, or by R. Bruce Wycherley, the Managing Director of the Abbey National, necessarily convince the purist.[110]

Doyle often said that Holmes had changed as the stories progressed and that he had become more human. In the same way the Darwinian fundamentalists (those who accept Bernard Darwin's theory of evolution) are quite happy in the belief that Holmes and Watson were in Upper Baker Street in 1881 and in York Place in 1894 and perhaps in Baker Street during some of the intervening years. The number stayed the same, but the house became larger and more comfortable.

Although a few of Mr. Holmes's correspondents are convinced that Abbey House is a museum dedicated to his memory, there were no memorials in Baker Street until the erection of the Abbey House plaque in 1985. But there have often been places named after him. Between 1962 and 1969 there was the Deerstalker Restaurant at 126 Baker Street, though beyond a few designs showing a deer-stalker, footprints, fingerprints, a magnifying glass, and a pipe, it did not excel itself in a Sherlockian way; its specialities, for example, were "Aunt Sarah's Apple Pancake" and "The Mermaid" scampi pancake. Next came My Dear Watson, which opened on 19 March 1970 at 119 Baker Street, and which deserved its title of "The Coffee House of Distinction" as it was in its way very distinguished. The menu included "The Cold Collation, left on the sideboard", "Food for the Baker Street Irregulars", and other such delicacies. There were also a few hot dishes. "At the suggestion of Mycroft Holmes," said the folded table-menu, "and to meet the preferences of visitors from Northern parts, Mrs. Hudson, housekeeper to Mr. Sherlock Holmes, has now arranged to serve two cooked dishes for High Tea daily". As well as the finely printed menu, place mats, and sugar wrappers, there was an attractive ashtray, which was so desirable that Mr. Holmes had advised the proprietors to offer them for sale to prevent their disappearance.

The Sherlock Holmes Hotel also opened in the summer of 1970. This is entered from 108 Baker Street and occupies the whole of the old Bedford House, that is the upper storey of 108 to 114 Baker Street and the large building behind, part of which forms the back of Sherlock Mews. It extends to Chiltern Street, on which there was the main entrance. Some attempt was made to give it character. The Dr. Watson Bar served both a "Dr. Watson" and a "Sherlock Holmes" cocktail; there was a Sherlock Holmes Coffee Shop (later renamed the Ristorante Moriarti!), and there was Moriarty's Den. "Sherlock, London" was its telegram address, and the Management quite properly urged their guests to "find time to settle down with a book and enjoy the immortal stories of Sherlock Holmes"; but "Mrs. Hudson's Gourmet Specialities" proved disappointing, and the designs used on the mats and tableware were of a low standard.

Further down the street, at 96, there was, from 1978 to 1983, the Sherlock Holmes Centa, formerly the Classic Cinema. And beyond the ticket barriers at Baker Street Station there is a pub bearing the name of Moriarty, a successor to the various refreshment rooms, cafés, buffets, and pubs in the station area which if not named after the great detective have at least had pipes and deer-stalkers in evidence. Baker Street Underground is now the main Sherlock Holmes showpiece. Since the end of 1979 there have been large platform murals on both of the Jubilee Line platforms from drawings by Robin Jacques. They show scenes from seven cases: "The Speckled Band", *The Sign of Four*, "The Red-Headed League", "The Lion's Mane", "The Solitary Cyclist", *The Hound of the Baskervilles*, and "Charles Augustus Milverton". Each one has a profile of the detective and a short explanatory note; thus for "The Red-Headed League": "You may earn £4 a week copying out the Encyclopaedia – provided you have red hair. Holmes finds it a 'three-pipe problem', ominous rather than eccentric, and takes Watson and the 'Yard' to the cellars of a London Bank where a shipment of gold has arrived from Paris. They await developments." In addition to these, many of the passages, stairways, and the platforms of the Bakerloo Line have since 1980 been adorned with ceramic tiles designed and made by Michael Douglas and Pamela Moreton; these have red, brown, and black silhouettes in bands or made up into large profiles.

Many of the businesses in Baker Street use Sherlockian motifs, such as the now defunct Baker Street Bookshop which also had one of the nameplates from the Sherlock Holmes locomotive. A little further afield, on the Marylebone Road, there is the site of the short-lived Sherlock's Discotheque, and going the other way there is a pizza house called Baskervilles. Although Madame Tussaud's has been slow to include Holmes and Watson in its Hall of Fame and has still not created an effigy of Professor Moriarty for the Chamber of Horrors, it did for a time have a panorama of *The Hound of the Baskervilles*. This was designed and made by Jane Jackson and showed the pursuit across the moor with Holmes emptying his revolver into the flanks of the hound. It was six feet wide, adorned with luminous paint, and lit by ultra-violet light. It went on display in the Diorama Room in 1961, remained there until 1967 and thereafter was given to the Royal Free Hospital (who subsequently mislaid it during their move to Hampstead).

The one other remarkable tribute to Sherlock Holmes is the pub bearing his name in Northumberland Street, just off Northumberland Avenue. This has a partial reconstruction of the sitting-room at 221b and a number of the original exhibits from the 1951 Sherlock Holmes Exhibition. When the exhibition closed on 22 September 1951, the exhibits were put into store while the Council decided what should be done with them. By the beginning of November an arrangement had been reached with Adrian Conan Doyle. He would buy everything that belonged to the Public Library and, with C. T. Thorne as organiser, would take it to America and exhibit it in as many cities as possible. Early in 1952 it was shipped to New York and it opened at the Plaza Art Galleries on 2 July. Although well received and in some ways better than the original exhibition, there was no great demand for it and it was returned to store. It remained there until 1956, when the suggestion was put forward that the material might be used as the basis for a "theme" pub. This was the idea of H. Douglas Thomson, who was a director of Whitbread's and a life-long admirer of Sherlock Holmes; he was also an authority on detective fiction, having, in 1931, written an excellent book, *Masters of Mystery*. Other theme inns included The Printer's Devil, near Fleet Street, and The Nag's Head in Covent Garden. The Sherlock Holmes, formerly known as the Northumberland Arms, was officially opened on 12 December 1957, and Thomson, who had prepared an informative catalogue of the collection which included choice extracts from the works of eminent Sherlockians, then answered the criticism that it was not in Baker Street by pointing out that it had once formed a part of the Northumberland Hotel, in which Henry Baskerville had stayed.

The pub has become a welcome landmark and, though many of the original drawings and manuscripts have now been replaced by facsimiles, it retains a distinctive atmosphere with its famous inn sign, its smoked-glass windows showing Holmes and Watson and their creator, and its cabinets of relics; while the restaurant or "grill room" upstairs is considerably enhanced by the corner of 221b, which is to be observed through a glass partition by those who are partaking of the "Chicken Sherlock Holmes" or the "Sherlock Holmes Veal Special".

The original sitting-room, designed for the exhibition, has been used again and again as the blueprint for television, stage, and cinema sets (its first use being in 1951 for the Alan Wheatley television series); it was also the basis for a second reconstruction at the Château de Lucens. This château, near Lausanne, was purchased by Adrian Conan Doyle in the early 1960s to serve as a Conan Doyle Foundation, and the new reconstruction opened there, in a cellar, in 1966. It was then a part of the Conan Doyle collection, but is now the sole survivor of it, as the collection has been dispersed and the château has passed into other hands.

While the Sherlock Holmes Exhibition was in progress, plans were afoot for the celebration of the centenary of the great detective's birth, which some felt would occur in 1952, but which most agreed would fall two years later (as Holmes had been described as being sixty in 1914). Early in 1954, therefore, the B.B.C., *The Times*, *John O'London's Weekly*, and other papers celebrated the happy occasion. That year also saw the publication of *The Exploits of Sherlock Holmes*, a series of twelve new stories written by Doyle's youngest son, Adrian, with the help in some cases of Doyle's biographer, John Dickson Carr. In the late fifties and in the sixties there were a number of new Sherlockian studies, also films, such as the Hammer colour production of *The Hound of the Baskervilles*, and new radio and television adaptations with Carleton Hobbs and Douglas Wilmer. There was a short-lived attempt to revive the *Strand Magazine*, and in 1967 came the two volume *Annotated Sherlock Holmes*, compiled by the great detective's biographer, W. S. Baring-Gould.

Billy Wilder's film, *The Private Life of Sherlock Holmes*, was released in 1970; a highly successful revival by the Royal Shakespeare Company of Gillette's *Sherlock Holmes* followed in 1974, and in 1975 there was Nicholas Meyer's *The Seven-Per-Cent Solution* involving Sigmund Freud. But the last decade would need a history to itself, for new books have proliferated and the number has grown to embarrassing proportions. Many of the more recent works, the studies, pastiches, gazetteers, quizzes, encyclopaedias, filmographies, cookery books, bridge manuals, and children's books will be familiar to the dedicated Sherlockian. The diversity and the quantity is such that one must perforce pick and choose. There are memoirs by Mycroft Holmes, by Moriarty, and most recently by Inspector Lestrade. It is now accepted that Holmes solved the Ripper murders – though there are three or more different accounts of how he did so, and he is known to have been involved in the Dreyfus case, and to have had dealings with Bertrand Russell, Theodore Roosevelt, Winston Churchill, Karl Marx, and others.

Although the standard varies, all are written with affection and the original works have not suffered, indeed since the expiry of the copyright many new editions have appeared and a book such as *The Hound of the Baskervilles* sells more copies today than it did when it was first published. Television has also provided interesting sidelights, with programmes such as *The Baker Street Boys* and *Young Sherlock*, and a major series starring Jeremy Brett. In 1985, Steven Spielberg produced a sequel to *Indiana Jones*, known in England as *Young Sherlock Holmes and the Pyramid of Fear*, and earlier the same year the detective had received the ultimate accolade when a mountain in Oklahoma was named after him.

RICHARD LANCELYN GREEN

I. EARLY WRITINGS (1887–1893)

———◆———

THE HAMPSHIRE POST

A Study in Scarlet

Under this title Dr. A. Conan Doyle, one of the Hon. Secretaries of our local Literary and Scientific Society, has composed a Christmas Annual which is certain to attract a host of readers.

Throughout Christendom the great religious festival of the Church is generally regarded as a period of peace and goodwill, of sensual gratification, and of profound benevolence. The seasonable thing to do is to enjoy ourselves, and to promote as far as possible the enjoyment of others. The literary tastes of the public at Christmas, however, are – if we may be permitted to judge of them from the productions of the ingenious gentlemen who cater for their entertainment – as far removed from tranquillity as may be. The weather is usually severe and inclement. The outward man needs to be protected by voluminous wraps; and the inward man fortified by liberal potations. It also seems as if the intellectual man requires to be stimulated and kept alive by repeated literary "eye-openers".

At all events, it is obvious that his reading at the end of the year bears a closer affinity to the acerbities of the Christmas weather than to the neutral greys of the Christmas sentiments. For a brief period love takes a back seat. Some time ago the writers of annuals indulged in premature resurrections. There was scarcely a castle in the country which had not its secret chamber, its horrible tradition, and its wandering ghost. Sometimes the intruder glared at the unfortunate denizen of the haunted apartment from the family portraits; sometimes it rustled past him on the stairs; and at other times it trespassed upon his private meditations and threw him into violent convulsions and cold sweats. Then the fashion changed. Quiet Christmas firesides were harrowed with narratives of ghastly accidents in the mine or on the railway, or of no less heart-rending wrecks at sea. Then we had a season of murder. Every page bubbled over with gore, with frightful revenges, and terrible deaths.

We still have bloody tragedies in plenty related for our Christmas enjoyment, but homicide is now combined with the achievements of the Detective. By these means the mind of the reader is enthralled by a two-fold charm. His interest is excited by the circumstances of the atrocity and the events leading up to it, and his attention is afterwards absorbed in following the marvellous steps by which the detective Nemesis pursues the murderer with the rare instinct of a sleuthhound. Of breathless recitals of this character we know of no more brilliant example than the little story which Dr. Doyle has just given to the world. Even the names of his publishers, Messrs. Ward & Lock, are vividly significant of the slow but certain retribution which dogs the feet of the evil-doer.

Differing from other learned authorities as to the ways of the world, who hold existence is of the iridescent nature of shotted silk, Dr. Doyle maintains that the skein of life would be colourless were it not for the scarlet thread of murder which runs through it. His recital is dominated by a thread of this distinctive colour; and the duty to which he devotes himself "is to unravel it, and isolate it, and expose every inch of it". Now, we think the author is to be cordially congratulated on the character of his murder, and also upon its originality.

In the first place the victim is a worthless scoundrel upon whom it would be a palpable waste of wholesome virtue to expend sympathy. The manner of his taking off is also in the highest degree peculiar. He is a powerful man – and yet there are no apparent signs of a struggle. He is discovered in a pool of blood – and yet it is not his own blood, as he is found to be unwounded. The blood, therefore, must be that of his assassin – and yet, again, the murdered man was unarmed at the time of his death. Here, then, is an abundance of mystery for the imagination to work upon. There is a second murder; but it is of no great importance, except to baffle the professional detectives and to throw a much needed light upon the circumstance attending the other.

We are told on the authority of Dickens that Godwin wrote his *Caleb Williams* backwards. He first involved his hero in a web of difficulties, forming the second volume, and then cast about him for some mode of accounting for what had been done. And in the whimsical account which he gives of the genesis of "The Raven", Poe relates that he first established in his mind the climax, or concluding query – the query in which the word "Nevermore" should involve the utmost conceivable amount of sorrow and despair. "Here then," he says, "the poem may be said to have its beginning – at the end, where all works of art should begin." Now we imagine that Dr. Doyle adopted the same principle of composition. He had a perfect right to perpetrate his murder in any way he chose; and he perpetrated it under such conditions as to harmonise with the train of subsequent events which he had marked out in his mind. In other words, the problem was derived to match the key which he held in his hand. With the exception of the criminal, he was the only spectator of the crime; and having witnessed its commission, nothing would appear easier than for him to keep Holmes upon the scent, and to lead the police upon a wild goose chase.

His detective is a marvellous creation, and the study of him which is given at the beginning is one of the most carefully elaborated portions of the book. As a painstaking delineation of abnormal activity Holmes is far ahead of the heroes of Gaboriau or Boisgobey. He is a profound chemist, though ignorant of the Solar System; and he has, furthermore, discovered a re-agent that is only precipitated by haemoglobin (whatever that may be), which he regards as a sovereign detector of blood stains. He is also possessed of a system of induction from which, by means of accurate and systematic observation which has become an unconscious mental operation, he arrives at startling conclusions. Nevertheless, when he sniffs sardonically at the mention of Gaboriau, calls Dupin an inferior fellow, and describes Lecoq as a miserable bungler, he appears to us to be somewhat ungrateful to his instructors. For Dupin, be it remembered, carried the analysis of perceptions to a science, and gloried in "that moral activity which disentangles". And whereas Sherlock Holmes could tell whence a man came, as well as identify a marine across the street, by an instantaneous process of generalisation, the Dupin of Poe had carried his keenness of observation to the extent of being able to actually read the thoughts of others.

Dr. Doyle's detective is able to tell the height of a murderer from his footprints, but Lecoq was able from the same evidence to describe, not only his height but his age. It is not, however, to "Monsieur Lecoq" that we would compare the *Study in Scarlet*, but to *L'Affaire Lerouge*. Tabaret and Holmes are both amateur detectives, and are only consulted when the professionals get befogged. Their methods of procedure are of the same character. Of the latter Dr. Doyle writes: "So engrossed was he with his occupation that he appeared to have forgotten our presence, for he chattered away to himself under his breath the whole time, keeping up a running fire of exclamations, groans, whistles, and little cries

60

suggestive of encouragement and hope." On the other hand, of Tabaret it is said that "as he came and went, he talked aloud, and gesticulated, apostrophed himself, called himself names, gave little cries of triumph, or encouraged himself". Both detectives discover that their respective quarries were smoking a cigar just previous to the commission of the murders.

It is also to be noted that the two tales have this resemblance in common, that combined with the main story is a second narrative, which, existing at first independently, becomes unexpectedly interwoven with the former. In the *Study in Scarlet*, this subsidiary thread is remarkably well written and intensely exciting. It deals with the awe-inspiring terrorism exerted by Brigham Young and the Council of Four among the community at Salt Lake, and will probably remind the reader of the Mormon incident in Mr. R. L. Stevenson's *Dynamiters*. The diction is vigorous and the local colouring realistic; while the state of suspense to which the author works the mind of the reader in the chapters dealing with the escape of the father and daughter and the pursuit of the fugitives is of the most breathless kind.

We must, however, confess that the Mormon element in the case is somewhat inartistically introduced. It jars upon the autobiographic method which characterises the other portions of the story. The jump from the account of the apprehended murderer being taken to prison in his own cab, to a graphic description of the Salt Lake valley and of the miles of saints on their way to take possession of their heaven-appointed home in 1847, is sudden and startling. Here we lose the acquaintance of John Watson, M.D., who is supposed to relate the story, and are indebted to the pen of the impersonal historian for a knowledge of what may be regarded as the motive of the crime. Had Wilkie Collins been the story-teller he would have thrown the whole of the Mormon incident into the form of a prologue, after which the adventures of the avenger and his detection would have followed as a matter of course. But we see no reason why Dr. Watson should not have been made to narrate the Ferrier episode from "information received" from the prisoner. Hope does indeed make a confession at the police station, but it is a continuation of the intercasted portion – obtained heaven alone knows how – and would be meaningless without it. In fact the prisoner takes it for granted that his auditors are perfectly conversant with his previous history, and begins his confession abruptly: "It doesn't much matter to you why I hated these men." What men? The auditors may know what miscreants are meant; but whether they do or not, there is no reason why Hope should accept their familiarity with the antecedent events as a matter of course.

61

He is inconsequential, too, in more respects than one. When apprehended he made the most strenuous resistance, but when fairly within the toils he regarded the whole affair with the utmost equanimity. His great revenge had been accomplished; and knowing that aortic aneurism had brought him to the brink of the grave, he was confident that he had nothing to apprehend from earthly justice. Would it not have been more dramatically consistent for the man who believed in the holiness of his mission of vengeance and in his approaching end, to have surrendered himself without a struggle?

In the course of the story an inoffensive lieutenant is taken up on suspicion of having committed the murder; and the naval service will probably consider it a slight to the profession that, although his innocence is ultimately demonstrated by the dénouement, the curtain descends upon his unmerited and hopeless imprisonment. And it is to be remarked that, notwithstanding all the amazing powers, cleverness, and acquirements of Sherlock Holmes, the detection of the murderer was owing almost exclusively to the exercise of ordinary common sense, an ingredient which is of far more importance in a detective than those phenomenal qualities with which the novelist is apt to endow his creations. Neither Holmes's chemical discovery, nor his preternatural gift of observation, was of any use to him in his pursuit of the criminal. At the beginning he did a very sensible thing, which no detective of ordinary intelligence would have omitted. He telegraphed to America, where the victim resided, and learned that he was in mortal terror of a man, named Hope, who was on his track. Convinced that the person who committed the deed was the cabman who brought Drebber to the vacant house, that he still pursued the avocation of a cabman, and that, however much he might disguise his appearance, he would, with the strange fatuity of criminals, conscientiously refrain from concealing his name, what more natural than for Holmes to dispatch the street Arabs to hunt him up at the livery stables, and to engage him to convey a portmanteau from the very house where resided the detective whom he knew to be on his trail, and whose astuteness he had had an opportunity of judging in the matter of the bogus wedding ring?

Verily, it is not so much the sagacity of detectives as the stupidity of the criminal classes which bring offenders to their doom. And after all that Dr. Doyle and Sherlock Holmes had done to bring the murder home to Hope, we are far from thinking that a jury would have convicted the prisoner on the circumstantial evidence accumulated against him. However, it is well for the sake of society that the text, "Be sure your sins will find you out", should be enforced by the novelist with a freshness and novelty bred of conviction and creative fruitfulness.

(LEADER)

2 December 1887

THE FLINTSHIRE COUNTY HERALD

Beeton's Christmas Annual

The writer – A. Conan Doyle – of *A Study in Scarlet* may be highly complimented on his success, as the tale, written in a style which captivates the reader, will certainly be read with profound interest. It has seldom been our lot to peruse pages which have such a strong charm; so much so, that the interest in the plot increases from page to page. The experiences and foresight of Sherlock Holmes, a private London detective, to discover the murderer of Enoch Drebber and Joseph Stangerson – two villains of the deepest cast – are remarkable proofs of the power of observation. This is the twenty-eighth season that Beeton's Annual has been published, but we doubt if any of its predecessors possessed such thrilling interest as is included in the pages of *A Study in Scarlet*.

2 December 1887

THE GLASGOW HERALD

Annuals and Christmas Numbers

Beeton's Christmas Annual (London: Ward, Lock & Co.) is now an old institution, and as regularly looked for as the holly and mistletoe. This year its contents are full and varied. The *pièce de résistance* is a story by A. Conan Doyle entitled *A Study in Scarlet*. It is the story of a murder, and of the preternatural sagacity of a scientific detective, to whom Edgar Allan Poe's Dupin was a trifler, and Gaboriau's Lecoq a child. He is a wonderful man is Mr. Sherlock Holmes, but one gets so wonderfully interested in his cleverness and in the mysterious murder which he unravels that one cannot lay down the narrative until the end is reached. What that end is wild horses shall not make us divulge. After the *Study in Scarlet* come two original little drawing-room plays. One is of the nature of a vaudeville, and is called "Food for Powder"; it should be effective as it is amusing. The other is "The Four-Leaved Shamrock", a drawing-room comedietta in three acts, also very good of its kind. The number is enriched with engravings by D. H. Friston, Matt Streetch, and R. André.

17 December 1887

THE SCOTSMAN

Christmas Numbers

The chief piece in *Beeton's Christmas Annual* is a detective story by Mr. A. Conan Doyle, *A Study in Scarlet*. This is as entrancing a tale of ingenuity in tracing out crime as has been written since the time of Edgar Allan Poe. The author shows genius. He has not trodden in the well-worn paths of literature, but has shown how the true detective should work by observation and deduction. His book is bound to have many readers.

19 December 1887

TIT-BITS

The Identity of Sherlock Holmes

BUTTONS wishes to know whether Mr. Sherlock Holmes, the detective genius, whose doings as recorded in the *Strand Magazine* by Mr. Conan Doyle have caused so much interest, is or is not an actual living person.

We cannot positively say. As a matter of fact we have not made the personal acquaintance of Mr. Sherlock Holmes, but we have read so much of his doings that we have made up our minds that if ever there is a mystery in connection with this office we shall endeavour to find out the whereabouts of Mr. Sherlock Holmes and employ him to investigate it, and if when that time comes we should find that no such person is in existence we shall then be very much disappointed indeed.

23 January 1892

New Sherlock Holmes Stories

Dr. Conan Doyle commands long prices. A new series of "The Adventures of Sherlock Holmes" has just been arranged for the *Strand Magazine*. The price paid will be £1,000 for the series of twelve stories.

25 June 1892

The Original of "Sherlock Holmes"

To the Editor

DEAR SIR, – Dr. Conan Doyle's interesting reminiscences, in the *Strand Magazine*, of his student days in Edinburgh, and of his professional "chief", recall to mind an incident in the life of Dr. Joseph Bell, which will show that his old pupil has not given an exaggerated picture by any means.

When Dr. Bell was young – entering on his career – diphtheria was a more obscure and novel disease than it is now. Its terrors were greater, because its treatment was not so well understood as at the present time. The famous surgeon, Syme, was performing wonderful operations in those days, and was the first (I am told) to introduce tracheotomy in cases of diphtheria.

In some cases of diphtheria the throat is so clogged that the patient cannot breathe, even when tracheotomy has been performed, and an attempt – occasionally successful – to clear the air-passages has to be made by someone sucking the exudature from the diseased tubes.

A little child suffering from that terrible disease was brought to the infirmary, and operated upon by Professor Syme, but the poisonous stuff had spread so far there was no way of relieving the patient except by suction.

Joseph Bell was Syme's assistant at the time, and he did the service required – risking his life, as he well knew, for that of the child. He took diphtheria very badly; it was scarcely possible to escape after such an action, and for a long time the young surgeon suffered from the deadly effects of it.

It is so common for medical men to do noble deeds that the public scarcely comment upon exceptionally brave (only "peculiar") cases. Yet titles and Victoria Crosses are given to men for less heroic actions than that which set Dr. Joseph Bell in a foremost place in his profession.

This incident, and what Conan Doyle calls his "remarkable individuality", make the popular "Joe Bell" (as the students affectionately style their favourite teacher) too picturesque a personality to escape the littérateur, and the diphtheria episode was utilised in a tale for students. More than once, besides, the "remarkable personality" has enabled the novel writer to describe a very acceptable hero without drawing on imagination, though only Dr. Conan Doyle has touched that side of the versatile character which had greatest attraction for him.

As an amateur detective Dr. Joseph Bell has earned the gratitude of many a troubled patient whose suffering the keen, kind grey eyes, which impressed his pupil so much, have traced to its true source in the mind.

Many a burdened life has had its care removed and its sorrow lightened through the ingenuity and sympathy of "Sherlock Holmes".

Yours faithfully,
ALGOUS

Edinburgh

10 September 1892

"The Sign of Four" in "Tit-Bits"

Next week we shall commence the publication in TIT-BITS of a story by Dr. Conan Doyle, entitled *The Sign of Four*. The work is founded upon the adventures of the celebrated Sherlock Holmes, which have attained such great popularity in the *Strand Magazine*. This story is considered to be equal to any of the others of the series, whilst it is considerably longer, and will extend through some seven or eight issues of TIT-BITS.

22 October 1892

H. – It is perfectly correct that *The Sign of Four* has been already published in book form. But it was done at a time when the great Sherlock Holmes had not made the brilliant reputation which now surrounds his name, and the sale was not of a very general character. We were delighted, therefore, when we were able to secure it for publication in TIT-BITS, and recommend every subscriber to read it.

29 October 1892

An Opinion from Scotland Yard

Those people who admire the remarkable detective creations of Edgar Allan Poe, and writers of the Gaboriau school, will be surprised to learn that experienced thief-takers entertain a profound contempt for the clever fictions these writers have invented. That M. Gaboriau was not a practical man in criminal investigation is proved by the fact that on more than one occasion he has signally failed to follow up a clue a professional detective has given him by way of experiment.

On the other hand, an experienced and able officer of the Criminal Investigation Department, at Scotland Yard, has a high opinion of the method of Dr. Conan Doyle, as described in "The Adventures of Sherlock Holmes". "Conan Doyle and Dick Donovan," this detective once remarked to the writer, "are more practical than writers of the Gaboriau school, and, at the same time, equally inventive."

29 October 1892

The Example of Sherlock Holmes

To the Editor

DEAR SIR, – Whenever I get hold of one of Dr. Conan Doyle's wonderful detective stories – be it in the *Strand Magazine*, in TIT-BITS, or in book form – I read it with the deepest interest.

On several occasions it has occurred to me that the science of minute and logical observation, as practised by Mr. Sherlock Holmes in the unravelling of the conundrums in crime placed before him, might be introduced into real life. To do this with effect, it would be necessary to raise the profession of detective to a much higher level than that upon which it at present stands. Salary and social status would be required to be raised to such an extent as would induce men of education to adopt the profession, in the same way as they go in for law, medicine, or the Church. A special course of training would be necessary. Attention would be given, in particular, to the development of the reasoning faculties and the power of minute observation, to such an extent as would qualify the student to form logical deductions from the smallest and most trifling details – details frequently overlooked, but which may prove of the utmost value. Witness the methods pursued by Sherlock Holmes.

Would it not be possible to apply those methods to the many mysterious crimes committed, the authors of which are never discovered? That there is something in the idea seems to me corroborated by an advertisement culled from a Scotch newspaper of this date, and which I reproduce. It reads as follows:

> SHERLOCK HOLMES. – Any persons thinking themselves capable of filling a post in a Modern Inquiry Office, which requires qualifications of the nature indicated in Dr. A. Conan Doyle's well-known stories, are requested to send testimonials, etc., which will be treated as confidential, to— (Office).

The above would lead one to suppose there are, at present, private detectives who have faith in the practicability of adopting the means used by Sherlock Holmes. If so, the sooner the idea is thoroughly ventilated and discussed, the better for the greater protection of law-abiding citizens, and for the prevention of the recurrence of such atrocities as the Whitechapel murders, or like cases, because in the detection of one criminal, with resultant punishment, may lie the prevention of other crimes.

I am, yours faithfully,
PUBLIC SAFETY

Partick.

26 November 1892

Sherlock Holmes and the Police

To the Editor

SIR, – I believe that the publication of the very powerful and interesting series of stories of detective skill, exemplified in "The Adventures of Sherlock Holmes", is likely to have an effect upon the English police system, which the author, Dr. Conan Doyle, had perhaps not anticipated, but which cannot fail to be beneficial.

With all due deference to those officers in the force who have shown an aptitude for the detection of the committers of crime, I deny that the majority of the men now vested with authority for the preservation of the peace are suitable or fitted to be pitted against the scheming rascals who do our most serious crimes. And this is not the fault of the men themselves, I hold, but of the system under which they are obliged to work, which has the effect of rendering them dull, official, and their manners so similar that they can be easily "spotted" by the men in opposition to whom their duties call them.

It may surprise the general public to learn that our officers are not selected because of their knowledge of the ways of the habitual criminal classes, or because they are men who have studied the business they are desirous of entering, or, indeed, have any aptitude for it at all.

For him to enter a police force, it is only necessary that a man shall be of good character – that is, that nothing shall be known to his detriment; that he shall stand a certain height, and have a certain chest measurement. Accepted, he is drilled into stereotyped mannerisms that he may for ever bear to the observant eye the warning label, "Police". It does not matter that he belongs to the uneducated class, that he can sign his name only with difficulty, and has to laboriously spell through the simplest paragraph.

Not at all. He is a big, sturdy fellow, who can tussle with the burly navvy and use his shoulders with advantage in a street row. He has no idea of using his intelligence: he is not paid for it; and so long as he can patrol the streets in regulation fashion and touch his hat in the correct style to his superior, he will be employed, and expected to cope with men who, unfortunately, make the successful commission of crime the object of their lives.

I believe that the organisation of our police system is radically wrong. The men selected for the very important task of protecting the public should be men of intelligence, men of an observant nature, who know the world and its people, and are prepared to meet them in their foibles. Perhaps it would be impossible to select entirely men equal in cunning,

68

resource, and ability with Sherlock Holmes, but he is a model on which our officers should be built, and the authorities might do worse than distribute volumes of his adventures amongst the members of the forces, for they would be instructive to the men.

Faithfully yours,
ONE INTERESTED

Lancashire.

17 December 1892

The Original Sherlock Holmes

A.C.L. sends us an advertisement of a London detective who is announcing himself as the original Sherlock Holmes.

As is known to most readers, the original of this remarkable character is Dr. Joseph Bell, of Edinburgh, and this London detective has no business whatever to bracket his name with that of Sherlock Holmes, and we are amazed at his audacity in doing so.

18 February 1893

"A Study in Scarlet"

We have pleasure in announcing that we have just concluded arrangements with Messrs. Ward, Lock, & Bowden to publish Sherlock Holmes's First Adventure, entitled *A Study in Scarlet*, by A. Conan Doyle, the opening chapter of which will appear in the Easter Holiday Number of TIT-BITS, dated 1 April. By this arrangement we are able to place before the readers either of TIT-BITS or the *Strand Magazine* every one of the Sherlock Holmes stories. Of course some of our subscribers have already read this most exciting story, but to the majority it will be quite new – and is worth reading again and again.

24 March 1893

A Self-Styled "Sherlock Holmes"

TIT-BITITE sends us the report of a recent trial, in which a detective who advertised himself as the original Sherlock Holmes was the prosecutor. He was coming back from the races, and allowed himself to be victimised to the extent of ten pounds by the three-card trick.

There appear to be several private detectives in this country who are calling themselves the original Sherlock Holmes, and we have had occasion to caution one of them, who undertook not to continue so styling himself. Of course, none of them are in any way connected with the eminent detective.

29 April 1893

An Examination in Sherlock Holmes

We are going to have an examination in Sherlock Holmes, open to anyone. Those who have read the Adventures of this eminent man, *A Study in Scarlet, The Sign of Four*, etc., will have an opportunity of displaying their knowledge of his methods. In an early issue, we hope next week, the questions will be published together with the conditions of the contest, and the prizes to be offered.

7 October 1893

Sherlock Holmes Examination Paper

We append below a number of questions as to the methods of Sherlock Holmes. For the best answers we offer: – First Prize, Five Guineas; Second Prize, Three Guineas; Third Prize. Two Guineas. Replies, marked "Sherlock Holmes" on the evelopes, to reach these offices by 4 November.

The Methods of Sherlock Holmes

I. Given two doctors' houses of the same date – how to determine which has the larger practice?

II. How to calculate that a train is going at the rate of fifty-three miles an hour?

III. What deductions as to the character of the owner did Holmes make from an inspection of a watch?

IV. How did the appearance of a man's pipe suggest: –

1. That he was left-handed?
2. That he was muscular?
3. That he had peculiar associations connected with the pipe?

V. How did Holmes deduce from the soles of Watson's slippers that he had had a cold recently?

VI. What indications of character might conceivably be drawn from bootlaces?

VII. How did Holmes deduce from the appearance of a man's stick that he lived in danger?

VIII. What appearance in a man dressed as a civilian led Holmes to deduce: –

1. That he was an old soldier?
2. Recently discharged?

3. From India?
4. In the Artillery?
5. A widower?
6. Probable cause of wife's death?
7. How many children (at the least)?
8. Their ages?

IX. What appearance in a felt hat led Holmes to deduce: –

1. That the owner's wife did not love him?
2. That the gas was not laid on in his house?

What other inferences were drawn from this hat?

X. How did Holmes know that a visitor waiting for him in the evening had only been in the room five minutes?

XI. By what process of reasoning did Holmes argue that because Watson's boots were very clean, therefore his practice was very busy?

XII. How did Watson's pocket-handkerchief prove that he had been accustomed to wear a uniform?

21 October 1893

The Prize of Five Guineas which we recently offered for the best set of answers to an Examination Paper on the methods of Sherlock Holmes has been awarded to Mr. Adam R. Thomson, 26 St. George's Avenue, Tufnell Park, N.

The Prize of Three Guineas has been won by Mr. J. M. Buckley, 57 Bedford Street, Liverpool; and the Prize of Two Guineas by Mr. Edward N. V. Moyle, St. Mary's, Isles of Scilly.

The following is Mr. Thomson's Competition:

I. By observing the steps at each house, those the more deeply worn indicating the larger practice. – 'The Adventure of the Stockbroker's Clerk'.

II. Having ascertained the distance at which the telegraph posts on the line are placed apart, note the time occupied by the train in travelling between any two of them, and calculate accordingly. – 'The Adventure of Silver Blaze.'

III. That he was the eldest son of the family and had inherited the watch from his father; that he was very untidy and careless in his habits; was left with good prospects, but threw away his chances; had lived for some time in poverty with occasional intervals of prosperity; had finally taken to drink and died. – *The Sign of Four*.

IV. Because, having been lit at lamps and gas-jets, the pipe was charred all down the right side, it being usual for right-handed persons to hold the left side to the flame; because the amber mouthpiece was bitten through, thus betokening that the smoker was muscular and energetic, and the possessor of a good set of teeth; because the pipe had been twice mended with silver bands, and each mend must have cost more than the article itself had done originally, thus showing that the owner valued it highly. – 'The Adventure of the Yellow Face'.

V. The soles of Watson's slippers, which were new ones, had become slightly scorched, and Holmes inferred that, as damp would have removed a circular wafer of paper bearing the shopman's mark that he noticed near the instep, this could not have been occasioned by the slippers having got wet and been subsequently burned in the drying. He assumed, therefore, that Watson had been sitting with his feet out-stretched to the fire, which a healthy man would scarcely have done in the month of June (his robust appearance showed the indisposition was a slight one). – 'The Adventure of the Stockbroker's Clerk'.

VI. Holmes refers to the great issues that may hang from bootlaces, and their condition certainly affords a tolerably reliable index both to the character of the wearer and the extent of his worldly possessions. In the former respect the following are some obvious deductions:

Leather laces indicate that the wearer possibly prefers strength to elegance; is economical; of a practical tendency; not imaginative, nor artistic, nor foppish; is careless of the opinion of others; given to much walking.

Leather laces in small, finely-finished, but old boots indicate that the wearer possibly is no longer able or willing to be as particular as formerly regarding his personal appearance.

Mohair laces indicate that the wearer possibly wishes to look neat; does not slavishly practise economy; is not given to heavy walking.

New laces in shabby boots indicate that the wearer possibly is anxious, as far as possible, to conceal his poverty.

Silk laces indicate that the wearer possibly is given to foppishness, vanity, self-indulgence, effeminacy, extravagance.

Odd laces indicate that the wearer possibly is careless; indifferent as to personal appearance; slovenly; lacking in self-respect; in foresight, not having a reserve stock of laces similar to the one he has presumably broken; wishes to be thought humble.

One lace mohair, the other leather, indicate that the wearer possibly has become more careful and economical than formerly, or *vice-versa* (according to the newness of the respective laces, and the age and style of the boots).

Laces coated with mud indicate that the wearer possibly is extremely slovenly, not having taken the trouble to tie the laces properly, lazy, in not stopping to tie them when they became loose; indifferent to discomfort, in having walked with them in this state; fond of country walks.

Laces of a different colour to the boots indicate that the wearer possibly is wanting in taste; is eccentric; likes at all cost to attract attention.

Laces tied up round the leg indicate that the wearer possibly is of a practical turn of mind.

Laces put through the boots crosswise indicate that the wearer possibly is more imaginative and artistic than if he had put them in in such a manner as to lace the boots horizontally.

Laces tied in a *negligé* knot indicate that the wearer possibly is careless, imaginative, artistic, hasty, untidy.

One lace broken and tied together indicates that the wearer possibly is given to hurry; lacks foresight in not having any spare laces to fall back upon; is indifferent to his personal appearance.

One or both laces broken and tied together, evidently some time since, indicate that the wearer possibly is extremely careless, indifferent, parsimonious, untidy, humble, or wishes to be considered so.

Laces not put through all the holes indicate that the wearer possibly is impulsive, untidy, careless; wants foresight not having bought laces long enough for the boots; lacks patience, self-respect.

– 'A Case of Identity'.

VII. Because the owner of the stick had taken some pains to bore the head of it, and had poured molten lead into the hole in order to make it a formidable weapon. – 'The Adventure of the "Gloria Scott"'.

VIII. His bearing; by his still wearing his ammunition boots; his sun-baked skin; because he had not the cavalry stride, yet, as shown by the lighter skin on one side of his brow, had been in the habit of wearing his hat on one side; his weight was against his being a sapper. His complete mourning, together with the fact that he was doing his own shopping; he had been buying things for children, and, as he carried a rattle, one of them was obviously very young, rendering it probable that the wife had died in child-bed; that there were at least two children was shown by the man having purchased a picture-book in addition to the rattle; from the nature of the toys. (Mycroft Holmes assisted in making the above deductions). – 'The Adventure of the Greek Interpreter.'

IX. The hat had not been brushed for weeks, and Holmes knew from the circumstances under which it had come into his possession that the owner could not be a bachelor; because the hat had five tallow stains upon it, showing that the owner must frequently have been brought in contact with burning tallow – probably owing to his walking upstairs with his hat in one hand and a guttering candle in the other. Holmes also inferred from this hat that the owner was highly intellectual; fairly well-to-do within the previous three years, but had latterly fallen upon evil days; that he had lost some of his former foresight – pointing to a moral retrogression which, taken with the decline of his fortunes, seemed to indicate some evil influence, probably drink, at work upon him; had, however, retained some of his self-respect; that he led a sedentary life; went out little; was entirely out of training; was middle-aged; had grizzled hair – cut a few days before; anointed the same with lime cream. – 'The Adventure of the Blue Carbuncle'.

X. By the state of the candle on the sidetable. – 'The Adventure of the Resident Patient'.

XI. Because he knew that Watson walked when his round was a short one, and took a hansom when it was a long one.

XII. From Watson's habit of carrying it in his sleeve. – 'The Adventure of the Crooked Man'.

The Sherlock Holmes Examination Papers have proved a very successful competition. A large number were equally correct in answering those questions which were drawn from the stories. The prize, therefore, came to be decided on the answering of the sixth question, which depends on the individual ingenuity of each competitor. Mr. Conan Doyle, who has taken an interest in the competition, has been kind enough to send autographed copies of *The Memoirs of Sherlock Holmes* to a number of the senders of the next best competitions.

16 December 1893

II. THE GREAT HIATUS (1893–1900)

———◆———

In Memoriam: Sherlock Holmes

We have had this week to chronicle the death of Sherlock Holmes, as we had not long ago sad occasion to record the death of Tartarin of Tarascon and of Mr. Stevenson's Pew. (One blushes to own a momentary forgetfulness whether Lecoq, Sherlock Holmes's great predecessor, did ever die.) Mr. Conan Doyle's astonishing detective became, even in his lifetime, so much a classic as to have been prescribed for educational purposes. He has well earned his retirement, and, unless the Queen shall command Mr. Doyle to show Sherlock Holmes in love, he may perhaps be permitted to rest in peace. Perhaps, we say – for in these days there is the publishing syndicate to reckon with, as powerful in its way as the Tudor despot.

Suppose someone, imagining himself to be "on the same intellectual plane" as Mr. Conan Doyle, should drag Sherlock Holmes to life again, what would be Mr. Doyle's remedy? Dickens's inventions used to be pirated so soon as ever they were published. Mr. Besant, greatly daring, wrote the other day a sequel to Ibsen. That, however, was controversy, not plagiarism. The famous instance is the sham Quixote of the spurious continuator, "Avellaneda". Cervantes makes – the provocation considered – very good-natured fun of him in his own Second Part, the conclusion of which had to be hurried to compete with and to correct the rival sequel. It was to prevent more personations that Cervantes consented to Quixote's death. Probably a similar consideration induced M. Daudet to slay the immortal, and make his Tartarin die a broken-spirited exile in Beaucaire.

75

An Involuntary Elegy

(In Memory of Sherlock Holmes)

So at the last he yields to Fate,
  And we lament a vanished friend,
Through thrilling pages that narrate
  The history of his tragic end.

Who solved with monthly stratagems,
  To win imaginary thanks,
Mysteries of pilfered diadems,
  And gunshot wounds and plundered banks.

Our recollection wanders o'er
  Black villainies by sea and land,
The Pair of Ears, the Sign of Four,
  The Twisted Lip, the Speckled Band.

And through them all that visage pale,
  Those hawk-like eyes, alert and bright,
That subtle wit that could not fail,
  Those theories that were always right.

Fare you, poor played-out fancy, well,
  We know you were absurd, untrue,
Yet have we met, we blush to tell,
  Heroes who bored us more than you.

Farewell; the modern novel's path
  Is pointing to a deeper Art,
And such a serious humour hath
  No place for your sensational part.

Yet, when we grapple with such tomes,
  In leisure hours on sunny lawns.
Perchance your memory, Sherlock Holmes,
  May lend a fervour to our yawns.

16 December 1893

The Death of Sherlock Holmes

G. and Very Many Others. – The news of the death of Sherlock Holmes has been received with most widespread regret, and readers have implored us to use our influence with Mr. Conan Doyle to prevent the tragedy being consummated. We can only reply that we pleaded for his life in the most urgent, earnest, and constant manner. Like hundreds of correspondents, we feel as if we had lost an old friend whom we could ill spare. Mr. Doyle's feeling was that he did not desire Sherlock to outstay his welcome, and that the public had had enough of him. This is not our opinion, nor is it the opinion of the public; but it is, we regret to say, Mr. Doyle's. The author desires to turn his attention now to other paths of literature, and for a time, at any rate, to leave detective stories alone. He has, however, promised us that he will, at some future date, if opportunity may occur, give us the offer of some posthumous histories of the great detective, which offer we shall readily accept.

In connection with this matter we have received the following interesting letter from SEEDY:

Now that we have heard of the decease of our friend, Sherlock Holmes, I would suggest that a "Sherlock Holmes Memorial Prize" be offered by TIT-BITS, under the following conditions: Competitors to state which they think to be the best of the series of "The Adventures of Sherlock Holmes", stating their reasons for so thinking. The "Adventure" receiving the greatest number of supporters to be considered the most popular; and the person sending in the best reasons for considering the successful one to be best to receive the prize. This should be a popular competition, and would prove a fitting tribute to the memory of our departed friend;

and in accordance with the above suggestions, we offer a prize of Ten Pounds under the conditions stated. Competitions, marked "Memorial", to reach these offices by Monday, 5 February.

6 January 1894.

Sherlock Holmes Memorial Prize

In the competition recently announced on "The Adventures of Sherlock Holmes", it was found that the most popular Adventure was that of "The Speckled Band". Next to it came "Silver Blaze", followed by "The Final Problem".

The best article on "The Speckled Band" was submitted by Mr. G. Douglas Buchanan, 9 & 11 Dundas Street (City), Glasgow, to whom the Prize of Ten Pounds has been sent for the following:

"The Adventure of the Speckled Band"

Having been a careful student of our friend Mr. Sherlock Holmes and his methods, since 1891, during which time I have read all the Adventures several times, I think that, of all the many problems which Holmes elucidated, none was more mysterious than "The Adventure of the Speckled Band", which appeared in the *Strand Magazine* for February 1892.

My reasons for thinking as I do, although perfectly satisfactory to myself, are somewhat difficult to explain. Holmes once said to Watson that the latter would probably find some difficulty in explaining the fact that "two and two make four", although he might have no doubt in his own mind that they did so, and I feel that I am in a similar position. Where all the stories are good, individual preference must account for a good deal of the favour one shows to any particular Adventure, and yet one can scarcely define the subtle charm which determines his choice.

I think that, in dramatic power, the long vigil in that chamber of death will compare favourably with any of the striking scenes in the other Adventures. Holmes and Watson never showed greater courage than when they braved the unknown horror in the darkness and silence of that early morning.

Then the death of the schemer by means of his own tool appears to me to be a veritable *coup-de-maître*.

To my mind, however, the examination which Holmes made of the room and its furniture, and which resulted in his discovering that the bell-rope was a dummy, is more impressive still. The very trivialities, on which the master-mind of Holmes based its deductions, interested me all the more on account of their being so apparently unimportant. The absence of all circumstances to heighten the effect of this afternoon's employment renders it all the more striking to me, because of its simplicity and lack of theatrical accessories. It was the preparation for the great and dramatic events of the ensuing night, and it seems to me to bring into due prominence the earlier links of the chain of causation. Usually, the ultimate and penultimate links are all that the reader of a novel is favoured with, but the glory of all "The Adventures of Sherlock Holmes" is that in them a due proportion is preserved of every link in the chain. In Holmes's examination of Miss Stoner's room, every action and every deduction appears, not

78

as an isolated phenomenon, but as one of a series of events, and the gradual evolution is, perhaps, the greatest charm of all to me.

Again, in this Adventure, the subtle and *outré* nature of the agency which Dr. Roylott employed to accomplish his nefarious ends, and his cunning and well-arranged method of procedure, made up a combination which afforded Holmes a unique opportunity of displaying his particular genius, of which he fully availed himself. His slight error at the beginning of his investigation put him on his mettle, and the acumen which he subsequently evinced was never surpassed in any of the other cases with which he was associated, none of which had the advantage of equally striking accessories.

Thus, inadequately, but to the best of my ability, I have endeavoured to explain why I think the most exciting of all Holmes's Adventures is "The Adventure of the Speckled Band".

17 February 1894

The Lessons of Sherlock Holmes

To the Editor

DEAR SIR, – Many tears have been shed over Sherlock Holmes's grave, and many have been the just praises showered upon the writer of his Adventures, for the pleasant reading with which he has delighted us in the *Strand Magazine*. But there is a far more salient point to be observed in these Adventures. There is, in fact, a most important lesson contained therein upon the necessity of cultivating the natural powers of observation which we already possess.

I do not think I could quote a better authority on the matter than Dr. Bell, of Edinburgh, who gave the following as his opinion to an interviewer, only a few days ago. He says:

> I should like to say this about my friend Doyle's stories, that I believe they have inculcated in the general public a new source of interest. They make many a fellow who has before felt very little interest in his life and daily surroundings, think that after all there may be much more in life, if he keeps his eyes open, than he had ever dreamed of in his philosophy.

What the words "Keep his eyes open" imply is more than I could attempt to explain here, but they are by themselves sufficiently suggestive to him who will take the trouble to ponder over them for even a short space of time. They may be applied to almost every action in a man's life, especially in these times, where every chance must be made the best of, where no man whose wish it is to succeed in life can afford to let the "tide" go by.

The necessary companion to useful observation is memory, without which its uses are but very limited, and it may be safely said that the better a man's memory the wider becomes his field of action in life, for of what use is observation to him if he does not remember what he has seen?

What I would suggest, therefore, is that parents should carefully cultivate in their children, both boys and girls, these two habits, namely, observation and memory.

The trouble is great, I know, but the reward is greater still; and I feel sure that children brought up with a goodly stock of these two qualities will have cause in their after life to thank those to whom thanks are due.

Yours faithfully,
A. H. B.

Wandsworth.

13 January 1894

ADVERTISEMENT

The Last Letter from Sherlock Holmes

DEAR FRIEND, – Mystery follows mystery; but the most mysterious thing of all is what has become of the part of my system which has almost taken the form of my second nature. I was especially cautious to provide myself with the indispensable before leaving home, but it has disappeared and I have lost all trace. I have unravelled many of other people's losses, but here is one of my own which has thrown me on my beam ends. I would not have troubled you, but in this benighted spot – although you will scarcely credit it – I cannot procure what I much need; so send by *first* post, as my movements are uncertain, one large box of Beecham's Pills. Note my assumed name and enclosed address, which I beg of you to destroy, as I do not wish my whereabouts to be known.

Yours,
S. H.

27 January 1894

TIT-BITS

The Death of Mr. Conan Doyle

S. B. G. – You are not the only person who, for some reason or other, has the idea that Mr. Conan Doyle is dead. This is happily untrue. He is very much alive. The impression seems to have got about from two causes. One, that his name has been confused with that of Hugh Conway, who died some years ago. The other because the great Sherlock Holmes, whose deeds Mr. Doyle chronicled, is at the present moment lying at the bottom of a precipice. We hope this contradiction will reach all who have made this mistake.

26 May 1894

The Shadow of Sherlock Holmes

G. W. R. has had a dream. He has recently been visiting Switzerland, and in his travels he found himself on a mountain pass overlooking a precipice, which seemed to him to be very similar to the picture, given in the Christmas number of the *Strand Magazine*, of the spot where Sherlock Holmes met his death. In his dream, he thought that he was walking along the pass once more, and what should come upon him but the figure of a man, who, from the many pictures which have been published of him, could be none other than the famous detective.

G. W. R. will see that someone else has been dreaming about the great man, and Mr. Richard Morton has turned his dream to practical use, having composed a clever and interesting song, entitled "The Ghost of Sherlock Holmes", which is to be found below. The author of "Ta-ra-ra-Boom-de-ay" has had many successes, and we hope that this one will equal the best of his others. Certainly it is far superior, so far as the words are concerned, to the average music-hall ditty.

Sherlock Holmes turns out to be one of those persons whom the world will not willingly let die. More people than one would care to count were shocked and grieved at his terribly sudden end. It is no exaggeration to say that the nation was sad for a space, for had it not learned to love and admire him, and to marvel at his mysterious ways?

Not only did the world take Holmes's death seriously to heart, but many people have felt constrained to try and fill the empty space that he once occupied in the public's mind. Imitators have been many; equals none.

One person has, however, gone beyond imitation. He has brought Sherlock Holmes back again into the world -- has raised his ghost, and holds him out to the public as the spectre of one of the most popular figures ever known in fiction.

Mr. Richard Morton has done this. Mr. Morton is the well-known song-writer, the author of Miss Lottie Collins's "Ta-ra-ra-Boom-de-ay"; of Mr. Eugene Stratton's "Dandy Coloured Coon" and "Susie Tusie"; of Miss Marie Lloyd's "Twiggy Yoo"; of Mr. R. G. Knowles's "Christopher Columbus" and "P'raps Not"; and, indeed, of a whole host of popular songs, grave and gay. Mr. Morton has recently been suffering from a painful illness, resulting in the loss of sight in the right eye. It was during his convalescence at Hastings that he dreamed a dream. He thought he saw the ghost of Sherlock Holmes! Presto! An idea!

In the morning Mr. Richard Morton sat down and wrote:

The Ghost of Sherlock Holmes

I

Don't start, and pray don't leave your seats,
　　There's no cause for alarm;
Though I've arrived from warmer spheres
　　I mean you all no harm.
I am a ghost – a real ghost!
　　That nightly earthward roams;
In fact, I am the spectre of
　　Detective Sherlock Holmes!

Chorus:

"Sherlock! Sherlock!" you can hear the people cry!
"That's the ghost of Sherlock Holmes!" as I go creeping by!
Sinners shake and tremble where'er this bogie roams,
And people shout, "He's found us out – it's the Ghost of
　　Sherlock Holmes!"

II

The man who plots a murder, when
　　He sees me flit ahead,
Forgets to murder anyone,
　　And "suicides" instead.
An Anarchist, with lighted bomb
　　To cause explosive scenes,
Sees me, and drops the bomb, and blows
　　Himself to smithereens!

Chorus.

III

The burglar who's a-burgling, when
　　He finds that I'm at large,
Gets scared, and says, "Policeman, will
　　You please take me in charge?"

The lady's who's shop-lifting tries
   To put her thievings back,
And says, "Oh, Mr. Sherlock, I'm
   A Kleptomaniac!"

Chorus.

IV

My life was more than misery;
   Compelled to strut the earth,
And be a spy at beck and call
   Of those who gave me birth.
But, now that I'm a spectre, all
   Their misdeeds shall recoil –
I'm going to haunt *Strand Magazine*,
   Tit-Bits, and Conan Doyle!

Chorus.

This is certainly something new in the way of comic songs, and shows the effect of detective literature upon the brain of an invalid. It is a huge success in the provincial music-halls and theatres, and within a few weeks will be heard upon the boards of some of the principal halls in the West End of London. The singer of the song is Mr. H. C. Barry, a clever young comedian, who has left the legitimate boards for variety-land. He has a distinct style of his own, and is very happy in his delineation of the awe-inspiring spectre of Sherlock Holmes.

9 June 1894

The Great Detective

C. W. O. writes: It may be interesting to you to know that Mr. Morton's clever song about the dear departed detective, Sherlock Holmes, would not have been the only song in existence about the gentleman in question, had he not met with an untimely and regretted death. The following is the first verse of a song written on the great Sherlock. The very next number of the *Strand Magazine*, after the song was commenced, contained the news of his demise. Little did Mr. Conan Doyle imagine that in killing off Sherlock he also blotted out the song of which this was the commencement:

A detective am I,
Wide awake, very spry;

I unravel at once any mystery.
  Slightest clue will suffice;
    Better no clue or plan,
  Then my acumen nice
    Gets to work, and I can
Of the darkest plot tell you the history.

Chorus:

    I find my clues
    In dusty flues,
  Or dig them up from musty tomes.
    The wicked quake,
    Wrong-doers shake,
When they hear the name of Sherlock Holmes.

23 June 1894

Oliver Wendell Holmes

H. L. – It is not true that Oliver Wendell Holmes was the father of Sherlock Holmes; as a matter of fact, they were not related at all.

27 October 1894

THE ST. JAMES'S GAZETTE

To the Ghost of Mr. Sherlock Holmes

When Sherlock Holmes, ingenious man, pursued his strange career,
We studied his Adventures with a sympathy sincere,
Although in time his victories monotonous became,
Because his base opponents never won a single game.

He caught his latest criminal, and then at last – he died;
"We mourn him, we lament him, but it's time he went," we cried;
Ah, foolish words! soon after we regretted him, dismayed
To find he'd left a family to carry on the trade.

They swarm in every magazine, each journal with them teems,
Detecting obvious criminals by very obvious schemes,
Adapting to their purposes devices long ago
Invented by that master-hand of great Gaboriau.

Their wisdom, too, is marvellous: the mud upon your boots
Informs them to a penny what your balance is at Coutts;
They know your mother's maiden name, what train you travelled by,
And if you've had lumbago – from the colour of your tie!

Yes! Sherlock Holmes is dead and gone; but still in other shapes
We meet the old detective whom no criminal escapes;
The hateful "Strange Occurrence" or "Mysterious Affair"
Still, still infests the magazines and drives us to despair.

O ghost of Mr. Sherlock Holmes, please mercifully kill
These shameless imitators of your own transcendent skill,
Or haunt the homes of editors, and pointedly suggest
That fictionary criminals might be allowed a rest!

11 February 1895

TIT-BITS

Conan Doyle's New Stories

Some fifteen months ago we received any number of remonstrances
from readers of this paper who were also readers of the *Strand Magazine*,
suggesting that we ought to specially request Mr. Conan Doyle to
continue his articles on the Adventures of Sherlock Holmes. Always
desirous of acceding to the wishes of readers of this paper and the *Strand*,
we brought to bear all the influences which we possessed, but with no
avail. Mr. Conan Doyle had made up his mind to stop this series, and
stop it he did. We did not consent to use the proverb that "a wilful man
must have his way", but rather remarked that an author must be
allowed to be the best judge of what he desires to write or to refrain from
writing.

Many people seem to think that we were in some way contributors to
the death of Sherlock Holmes, and have felt indignation against us that
we should be accessories to the tragedy. As a matter of fact, we pleaded
for his life with great but unsuccessful zeal. Happily, now, those who
enjoy following Mr. Conan Doyle's delightful ingenuity have brought
before them a character which will probably turn out to be a greater one
even than Sherlock Holmes. In the April Number of the *Strand Magazine*
commences a series of stories entitled "The Exploits of Brigadier
Gerard", which though not of the detective type will, judging from those
which have already come to hand, be superior to any detective stories
which we have ever read.

20 April 1895

A Student of Sherlock Holmes

F. W. B. has lately been reading a number of detective stories, and has
specially been studying the immortal Sherlock Holmes. He has been

applying the principles of this great detective in various matters connected with actual private life. He says, and we have no reason to disbelieve him, that he has been very successful, with the result that he has been fired with the desire to become a detective by profession.

If he were to succeed, it would not be, by any means, the first time that a reader had discovered his true calling by the perusal of TIT-BITS and the *Strand Magazine*. He cannot, however, become a Scotland Yard detective, which is his special desire, until he has served as a constable in the Metropolitan Police Force. A letter to that celebrated "Yard" will bring full particulars.

8 June 1895

Brigadier Gerard

E. T. L. writes: "I was one of the loudest in my protest that Sherlock Holmes was allowed to be killed. I beg to say that I now rejoice in his death, because it has been the means of bringing to life the delightful Brigadier Gerard."

8 June 1895

The Model for Sherlock Holmes

AMY suggests that we should offer a prize to the person who most resembles in features our old friend, Sherlock Holmes. Amy has recently been at the seaside, where a gentleman was stopping, and whenever he walked about, it was a constant source of the remark, "How like he is to Sherlock Holmes."

We are much obliged for the suggestion, though we scarcely think it is a fitting subject for a competition. As a matter of fact, we believe that the gentleman who sat as the model of Sherlock Holmes, for the pictures of the great detective which appeared in the *Strand Magazine*, was the brother of the artist who drew them.

Another correspondent writing on this subject asks whether the cessation of the Sherlock Holmes stories was not a considerable loss to the *Strand Magazine*. Undoubtedly we were very sorry when the stories ceased, and made every effort to get Mr. Conan Doyle to continue them. But it is a pleasing fact that the circulation of the *Strand Magazine* is now greater than ever it was during the publication of the celebrated Sherlock Holmes series.

21 September 1895

The Reichenbach Falls

P. sends us the interesting information that a few weeks ago, when holidaying in Switzerland, he visited the famous falls of Reichenbach, into which the late-lamented Sherlock Holmes and the not-so-much-regretted Moriarty fell after their never-to-be-forgotten struggles. He says Dr. Conan Doyle's description of the awe-inspiring place brings it to the mind "like a picture", for, as far as he could see, it is absolutely correct. Already, the falls are the resort of visitors anxious to inspect them, and many are the discussions which ensue as to what became of the famous detective. Indeed, the guides are beginning to point out the Reichenbach Falls as the actual place where Holmes was killed, and doubtless, if they are given a few years' time, they will weave as pretty a legend round Conan Doyle's creation as they seem to have done in William Tell's case.

28 September 1895

The Perspicacity of Criminals

S. P., in reading an account of some recent crimes, was greatly impressed with the amount of skill and ingenuity displayed by the perpetrators. He cannot help thinking, he says, that though detectives may be lacking in the abilities of a Sherlock Holmes, there are several of our present-day criminals who seem almost equal to the great detective in perspicacity.

Undoubtedly, the way in which many crimes are committed goes to prove that there are sufficient ingenuity and ability exercised to make an honourable fortune if they were employed in more laudable enterprises. Unfortunately, however, it frequently happens that in many of these cases the possession of shrewd intelligence is combined with an inherent criminality, which appears to be so powerful as to effectually prevent the ability from being exercised in an honest manner.

3 April 1897

"The Man with the Twisted Lip"

Dr. Conan Doyle once made a curious little slip in one of his inimitable series of "Sherlock Holmes" stories. In the bewildering story of the beggar who is arrested on suspicion of having murdered himself, we learn that the accused was remanded to Bow Street, where he is visited whilst under remand. Considering the important part which that famous police-court has played in fiction for the past century at least, the error was a natural one. As a fact, however, accused persons on

87

remand are sent to one or other of the prisons until the day of their re-examination.

19 February 1898

A Chronic Complaint

THREE CASTLES comes along with another long-continued – shall we say? – chronic complaint against Mr. Conan Doyle, that he does not give us a new series of Sherlock Holmes. Three Castles does not employ any arguments, nor do any of our correspondents who desire the same thing, which we have not already put before Mr. Conan Doyle. After all, the author is the best judge of what work he wants to do, and in any case he is the deciding factor in the matter. We hope that he will continue the series at some time, but when – or if ever – we cannot at present say. In the meantime we are publishing his "Sherlock Holmes", both the *Adventures* and *Memoirs*, as well as *The Sign of Four* in book form at sixpence each.

1 April 1899

THE BOOKMAN

From a Physician in Baltimore

To the Editors

In the February BOOKMAN you allude to the parallel between Rudyard Kipling's "Explanation" and Flecknoes's "Fable". Have you ever noticed that between Conan Doyle's Sherlock Holmes and Edgar Allan Poe's Monsieur Dupin? Both were house-mates, if not room-mates, of their respective writers. Both won success through their peculiar powers of analysis. Both were consultant detectives, so to speak, and had the same contempt for the regular detective force and for newspaper men in general. When M. Dupin had eliminated by exclusion all the familiar nationalities in "The Murders in the Rue Morgue", he drew out his convenient copy of Cuvier and read a description of the orang-outang, and left no doubt in the mind of his listener as to the author of the crime. When Sherlock Holmes had excluded all races known to his listener, he took down a volume of his cyclopaedia and read a description of the savages of the Andaman Islands, and his listener knew at once who was the accomplice of the one-legged man in the murder of Major Sholto.

And by the way, there is something of a parallel between the one-legged man in *The Sign of the Four* and the one-legged man in Robert

Louis Stevenson's *Treasure Island*. In both there are a hidden treasure, a diagram, a contract and a sign. In one the sign is the "black spot", in the other it is the "Sign of the Four". The same terror of a one-legged man that was exhibited by the Captain at the Benbow Inn was exhibited by Major Sholto at his home. When the Captain at the Benbow died, the sign of the "black spot" had been served on him; when Major Sholto died, the "Sign of the Four" was found on his person.

There are many other points of resemblance, and I should like to know what others, better informed than myself, think of it.

October 1899

TIT-BITS

Mr. Justice Day

L. E. B. has recently been shocked – "thunderously pulverised, pounded, and crushed", he calls it. Whilst attending a trial amid the solemn precincts of the law courts on a recent occasion the learned judge startled the assembly by anxiously inquiring, "Who is Sherlock Holmes?" He was informed that the gentleman was a certain person created and made notorious by Conan Doyle. "Ah," said the judge, "who is he?" "Really," continues our correspondent,

> it was bad enough for other gentlemen of the Bench to set the ball rolling by asking "Who is Connie Gilchrist?" "Who is Corney Grain?" but these are comparatively pardonable to this later confession of innocence. The offender this time was Mr. Justice Day, but surely he is anxious for the public to believe him benighted. Don't you think it's about time some pupil teacher were told off to impart a little knowledge of men and things to those who have been made judges over us?

Don't worry. If the learned judge has not already made the acquaintance of Sherlock Holmes and Conan Doyle, there is a great treat in store for him. The adventures of the world-famous detective are now being re-published from these offices at a price well within the income of most gentlemen of the Bench. We are confident that if Mr. Justice Day will devote a couple of hours of his scanty leisure to the perusal of this work he will be amongst the first to admit that he never made a better investment of 6d. in his life.

1 September 1900

III. *THE HOUND OF THE BASKERVILLES* (1901–1902)

---◆---

TIT-BITS

The Revival of Sherlock Holmes

Very many readers of the *Strand Magazine* have asked us over and over again if we could not induce Mr. Conan Doyle to give us some more stories of this wonderful character. Mr. Conan Doyle has been engaged on other work, but presently he will give us an important story to appear in the *Strand*, in which the great Sherlock Holmes is the principal character. It will appear in both the British and American editions. In America the play founded upon the career of the great detective has run for many months with enormous success. It is going to be produced in London in about three months, and at the same time the new Sherlock Holmes story will commence in the *Strand*. It will be published as a serial of from 30,000 to 50,000 words, and the plot is one of the most interesting and striking that has ever been put before us. We are sure that all those readers of the *Strand* who have written to us on the matter, and those who have not, will be very glad that Mr. Conan Doyle is going to give us some more about our old favourite.

25 May 1901

"The Hound of the Baskervilles"

We have very great pleasure in stating that in the August Number of the *Strand Magazine*, ready next Thursday, another adventure of Sherlock Holmes will appear, entitled *The Hound of the Baskervilles*. This is a powerful story of the great detective's work, and is perhaps one of the most interesting and exciting experiences that ever befell him before that fatal fall over the precipice. Mr. Conan Doyle himself says that

90

until Sherlock's death he had no idea of the great interest he had created. He received letters from all parts of the world remonstrating at Sherlock being killed, some of them in no unmeasured terms. One of them from a lady commenced affectionately as follows: "You brute!" For a long time Mr. Conan Doyle has been engaged on other work. We are sure it will to the delight of everyone that he is now returning to the ingenious practices of our old friend. The new adventure will continue for several months in the *Strand*.

27 July 1901

George Newnes, Limited

[The fourth annual general meeting of George Newnes, Limited, was held on 31 July 1901; the Chairman, Sir George Newnes, Bart, M.P., moved the adoption of the report.]

Dealing with the *Strand Magazine*, Sir George naturally congratulated the shareholders on the fact that the firm had been able to resuscitate their deceased friend Sherlock Holmes. This they had been trying to do for a number of years, but Mr. Conan Doyle had been a little obdurate. At last, however, he had revived that eminent detective, and in a series of numbers of the *Strand Magazine* was giving them an account of one of Sherlock Holmes's most exciting and interesting adventures. Those who had seen it thought that *The Hound of the Baskervilles* was not only as good as but better than any of the Sherlock Holmes stories. The Company had been offered a very substantial sum for the American rights, but they had refused the offer, because the Directors wished the *Strand Magazine* in America to continue to increase in popularity as it had been doing.

10 August 1901

HARPER'S WEEKLY

Notes of a Bookman

The Resuscitation of Sherlock Holmes

The Resuscitation of Sherlock Holmes is an accomplished fact – *vide* the August *Strand*. In view of the reappearance of this distinguished character I submit the following documents and correspondence in the case:

From the London *Daily Mail*, 19th July

Zermatt, *Friday*

An extraordinary rumour is circulating here that Mr. Sherlock

Holmes, the eminent criminal investigator, whose tragic death in a crevasse was reported circumstantially several years ago, creating a great sensation all over the world, has recently been seen in Zermatt. A well-known guide, Andrew Breen, has made affidavit before a notary that on Thursday last he saw Mr. Holmes in a café. Breen maintains that there could be no mistake about his identity, though he was obviously taking every precaution to keep himself as much out of the public gaze as possible. It may be remembered that when Mr. Holmes and Professor Moriarty were first reported to have fallen into the crevasse, the story was received with incredulity, and the suggestion made that it was merely a ruse on Mr. Holmes's part with some ulterior object. This was denied at the time, but Breen's story now justifies the scepticism of several years ago.

From the London *Daily Express*, 20th July

As our Mr. Hesketh Pritchard has just returned from his search for the Giant Sloth, which he was unfortunately unable to discover, though he met with indubitable traces of its existence, we have determined, regardless of expense, to despatch him forthwith to Switzerland, where the reappearance of Sherlock Holmes is reported. Holmes is said to have been seen as late as last week at Zermatt. We always suspected that he was not really dead, and venture an hypothesis that he did not fall to the bottom of the precipice when he fell over the ledge with Professor Moriarty. He was doubtless caught by a clump of trees twenty or thirty feet below, and, fearing pursuit from some other members of the Moriarty gang, he allowed the report of his death to go unchallenged, hiding himself for that time under another name in one of the Cantons. If our Mr. Pritchard is as successful as he hopes to be, he will bring the Great Investigator back to London to score greater triumphs than ever in the interest of truth and justice.

From *Le Journal de Genève*, 19th July

What we maintained in face of the whole world's Press some years ago has at last been proved correct, and the notorious Sherlock Holmes is proved a greater liar and fraud than even we ventured to suggest he was. It will be remembered by our readers that Holmes, while on a wild goose chase over the Continent, found his way to Switzerland, and was stated (with many plausible details) to have fallen from the ledge of an Alpine pass, along with a scoundrel of the Dynamite English party named Moriarty. The story was circulated everywhere, and the result was that Alpine-climbing was rendered very unpopular for two seasons. From the very first we disbelieved the story, which had many suspicious elements in it. The only witness of the extraordinary and inexplicable accident whereby the two men were said to have lost their lives was one Watson, a friend of Holmes, who, so far as we have been able to ascertain, earned his living by narrating the exploits of Holmes. That Watson was in a state of intoxication when he returned from the mountain to ask for a search expedition was well known at the time, though delicacy prevented us from mentioning the fact. The search party, consisting of nineteen guides, went all over the pass, and left not a yard of it unexplored, but they failed to find a scrap of evidence in support of Watson's story. This of itself would have been sufficient to throw grave doubts upon the story, but two days later, Watson, pretending to go out for a toothbrush, eluded the vigilance of the genial proprietor of the Bear of Berne Hotel (whose advertisement will be found on page 4), and decamped from the district, leaving his bill unpaid. Influenced by the serious injury which was done to the popularity of mountaineering by the narratives of Holmes's death, we boldly expressed a doubt of the whole affair, and were threatened with an action for damages by the English canon named Doyle, who appeared to be a relative of Watson or Holmes. At the time we apologised to Canon Doyle for suggesting that the story was false, but now we withdraw our apology, and brand Holmes and Watson as unprincipled ruffians. We hope soon to be able to lay bare the plot whereof this cock-and-bull story was an essential part.

Letter from Holmes to Watson

Zermatt, *5th May*

Don't you think it is about time I was permitted to leave this confounded place? I'm sick of it. It is all very well to maintain that the longer I stay away the keener will be the interest in my return to active work again; but I am not blind to the possibilities of a generation rising "who know not Joseph". I hear about a new fellow called Captain Kettle, who seems to be a little in our line. I hope you are not ass enough to let him get a position we cannot easily bounce him out of. But, first and last, I'm sick of this d—— place. And the fleas!

From Watson to Holmes

London, *8th May*

On no account venture into the open for a while yet. Doyle's far too busy to have anything to do with us at the moment, for he's over head and ears in the war movement. There's nothing at all in the Kettle story. Kettle is simply a low, maritime bully, who could not maintain the regard and affection of the British for more than six months. Besides, he's given up that business, and has been cavorting in *The Messenger Boy* at the Gaiety for a year back. I believe he has started a farm somewhere about Hythe lately. There was never the slightest danger that Kettle would interfere seriously with your position. Why – you are unique, my boy, unique! There has been nothing like you since old Lecoq, and if you stayed away ten years you would be hailed like an emperor on your return. But make no mistake: if it is "oof" that is wanted I will send it. I can't see that the work of a waiter at a Swiss hotel is any harder for you than investigating, and if you continue to wear the false whiskers you'll never be discovered. In any case, it's not the time to come back here. We're all in a mess over the war; money is tight, and our particular form of entertainment would scarcely go, I fear.

From Holmes to Watson

Zermatt, *3rd June*

False whiskers! That's the confounded thing. The boss of this place insists on my shaving, and if my hirsute adornment goes it's all up with us, for I'll be spotted, sure. And you say I'll "never be discovered". I begin to fear that is what you want. Why, man, I long to be discovered. Discovery, let me remind you, Watson, was my business. It is all very well for you and Doyle to live like lords on the strength of my alleged reputation, but I'll be hanged if I stay here any longer waiting on Cook trippers and hunting Swiss fleas. Unless you send me enough money to get back to London comfortably, I shall blow the gaff. That's flat!

Telegram – Watson to Holmes

5th June

For Heaven's sake don't! Will see what Doyle says. Newnes encourages the idea, but I think it suicide.

Telegram – Holmes to Watson

5th June

I'm off. Will be in London this week.

Extract from Letter
By Lord Rosebery to the London City Liberal Club

The paralysis of Liberalism is due to a fundamental and incurable antagonism of principle with regard to the Empire at large and our consequent policy. More vital than that is the fact that we want a Man – a Mind sufficiently strong to influence the warring elements of party; to placate the Opposition, now howling like wolves out of all harmony. In the great crises of history the hour has almost invariably brought such a Man, and I need scarcely recall to you the case of Napoleon, who took the scraps of Empire and welded them to his mighty purpose. But where are we to look for such a Man? I have in my mind at the moment the name of one who, it seems to me, is alone able to save the party, whose name some years ago was on every lip, though since then there has been an interregnum of mysterious silence. Need I say that I allude to Mr. Sherlock Holmes? If there is one in Europe to-day who could discover the mind of Liberalism, who could see what lies at our hearts as a party, it is this great and world-eminent investigator. It could not fail to gratify many of you to learn that Mr. Holmes, whose death in Switzerland some years ago we were led by some as yet inexplicable events to deplore, has within the past fortnight been reported alive and well. If that is so – and there is every reason to believe it is so – we have in Mr. Sherlock Holmes the Man and the Mind. I myself shall never voluntarily return to public life associated with any party; but I have the utmost confidence in recommending Mr. Holmes to your notice.

From the Agony Column, London *Times*

20th July

Sh-r-ck H-lm-s. – If you are in town, come to us at once. All will be forgotten and forgiven. – W-ts-n.
W-ts-n. – Rats! Simply Rats! It's all over between us. Have seen Sir George and C.D., and we propose to leave you out of the show altogether. – The Ex-Waiter, Soho.

From the London *Star*, 19th August

Sherlock Holmes is said to be back in London again, and residing in

Soho. He is described as looking younger than ever, and we see, indeed, little reason why the suggestion of Lord Rosebery should not be followed, and Mr. Holmes be entrusted with the discovery of the Liberal Party.

Dr. Doyle Interviewed –
from Literature, 2nd August

"So it really is the case that Mr. Sherlock Holmes has been discovered alive?"

"I do not commit myself in any way upon that point," said the distinguished author. "You have seen, doubtless, as much of the evidence as I have. I know that my friend Mr. Watson is a most trustworthy man, and I gave the utmost credit to his story of the dreadful affair in Switzerland. He may have been mistaken, of course. It may not have been Mr. Holmes who fell from the ledge at all, or the whole thing might be the result of hallucination. I confess the stories now being published seem circumstantial enough, and that Holmes may be alive. But I have not seen him. There has been an advertisement in *The Times* suggesting that I have, but it is not true; I have never seen Holmes. Watson, however, lately came on certain old documents dealing with a part of the career of Holmes's early in life, and I propose to publish these. They may be interesting; they may, indeed, induce Holmes, if he is really alive, to manifest himself again.

JAMES MACARTHUR
31 August 1901

THE CAMBRIDGE REVIEW

"The Hound of the Baskervilles" at Fault

An Open Letter to Dr. Watson

DEAR DR. WATSON, – Before the appearance of the February number of the *Strand Magazine*, it is my desire to draw your attention to one or two points in your story, *The Hound of the Baskervilles*, in which the world was rejoiced to welcome the reappearance of the late Sherlock Holmes. Whether you can escape all the charges of inconsistency which I shall bring against you, without straining the bounds of literary morality, is to me, and I hope to others, an important question.

From your first chapter the fundamental deduction can be made, that the year of your story is 1889. ("He left five years ago," says Sherlock, looking at Dr. Mortimer's stick, engraved with the date 1884.) Now Sir Charles Baskerville's met his death on 4 May in that year, the night before leaving the Hall for a sojourn of some months in London. A short calculation, or reference to a diary, shows us that 4 May 1889 was a Saturday. Did Sir Charles mean to go from Devonshire to London on a Sunday? Again, in Chap. XI, Mrs. Laura Lyons says that she "saw his [Sir Charles's] death in the paper next morning". That was quick work anyhow, as Sir Charles was not discovered till midnight on Saturday; and are local Sunday papers so common in villages such as Coombe Tracey?

You give no precise dates (of the month) till Chap. VIII, which contains your first report to Sherlock, dated 13 October (which was a Sunday, though you do not seem to know it). At the beginning of that report you say that a fortnight has passed since the flight of Selden, the escaped convict. Now you, Sir Henry, and Dr. Mortimer came down to Baskerville Hall from London on a Saturday, upon the evening of which Perkins the coachman told you that the convict had "been out three days now", that is, he must have escaped on a Wednesday or Thursday. From these data, I conclude your "fortnight" is only approximate, and that Selden escaped Wednesday, 2 Oct. or Thursday, 3 Oct., and that you arrived in Devonshire on Saturday, 5 Oct.

At least you must confess that your first day on the moor was a Sunday, whatever the day of the month was. Now on that first Sunday you went to Grimpen to make inquiries of the postmaster, concerning the test telegram sent by Sherlock to Barrymore. And you found the postmaster, "who was also the village grocer", at home. Then you met Mr. Stapleton, the naturalist, out for a Sunday walk, with the net which you justly call "absurd" in another place; and later in the day he came over to call on Sir Henry.

Of the interval between this Sunday and 13 October, also a Sunday, when you first report begins, you give us only two dates: – "the very next morning" after the Sunday call on Sir Henry paid by Stapleton, the latter took you both to show you "the spot where the legend of the wicked Hugo is supposed to have had its origin". The other date is a Thursday, when Dr. Mortimer lunched with you. This must have been 10 October.

Now your report accounts for the following dates: 12 October, when you first saw Barrymore on his nightly excursions; 13 October, when Sir Henry seized the opportunity of it being a Sunday to meet Miss Stapleton on the moor and propose to her under your eyes and those of her alleged brother; and when you and Sir Henry sat up for Barrymore the first time; 14 October, when you again sat up for and caught

Barrymore, heard his (or rather his wife's) explanation, went to catch the convict, and saw "the man on the Tor".

But of 15 October you give no account beyond mentioning that "to-day we mean to communicate to the Princetown people where they should look for their missing man". The extract from your diary in Chap. X begins on 16 October, which you call "the morning which followed our abortive chase of the convict". It was not. Your "abortive chase" was on the night of 14 October, as is proved by your writing the diary of it on the 15th. This you cannot escape. It is true that you say (Chap. VIII, init.) "one page is missing" from your letters to Sherlock Holmes, which may account for 15 October; but is this an intentional subterfuge?

In Chap. XI, which is the present limit of your tale, you are discovered, by one who can only be Sherlock himself, sitting in a neolithic hut, at sunset. A careful calculation reveals that this day is Friday, 18 October, which is the day on which you and Sir Henry "are to dine at Merripit House as a sign" of the healing of the breach between Sir Henry and the Stapletons. I hope you will get back in time to dress, but I doubt it.

Lastly, and worst of all, you cannot have been living with Sherlock Holmes in Baker Street at the date of the beginning of this story. In *The Sign of Four* you became engaged to Miss Mary Morstan in September 1888, and you were married "a few months later". How then in September 1889 were you still a bachelor in Baker Street?

The identity of Murphy, the gipsy horse-dealer; the so-called "death" of Rodger Baskerville in that vague place where all black sheep die (especially if they are younger sons), namely, Central America; and the evidence that you are a minor poet; – these are points about which I may say more another time.

FRANK SIDGWICK
23 January 1902

THE BOOKMAN

Some Inconsistencies of Sherlock Holmes

A recent number of the *Independent* contains a paper on Sherlock Holmes, in which the claim is made that his creation is a distinct addition to English literature, and that the stories in which he appears are better than the stories by Gaboriau and Poe, with which they have been often compared. The reason for this is found in the fact that the human element enters very decidedly into the Sherlock Holmes cycle, whereas it has little to do with the narratives about M. Lecoq and M. Dupin. Gaboriau's detective stories are, indeed, mere Chinese puzzles. Poe's are mathematical problems, or perhaps we should say problems in chess. Conan Doyle, however, has made us feel an interest in Sherlock Holmes, and in Watson, and in Gregson and Lestrade and Mycroft Holmes, as human beings with very distinctive and definite characteristics.

There is one little inconsistency in the portraiture of Holmes which we are surprised that no one has yet mentioned. In *A Study of Scarlet* Watson catalogues Holmes's limitations, and among other things says that his knowledge of literature was nil. "Of contemporary literature, philosophy and politics he appeared to know next to nothing. Upon my quoting Thomas Carlyle, he inquired in the naïvest way who he might be and what he had done." This is pretty specific as a statement, and therefore one is naturally surprised to find in the very next book (*The Sign of the Four*) Sherlock Holmes recommending Watson to study Winwood Reade's *Martyrdom of Man*, citing French aphorisms, quoting Goethe in the original German, referring to Jean Paul in relation to Carlyle! reverting once more to Winwood Reade, and winding up at last with another bit of Goethe. Elsewhere he shows a familiarity with George Sand, and in "A Case of Identity" gets in both Horace and Hafiz in a single sentence. Indeed, in the matter of quotations and allusions, we think that the later Sherlock Holmes could run Mr. Mabie pretty hard.

We believe that the interest of the reading public in Sherlock Holmes is increasing rather than diminishing as time goes on. One proof of this is found in the fact that Dr. Doyle has been absolutely forced to write another Holmes story, and that the serial publication of it in the *Strand* has made the issues of that magazine jump to thirty thousand copies beyond its normal circulation. We are reading *The Hound of the Baskervilles* ourselves, and it is the first story that we have read in serial form for more than ten years. We should like to publish some guesses here as to how it is going to turn out, but we prudently abstain. The thing indeed is growing so fearfully complex as to seem scarcely to admit of any solution whatever; yet experience has shown that when the explanation does come, it will be so absurdly simple as to make one fairly gasp at not having seen it from the beginning.

January 1902

The Footprints of the Baskerville Hound

Very few people, we think, who have been reading the new Sherlock

Holmes story have as yet been able even to guess at what will be contained in the closing chapters. Five instalments have now appeared; it is three months since Holmes has played any part in the narrative; and as a result everything seems to be in a chaotic state. Any guess as to the outcome, in consequence, must be based on the events which were narrated in the first two instalments. As a rule, almost everyone with whom we have discussed the story has confessed himself or herself utterly at sea; yet we have heard one theory, which, though it is hardly likely to prove the right one, has the merit of a certain weird ingenuity. Then, too, it can be made to fit all the circumstances, and in connection with this we must remember the adage of Holmes himself on a former occasion: "When you find a theory that fits all the circumstances, no matter how improbable that theory may seem, it is the right one." The author of the hypothesis originated it after reading four instalments of *The Hound of the Baskervilles* as it is appearing in the *Strand Magazine*. At the time he had not seen the chapters which appeared in the January Number, and which dealt with the confrontation of the butler Barrymore by Sir Henry and Watson, and the subsequent expedition over the moors in search of the escaped convict. But this last instalment, it must be said, does nothing either to destroy or confirm the original theory.

According to the idea of this theorist, one of the few incidents of vital importance and meaning was that of the theft of Sir Henry Baskerville's shoes in the hotel in which he was staying at London. To any one acquainted with the methods of Sherlock Holmes, or perhaps it should be said of the methods of the Sherlock Holmes stories, it was evident that this at least was no false clue introduced for the sole purpose of leading astray the mind of the reader. What, then, was the significance? What impression was to be compared with that made by Sir Henry's boots? It was while mulling on this line that there occurred the strange thought that those who had stolen the shoes had done so not for the purpose of studying the outside; *they wanted to examine the inside.* And from that the theory which builded itself was something as follows:

The Sir Hugo Baskerville who met his death in so horrible and yet so well-deserved a manner and bequeathed such a curse to his descendants had a wife who had followed him in secret on the eventful night with which the opening instalment of the story deals. (If he had not a wife, the brother through whom was traced the descent of the family had one, and so the matter is much the same.) At any rate, this wife was a witness to the hideous scene of the hound plucking at Sir Hugo's throat. Some months afterwards she gave birth to a child which was found to be physically perfect with the exception that it had the feet of a hound, and in every generation or every other generation of the family since that day there had been born a child cursed with this hideous deformity.

Improbable as this hypothesis seems, if you will go over the back numbers, you will find that everywhere it can be made to fit. The footprint found close by the dead body of Sir Charles was not that of a hound, but of a Baskerville. Sir Henry's shoes were abstracted (and it must be remembered that two pairs were taken because the first pair was too new to tell any story), in order that those interested could see whether the impression left within was that of the foot of a man or of a hound. Perhaps it was Holmes himself who wished to see whether it was Sir Henry who had stood beside the dead Sir Charles. Perhaps it was the emissaries or the fellow-conspirators of the criminal Baskerville who wished to know whether Sir Henry himself was afflicted in the manner described, because if such were the case, he would certainly guess at the real solution. The actions of the butler, Barrymore, are thus explained, because he was a repository of at least part of the secret. The convict Selden was perhaps the arch criminal – he may have been the lost Rodger Baskerville himself. But as to Stapleton and his sister and the hideous noise which arises from the moor, and the black-bearded man who followed Holmes and balked him in London and the various other mysterious details of the story so far as we have read it, the theorist has nothing definite to say.

February 1902

Raffles and Sherlock Holmes

The theory advanced in the February BOOKMAN about the footprints of the Baskerville hound has brought to this office a number of letters, some of which contain theories far more ingenious than our own. Our chief regret in the matter is that we did not use the idea in the January Number so that we could have discussed some of the resulting letters in the February issue, because we have an idea that the March instalment of *The Hound of the Baskervilles* (these lines are being written on 10 February) is going to tell us what it is all about. So we feel that we shall have to take leave of Sherlock Holmes for a little while and turn our attention to another gentleman with whom we occasionally hear him contrasted and compared.

The first time that Mr. E. W. Hornung put an apparent end to Raffles, the amateur cracksman, it was with a very obvious hesitation. The author seemed to be saying: "This chap seems to be becoming somewhat of a bore, so here goes. But as it may be convenient to bring

him back, I may as well throw in the suggestion that although he undoubtedly jumped overboard he did not necessarily drown." It was
much the same way with Sherlock Holmes. Dr. Doyle protested, and
very loudly protested, that if he did not kill Sherlock Holmes, Sherlock
Holmes would certainly kill him. But when it came to the point, and
Professor Moriarty was made to throw the detective over the Alpine
precipice, the author saw to it that nobody ever found the body. Nor did
he throw out any hint that all the stories preceding the catastrophe had
been told. On the contrary, in the course of former narratives, allusions
were made to other stories, among them "The Adventure of the Tired
Captain" and "The Adventure of the Second Stain", with a promise
that they should appear in print at a later and more favourable day.
Raffles's second "finish", however, was very emphatic and decisive,
and, consequently, it is with considerable curiosity that we await his
next reappearance.

March 1902

A Sherlock Holmes Number

We might as well inform our readers in advance that the next Number of
THE BOOKMAN is going to be distinctively a Sherlock Holmes affair. It
will celebrate the completion of *The Hound of the Baskervilles*, and the
Editors of this magazine intend to enjoy themselves hugely over the
whole thing. We don't mind admitting confidentially that the Editors
are not always quite in sympathy with each other's individual tastes and
preferences and fads – which is a good thing for THE BOOKMAN, since it
ensures variety. When the Senior Editor, for instance, stirs around in
European politics, or dwells with fondness on some singularly interesting diplomatic complication in South America, the Junior Editor settles
down very low in his chair and looks out of the window as far up the
street as he can see, and hopes that somebody will come in, or that
something will occur to end the agony. Likewise, when the Junior
Editor thinks that he has got an entirely new and illumining revelation
about something in the writings of Alexandre Dumas *père*, or when he
successfully works off baseball intelligence, in the guise of literary
comment, the Senior Editor descends softly into the basement and
mopes and moans all by himself. But when it comes to Sherlock Holmes,
then –! A brisk hum of confluent voices penetrates the inner office. The
latest number of the *Strand* has arrived, and each Editor suspends all
work for the remainder of the day. Grinding toil is forgotten, and Fancy
holds full sway. The whole Baskerville mystery is traced back to the
beginning. The back numbers are hunted out, so that each incident may
be restudied, each phrase reweighed, and each apparent clue retested in

the light of the new chapter. All the past literature on Sherlock Holmes is again gone over; even the other stories of Dr. Doyle are quoted and turned inside out for purposes of comparison. Why were Sir Henry's shoes stolen? Was the Barrymore episode merely a blind to throw the reader off the scent? Who cut out the words from *The Times* and pieced them together into a letter of warning? Who was the man in the cab? Was there a real hound? Who was Stapleton? And how much of the story is Fletcher Robinson's and how much Conan Doyle's? Discussion waxes hot. Both Editors are violently stirred. Both talk at the same time – interminable, impatient, dogmatic, delighted. They go out at last to finish the argument at dinner. Midnight finds them still comparing Lecoq, Dupin, and Sherlock Holmes, and insisting on the inaccuracy of each other's quotations. It is exhilarating to the last degree, and naturally it has all got to be reflected, sooner or later, in the pages of THE BOOKMAN. Hence, the May Number, as we said in the beginning, will be distinctively a Sherlock Holmes affair. To tell the truth, we wish it were out now, as we are simply consumed with anxiety to read it ourselves.

April 1902

More Sherlock Holmes Theories

It was only a few months ago that we were discussing in these columns the subject of the serial, contrasting the average illogically chopped-up narrative of to-day with some of the real serials of forty or sixty years ago. A book which is in many ways a notable exception to what we said is the widely exploited *The Hound of the Baskervilles*, which, while not so very extraordinary as a complete story, was in a minor way a really great serial. In fact, in that form it has proved the most successful book since *Trilby* came out in parts in *Harper's Magazine*. After reading the tale as a whole in book form, one can look back and realise how cleverly devised each instalment was, and how, with one or two exceptions, the closing paragraphs of each month's part were worked up so as to stimulate to the highest degree the reader's excitement and curiosity. The opening instalment appeared in September, and the closing lines were a positive triumph in that they instantly won and held the attention of every reader, and left him unsatisfied to the very end. The head of the Baskerville family had been found dead under peculiar circumstances. The story of an old legend of a gigantic hound which, more than two centuries before, was said to have worried to death the wicked Baskerville of that day, and afterwards to have followed the family as a curse, was told. And after the plain facts and the supernatural legend had been placed side by side, they were linked into one thrill of wonder and horror by the information that, although nothing had been said of it at the coroner's inquest, there had been found near the body of the dead Sir Charles footprints, not of a man nor of a woman, but "the footprints of a gigantic hound".

By this time the whole story is known to those who have read it either in book or serial form. Perhaps there are some who are more or less disappointed in the manner in which the tale was worked out, and indeed there are some explanations which strain the credulity. Some months ago, when only two or three parts had appeared, a theory as to the solution was printed in THE BOOKMAN. This theory proved very far wrong; but the number of letters which came to this office, contradicting or affirming it, served to show how widespread was the interest in the serial. We should like to print them all, because even now they are entertaining, but it is very obvious that we could not. However, we are going to give two, which show to a certain extent the tone of all the rest.

Sir Hugo Baskerville and the Yeoman's Daughter

To the Editors

Your speculations on the outcome of the new Sherlock Holmes story have interested me very much, especially the ingenious theory given in THE BOOKMAN for this month. Merely as a matter of passing interest might I call your attention to another phase of that same theory? Taking it for granted that there is in the neighbourhood of Baskerville Hall some person with feet like a hound, does it not seem more probable that this person is a descendant of the girl whom Sir Hugo Baskerville wronged? She was lying prostrate when Hugo's companion saw the hound tear out his throat, but her death is nowhere insisted on – Dr. Doyle does not "produce the corpse". That any woman of the Baskerville family should have followed in that wild gallop across miles of moor seems improbable. But let it be given that this girl had only fainted, and that she lived to give birth to a child (whether or not an illegitimate Baskerville), and one or two more points in the story seem to be solved. For instance, there is good reason for a bitter family feud between the hound-footed descendants of the Baskervilles – no one can blame a man for feeling a little peevish towards a family one of whose members has cursed him with such inconvenient extremities. Or allow that a sort of insanity accompanies the malformed feet. That is not an impossibility in the realm of fiction. And many of the Baskervilles have died sudden deaths. Why may not this account for the peculiar actions of the butterfly-chasing Stapleton? He is the dog-toed one, I am convinced (for the moment), and the escaped convict Selden is innocent of everything save an entirely extraneous murder. The hideous sound heard on the moor is some natural phenomenon connected with the Grimpen Mire. The original hound was one of Baskerville's pack which turned on him for some reason, and whose size was magnified by the frightened shepherd and the tipsy companions. The animal seen by Sir Charles was really a black calf. And, last of all, the typewriting lady interviewed by Dr. Watson has nothing to do with the case – nothing important, at least – but is merely another one of those false scents and ridiculous blunders that the ingenuous Watson is always falling into for the greater glorification of Sherlock Holmes.

The Identity of Selden

To the Editors

I have very much enjoyed reading in the current BOOKMAN your comments upon the outcome of *The Hound of the Baskervilles*. I have read this Sherlock Holmes story with great interest, and had also the club-footed theory. However, I carried the theory a little farther, trying to account for the other characters. Assuming that the escaped criminal, Selden, is in reality Rodger Baskerville, and that this Rodger had met Sir Charles at the trysting-place at the yew hedge on the night of the latter's death, it is probable that Sir Charles, expecting to meet Laura Lyons, had died of fright at beholding Rodger, against whom he had probably committed some great wrong. This was Rodger's revenge. Rodger, of course, in order to approach noiselessly, had removed his shoes, which accounts for the footprints near the dead body. Rodger has used Laura as an unsuspecting tool. Laura, shocked at the terrible outcome of her friendship with Rodger, instead of revealing her connection with the death of Sir Charles at the time of her appointment with him, had never revealed anything about it, through fear of incriminating herself. This, then, was her secret. Now for the other suspicious characters, Stapleton and Barrymore. Both are in the plot with the convict; Stapleton more than Barrymore. Mrs. Barrymore is innocent, as was shown by her plausible confession to Sir Henry and Dr. Watson. She had been told this story and led to believe it was really true. Barrymore may be as innocent as his wife, though more likely he is more closely connected with the crime. Stapleton is hand in glove with the convict, as is shown by his lack of fear of living on the moor while the convict is still at large, although we know that Stapleton is of a nervous and irritable disposition. His sister has in some way learned something of the plots of her brother and the convict, and is filled with sympathy for Sir Henry, with whom she afterwards falls in love. Her brother, however, has some powerful influence over her. Stapleton was the agent of the villain in London, and Miss Stapleton (who was there with him, for he did not dare to leave her out of his sight) was the person who sent the warning, made up from the newspaper, to Sir Henry, not daring to use her own handwriting, through fear of being discovered by her brother. Then, when on the moor with Sir Henry, she again warns him, and Stapleton's anger at discovering them together was caused through fear that she might know something of his plots and be revealing them to Sir Henry. Miss Stapleton does not know what the plot is, but only suspects its existence. The supposed barkings of the hound can be attributed to merely physical causes, such as the escaping of gases on the moor.

Probably this is but little more than you have already expressed in your columns, but I hope that it may be of some interest to you.

May 1902

THE NEW YORK SUN

The Doyley Dialogues

By Samuel Hopkins Adams

I

The Messenger Boy

Observe the Messenger Boy, how he runs. *Is not this unusual?* It is positively abnormal. *And its cause?* He goes on a Hurry Call for a man – *To fetch a doctor?* To fetch a book. *What book?* THE HOUND OF THE BASKERVILLES. *How surprised and gratified the man will be to get his book so soon.* He will not. *Why so?* The Messenger Boy has heard of that book. *Well?* He will dip into it. *Yes?* And see the name of Sherlock Holmes. *And then?* He will seat himself on a mossy kerb. And he will read. And read. And read. *But the man. What of him?* He will tear his hair and cuss. *Is that all?* No. Presently he will rake up another $1.25 and will hustle to the bookstore himself. *Wise man!* Happy Messenger Boy!

3 May 1902

II

The Policeman

Consider now the Policeman. *Is the Policeman alarmed?* Bless you, no!
Why, then, so Pompadour an aspect? That shows absorbed interest. *And the
two persons operating upon a third?* Oh, that's a mere detail. *What manner of
men are they?* They are thugs. *Will not the cop butt in?* Not he. *Why not?* He is
engaged on a more important case. *Which is?* The Mystery of THE
HOUND OF THE BASKERVILLES. *How does the cop figure?* He is assisting
Sherlock Holmes. *To do what?* To catch the Hound. *And will the obliging
Policeman catch the Hound?* Probably not. But you can. *How so?* By
following the trail to a book-shop and surrounding him with $1.25 in
coin of the realm.

10 May 1902

III

The Christian Gentleman

Why does the Heathen rage? It is not a Heathen. It is a Christian
Gentleman. *Why does the Christian Gentleman rage?* He has just heard the
guard chant his lay. *Which lay?* "Hundernumptysinxt! Allout!" *Does not
the Christian Gentleman wish to get out?* He does, indeed! He wished to get
out at Forty-Second Street. *What prevented?* He was dead to the world.
What a curse is inebriety! Certainly. But that is not his trouble. *What is it,
then?* He was reading THE HOUND OF THE BASKERVILLES. *And forgot his
station?* Even so. And all the world, besides. *What will the Christian
Gentleman do now?* Buy another ticket. *And go back to Forty-Second Street?*
More likely to South Ferry. *Why so?* Because that is the other end of the
line. *And will the Christian Gentleman never get home?* Oh, yes. When he has
finished the book.

17 May 1902

IV

The Peaceable Citizen

Aha! A warrior of old! Not at all. It is an ordinarily Peaceable Citizen.
Why, then, the war-path rig? He has something on hand. *What is his little
game?* He is about to commit justifiable homicide on an intimate friend.
Why such extreme measures? The I.F. butted in on him as he was reading
THE HOUND OF THE BASKERVILLES. *And interrupted?* No; the reader was

107

too deep in the story. *What harm, then?* Just then the phone buzzed. *Ah!* That's what the friend said as the other went – *To answer the phone?* No, to choke off the bell. *Then?* He seized on the book. *And began the story?* In the middle. When he had read to where Sherlock Holmes finds the mysterious footprints – *Footprints of what?* Just then he heard the other man returning. *And dropped the book?* He couldn't. He borrowed it very informally and fled. *What did the owner do?* Observe the picture above. *And what became of the I.F.?* Observe the picture below. *He seems in terror of his life.* Worse than that. *What could be worse?* The fear of being cut off in his prime before he reaches the solution of the mystery!

24 May 1902

V

The Bridegroom

Consider the lily of the field. *Verily, he out-Sols Solomon.* He has due and proper cause. *Is he to be Queen of the May, mother?* No; but it is his wedding day, tra-la, tra-loe! *And he hastens to church?* Not he. *Why not?* The matter has escaped his mind. *Careless mind!* He is very busy. *Learning his part?* No; following a hot trail. *Trail of what?* THE HOUND OF THE BASKERVILLES. *What of his marriage?* Sh! You'll disturb him. *But the bride?* Don't worry. She's busy, too. *What! Has she also a copy of the book?* Just so. *And there will be no wedding?* Not to-day. Some other day. *When both have finished the story?* Go to the head.

31 May 1902

VI

The Bookseller

Behold the man at the counter. *Quite so. He seems engrossed.* Yes; he is deducing things. *Is this, then, the famed Sherlock Holmes?* No; only a meek and humble disciple. *And what is he deducing?* A conclusion from a book. *Is it difficult?* Not at all. He observes the title. *Which is?* THE HOUND OF THE BASKERVILLES; and under the title a picture of Sherlock Holmes. *What then?* From this he deduces that it's a good thing and he can't afford to miss it. *Is the other person also a practitioner of deduction?* He is. He holds a $5 bill. *Well?* From this he makes a deduction of $1.25. *Ah, a commercial transaction?* A mutually satisfactory one. The Bookseller rejoices because this is the thirteenth copy of the book he has sold in an hour. *And the purchaser?* Is gleeful because he has bought $125.00 worth of enjoyment for $1.25. *What, then, do we deduce from this?* That it's a good proposition

108

which benefits both sides. *Ah! How simple is deduction when you once know how.*

7 June 1902

TIT-BITS

"Sherlock Holmes" at the Lyceum

R. S. and Others. – We are very glad to say that the success of the play, *Sherlock Holmes*, is very great indeed. The Lyceum Theatre is crowded every night from floor to ceiling, and it looks as if the play would run there well into next year. Mr. William Gillette's performance in the character of Sherlock is a splendid one. He hits off the great detective as we know him in Conan Doyle's stories to the very life, and at times when he is just on the point of discovering something, or when he himself is in physical danger, the house is electrified into dead silence. It makes it the more interesting that his old enemy Moriarty comes into the drama, and this part is well played by Mr. Abingdon. Mr. Gillette, whom we believe took leading parts in his own plays after he had been on the stage less than a year, is a fascinating actor. The scene at the end where he is trapped by Moriarty into a den where he is to be put to death by means of gas is a very striking one, and the way Sherlock escapes arouses the excitement of the audience to the highest pitch.

12 October 1901

Should a Public Monument be Erected to Sherlock Holmes?

Supposed to be written by Dr. Watson

To those millions of readers who have been with us, so to speak, in so many of our adventures, it will be readily conceived that this question is to me of profound interest. Ever since the tragic circumstances which at one blow ended the career of my deeply lamented friend Holmes and robbed the world of its greatest genius in the detection of crime, I have felt assured that sooner or later I should be called upon to convey to a sympathetic public the message which he intrusted to me.

I dropped into his rooms at Baker Street one evening in the month of August. The heat during the day had been up to 92° in the shade, and I was not surprised to find him lazily stretched out on the sofa. It was the first time I had seen him after the Croydon Cardboard Box Case. He seemed particularly pleased to see me, and as the evening advanced we talked upon all manner of subjects. At one time it would be the structure

109

of the teeth of Polar bears; at another we would discourse on the discovery in Assyria of a tablet bearing an account of the conquest of Babylonia by the Elamites. Finally we drifted to the discussion of monuments in general and public memorials in particular.

"You take it from me, Watson, that a public memorial is entirely a superfluity. Now, take my own case. I have no doubt that when I am gone there will be some public regret expressed in the newspapers, after which the B.P. will, with the best intentions, want to associate my name with one of these lifeless things. If need be, Watson, you tell them that I would have none of it."

"But surely," I broke in, "you would never suggest that the British public should deny themselves the privilege of erecting a monument to commemorate your work, when such a consummation is often accorded to less and seldom to more worthy subjects?" In sincerity I would have substituted the word "never" for "seldom", but Holmes had no ear for flattery.

As was his wont when about to deliver himself of something which he particularly wished me to remember, Holmes looked hard at me and brought the tips of his fingers together.

"Don't you make any mistake, Watson. When this project is mooted, if you are spared, simply tell them that from Holmes's own lips you knew that monuments were viewed by him with strong abhorrence, and with emphasis. Don't forget the adjective."

"And your reasons?" I ventured to ask, taken aback by the sudden change to energy which his tone and manner betrayed. I did not remember to have seen him speak with so much vigour and decision.

"A proper question – there should always be a reason for every statement. And yet you, Watson, have seen so much of my work that it must be clear to you that I need no greater memorial than the record I shall leave behind me."

He transferred his gaze to the ceiling, and with a half-dreamy air, as though living once more in the past, he continued:

"There is scarcely a crowned head in Europe but has reason to thank me for unravelling some personal mystery that was eating away their life and happiness. My clients will hand down my name as a 'blessed memory', whilst criminals will utter it with bated breath. What better memorial than this? I doubt not that your own chronicles of my adventures will of themselves become historical."

"But what would Trafalgar Square be without its Nelson, or Princes Street, Edinburgh, without its Scott, not to mention –"

Holmes interrupted me with a gesture of impatience. "There you've hit it, Watson. It is true Trafalgar Square would be robbed of an object of interest and that Princes Street would be deprived of the greatest literary monument in the world; but do you think either Nelson or Scott would pass into oblivion if the monuments had never been?"

I was compelled to admit that they would not. Holmes proceeded:

"Monuments don't always signify merit, my dear fellow. Almost any mediocrity of municipal life, particularly if he is blessed with a fair share of this world's goods, can command his monument. The work of real men of genius is oftener left to stand unaided the test of posterity. I much prefer to abide by that test."

I was wondering at what point to renew the assault, when there came a loud knock at the hall door. Whilst the boy in buttons was answering the call Holmes remarked: "If I mistake not, this knock comes from a gentleman interested in the Manchester Ruby Case."

These were the only words that ever passed between us on the subject, but Holmes was emphatic enough, and, whatever my personal wishes may have been, I cannot do less than make known his views. There are times even yet when I feel that in this Holmes erred. It may have been due to that sense of modesty which was inseparable from him.

J. H. BREARLEY
28 December 1901

THE PLAYGOER

Sherlock Holmes on the Continent

Sherlock Holmes in Dutch, performed at the Grand Theatre, Amsterdam, on Sunday night, 12 January, made an emphatic hit. The piece was produced by A. Van Lier Freres; the scenery, identical with that used by Mr. Gillette at the Lyceum, was built in London; and the electrical appliances were sent to Amsterdam from America. This is the first of the Continental productions of *Sherlock Holmes* now running at the Lyceum, but companies are about to play the piece in Austria, Denmark, Hungary, France, and Germany. The play has been translated into Russian by Countess Bella, and will be put on at the Imperial Theatre, St. Petersburg, on 1 March.

February 1902

PUNCH

Our Happy Holmes

Sherlock Holmes is a prodigious success. While running at the Lyceum it is keeping itself going, at the same time, in various theatres here, there and everywhere. It is to be played in French, Chaldaic, German, Italian, Phœnician, Greek, Double Dutch, and Egyptian. It will be produced in the fine theatre now in process of construction in the Undiscovered Islands. Several rival Indian tribes are on the war-path with it. One performance was given before His Majesty of the Anthropophagonian country, who was so delighted that he insisted on the entire troupe being presented to him *before supper was prepared*. Although the company accepted His Majesty's most gracious invitation, they were compelled to leave hurriedly some hours before the time appointed. Scandinavian-speaking players will act it at Stockholm. This last-mentioned troupe will be known as "The Stock-Holmes Co.".

12 February 1902

Authors at Bow Street

The first sitting of the newly constituted Literary Bench was held on 29 February 1902. The Court was crowded. The Magistrates present were Mr. Watts-Dunton, J.P., Mr Edmund Gosse, J.P., and Dr. Robertson Nicoll, J.P. Mr. C. K. Shorter acted as Magistrate's Clerk. One of the principal cases is reported below:

Arthur Conan Doyle, forty-two surgeon, and William Gillette, forty-four actor, two able-bodied men, were flung into the dock charged with the exhumation of Sherlock Holmes for purposes of gain.

Mr. James Welch, K.C., prosecuting for the Crown, said that not since the days of Burke and Hare had so flagrant a case been heard of. Long after the death of Mr. Holmes, who had been in his day a detective of some skill, though not attached to Scotland Yard (*sensation*), the prisoners had exhumed him, and were charging, at the Lyceum Theatre, considerable sums to persons who wished to view the body. Sir George Newnes, proprietor of the *Strand Magazine*, gave evidence of Sherlock Holmes's death.

19 February 1902

THE BOOKMAN

Coronation Honours

We salute and cordially congratulate Sir Arthur Conan Doyle, Knight Bachelor, upon the recognition which he has received from his sovereign lord, the King. His new honours were, to be sure, given him for his defence of the British policy in South Africa, and not for the creation of

Sherlock Holmes, Mycroft Holmes, the good Dr. Watson, the obtuse Lestrade, the fatuous Gregson, and the Gigantic Hound. If the King had been recognising these things, he would have had to give Sir Arthur a peerage.

We have never until now experienced any desire to be King of England; but we are beginning to see that there are possibilities in the kingship which we had not recognised before. If, for instance, we were occupying the English throne, we should cause it to be intimated to Sir Arthur Conan Doyle that he might become a baronet as soon as he should write "The Adventure of the Second Stain", which he has so exasperatingly mentioned in one of his other tales, and which seems to us one of the most piquant, mysterious, and altogether tantalising titles that anyone ever invented. We should also cause it to be understood that a story as good as *The Hound of the Baskervilles* would gain for its author the rank of baron; a story as good as *The Sign of the Four*, the title of viscount; and one as good as *A Study in Scarlet*, the title of earl. A book like the *Memoirs* would deserve a marquisate; and if it is conceivable that anyone should again produce so fascinating a volume as the *Adventures*, it is perfectly obvious that such a person ought to be a duke.

August 1902

Dr. Watson's Wedding Present

We don't mind admitting to our readers that there is trouble in the office of THE BOOKMAN. In fact, the relations between the Junior Editor and the Senior Editor are seriously strained. It all came from a remark of the Senior Editor, who happened one day after some hours of reverie to ask, apropos of nothing: "I wonder what Sherlock Holmes gave Watson for a wedding present?" Now that is an interesting question. You see, when Watson announced that he was going to marry Miss Morstan, Holmes expressed his regret, because on general principles he didn't believe in marriage. Still, Watson was his one intimate friend, and indeed had met Miss Morstan through Holmes, as is written in *The Sign of the Four*. So it is not to be supposed that Holmes gave him no wedding present at all. Yet what sort of wedding present would a man like Sherlock Holmes hit upon? It is a very subtle question and needs much thought. But the Junior Editor answered it right off, as though it were quite simple. He said that weddings and such things being wholly out of Holmes's line, he probably went to some big shop in Bond Street and handed out a ten-pound note to the first clerk he met, and said: "Please choose a wedding present for me to give to a friend." The Senior Editor had to admit that this theory has the merit of definiteness; yet somehow or

113

other it doesn't seem satisfactory nor quite like Sherlock Holmes. Still, he hadn't any explanation of his own to offer, and so he goes around in a most dispirited way, while the Junior Editor moves briskly about the office with an air of conscious superiority, rattling his golf-sticks and grinning in the most exasperating fashion whenever he catches the Senior Editor's eye.

December 1902

From a Lady in Berkeley, California

To the Editors

Just a word regarding Sherlock Holmes's wedding present. The idea of "the editor with golf-sticks" is certainly crude. Would it not have been truly characteristic if Holmes had contrived in his own ingenious fashion to find what Dr. Watson and his bride had most wanted for their new home, but had been forced to cut from the list, since the doctor's purse was not over-plethoric? You will probably think that this is begging the question, after all.

January 1903

The Partial Solution of a Mystery

[Observing that Watson was about to be married, Sherlock Holmes offered him the Hound of the Baskervilles. This was refused. He could not do as other men would and seek advice from a Bond Street store as his public would flock to Watson's house to see what had been chosen, but he promised to find a suitable gift.]

From the Narrative of Dr. Watson

Sherlock Holmes fulfilled his promise and sent a present, which made everyone think of the great detective, who had unwound so many tangled skeins. It was an enormous ball of worsted, five feet in diameter, and red and black in colour. With it was a note:

My Dear Watson, – I send you this ball, which is like an interesting case, for there is a great deal of unravelling to do before one reaches the heart of the mystery. At irregular intervals you will find clues that will help a truly logical mind to deduce the final outcome.

This is the longest yarn I have ever been connected with. The present is worsted, but I am not; for, long before the last piece shall have been unwound, the public will have forgotten I ever gave a present; and so they cannot say, "How commonplace!" Therefore,

114

my reputation for wisdom is saved.

That all your fondest hopes may be realised, is the earnest wish of,

SHERLOCK HOLMES

P.S. All the wool must be knit as it is unwound, though part of it is already crowshade. – S. H.

Perhaps Holmes's "public" would like to guess the ending of his wonderful yarn. If they would not, I will tell them – when I find out.

J. ALSTON COOPER
February 1903

On Secret Writings

An interesting chapter in the life of Edgar Allan Poe, which seems to have been forgotten by most people, although it is curiously illustrative of one important side of his genius, is that which showed his great power in the matter of unravelling and deciphering secret writings.

One of the principal means of devising a cipher, as Poe pointed out, is to take as the key some phrase or name or title containing just the number of letters of the alphabet, and then for "a" to use the first letter of the phrase, for "b" the second, for "e" the fifth, and so on. For instance, if we were to propound the cipher: "RMEEHMEER-RIEOKIRCEEHTOETOETFCIEOFEEORTH" in THE BOOKMAN, all our astute readers (and that of course means them all), after a brief, superficial study, would discover that we were at our old tricks again, that we had taken as a key *The Memoirs of Sherlock Holmes*, a title which happens to contain just twenty-six letters, and would glibly read out the cipher: "If you decipher this you are a real Sherlockian."

March 1903

Un-Sherlockian Business

To The Editors

Again Sherlock Holmes. Fine as Mr. Gillette's Sherlock is, he does seem to have made a slip in assuming that Moriarty would not have tried to get the pistol if he had had another. But how about Moriarty's failure to see Holmes remove the cartridges, as shown by his afterwards snatching the pistol and trying to fire it? Is this up to the standard of the Doyle Moriarty?

I have wondered if anyone else regarded this incident in the play as a lapse of Moriarty's usual alertness.

A BOOKMANITE

Honesdale, Pennsylvania.

Moriarty deserves no censure for failing to see Holmes remove the cartridges. Of course Moriarty was a genius, but of course, also, Sherlock Holmes was a still greater one. Holmes didn't want Moriarty to see the removal of the cartridges, and naturally he didn't let him see it. Had Moriarty detected him, Moriarty would have been cleverer than Sherlock Holmes, and surely, *that* would not be the Doyle Moriarty.

May 1903

The Reigate Puzzle

To the Letter-Box

Still again – though I trust not finally – Sherlock Holmes. (Surely you can blame no one for keeping that subject to the fore!) "The great detective" is quite apparently a quack of quacks, deserving to rank as a minor satellite of Cagliostro's; his creator stumbles perpetually, falling often. For proof, select any one of Holmes's adventures or memoirs at random – say "The Reigate Puzzle".

Of course, you recall how the fragment of a note furnished Sherlock his principal clue. He discovered that the two Cunninghams constructed this note, each writing a word in alternation, so as to avoid the missive's identification. Yet – O absurd improbability! – neither made the slightest effort to disguise his own hand. Had they been the ordinarily intelligent beings Doyle sought to make them, it is manifest that they must have written – the old man in imitation of Alec – as differently from usual as possible – which would have rendered Holmes's "wonderful deductions" impossible. I suppose even the merest tyro can do something towards the forgery.

Of course, that one man wrote all his words first might still show, but it is doubtful if the stronger and weaker (elder and younger) could now be determined; and it is certain that a blood-relationship between the writers could not now be deduced from the fact that "both used Greek *e*'s".

Isn't it perfectly evident that, explaining, Holmes realised the childishness of his efforts at this point, and, as in the case of the nervous attack which prevented Inspector Forrest's revealing the clue to the criminals a few hours before, he hastily sought to gloss over the foozle he had made, by modestly remarking that "there were twenty-three other deductions which would be of more interest to experts than to you" – plainly, a not creditable bit of charlatanism.

SOL STICE

This is a bit of very specious special pleading. The writer has ignored the following facts: (1) That the Cunninghams were not experts in crime, but amateurs; (2) that they supposed that only the murdered man would ever see the letter, for Alec expected to recover it from the dead body; (3) that Holmes did not depend entirely upon the evidence of the letter, since he had detected the Cunninghams in two distinct lies – one relating to the alleged struggle, and the other relating to the place where the alleged murderer had made his escape; and (4) that Holmes was aware of the singular and apparently fruitless burglary which had been committed in the house of the person towards whom the Cunninghams felt a bitter animosity. In view of these facts, our correspondent's strictures upon Sherlock Holmes seem to be utterly unwarranted.

June 1903

IV. SHERLOCK HOLMES REDIVIVUS (1903–1910)

————◆————

The First Announcement

[The sixth annual general meeting of George Newnes, Limited, was held on 30 July 1903; the Chairman, Sir George Newnes, Bart, M.P., presiding.]

The Chairman noted that both TIT-BITS and the *Strand Magazine* had retained their hold upon the public. He went on to say:

> Another interesting announcement I have to make with regard to the *Strand Magazine* is that an old friend of ours, long supposed to be deceased, has been discovered to be still alive. I refer to the greatest detective of modern and ancient times, Sherlock Holmes. You will remember that great fight he had on the Swiss mountain, when both he and his enemy were supposed to have come to a terrible death, and it was thought that we should hear no more of him for ever. His loss was deeply mourned by thousands of people, for it is no exaggeration to say that thousands of letters saying so were received by us from people both in this country and wherever the English language is spoken. I am sure that those thousands of people will rejoice to know it has been discovered that he was not dead at all. How he miraculously escaped, where he went to, and what he has been doing since will be set forth in the pages of the *Strand Magazine* commencing in a couple of months. I have no doubt there will be a great rush for the October Number to read the account by the faithful historian of this detective, Sir Arthur Conan Doyle – the account of the wonderful escape and subsequent events.

8 August 1903

118

The Return of Sherlock Holmes

Next week the great Sherlock Holmes returns. As a matter of fact he has been back some time, but it is not until the October Number of the *Strand Magazine* that the first accounts can be read of what has occurred since he departed from the gaze of the British public. It is extraordinary the interest that is taken in this gentleman. The advance demand for the October Number is such that it will tax our resources to be able to supply all that are wanted in time. "The Adventure of the Empty House" is the first story that Sherlock Holmes gives us on his return, and we are sure the reading of it will make everyone glad that he has come back safe and sound.

26 September 1903

"The Adventure of the Empty House"

We wish to call the special attention of our readers to the fact that the great Sherlock Holmes is not dead after all. He reappears in the October *Strand Magazine*, which is now ready. The story of how he escaped and what he has been doing since is told by Sir Arthur Conan Doyle, the faithful chronicler of the life of this truly wonderful man. "The Adventure of the Empty House" is the first story of the new series. The news of the supposed death of Sherlock Holmes was heard with regret wherever the English language is spoken. The news of the return of Sherlock Holmes will be welcomed in tens of thousands of homes.

3 October 1903

TIT-BITS

The New Stories

H. R. and Others congratulate us upon the return of Sherlock Holmes. H. R. thinks that "The Adventure of the Empty House" in the October Number of the *Strand Magazine* is the best of the Sherlock Holmes stories.

That, of course, is a matter of opinion. It certainly is intensely interesting. Other stories are coming along which, we believe, will make the reappearance of the old favourite more and more welcome.

17 October 1903

The Sherlock Holmes Picture Post-Cards

The "Sherlock Holmes" picture post-cards have become the fashionable craze. They form an interesting collection of six beautifully printed pictures of Sherlock Holmes pursuing his marvellous investigations. Drawn by Mr. Sidney Paget, these picture post-cards will interest you and your friends in connection with "The Return of Sherlock Holmes", a new series of remarkable stories commencing in the October issue of the *Strand Magazine*. Each Set will be mailed in a specially-designed envelope. Post Free, 7d.

17 October 1903

PUNCH

Justifiable Homicide

Sherlock Holmes, by kindly fate
    Rescued from a frightful danger,
Once more to investigate
    Other mysteries, and stranger.

Still as perils, dread and vast,
    Close you round, but cannot hurt you,
Each unravelled thread at last
    Scores another point for virtue.

While new villains to arrest
    Gives you sport and occupation;
Just one crime we might suggest
    For your speedy perpetration;

Yes, though still your subtle brain
    With its old adroitness plots on,
Double merit you might gain
    If you'd only strangle Watson.

21 October 1903

TIT-BITS

"The Adventure of the Norwood Builder"

"The Return of Sherlock Holmes" in the *Strand Magazine* has been hailed with delight in all parts of the English-speaking world. The second story of the new series, entitled "The Adventure of the Norwood

Builder", appears in the November Number of the *Strand Magazine*.

7 November 1903

The November Number of the *Strand Magazine* contains the second of Conan Doyle's new series of detective stories – "The Return of Sherlock Holmes". The story is one of intense dramatic interest, and the solution is made to hinge upon so simple a clue as that of a man's thumb-print. It is a tale of mystery, so deep that the reader feels certain after he has read the first half of the story that even Sherlock Holmes will not be able to unravel so tangled a web. But the great detective is not to be thwarted yet, and once more Inspector Lestrade is forced to concede his admiration for the wonderful methods of Holmes.

The October *Strand* contained "The Adventure of the Empty House", and the stories will be continued from month to month.

14 November 1903

The Conduit Street Jewel Robbery

The four dramatic arrests in connection with the jewel robbery in Conduit Street come in rather startling sequence to the Sherlock Holmes story in this month's *Strand Magazine*. In Conan Doyle's tale, as in the case of the clever Inspector Drew, the only clue was a finger-mark, which, when enlarged by photography, furnished the necessary means of identification. The Scotland Yard authorities would seem to have been studying "The Adventure of the Norwood Builder", so identical were the methods adopted; but the novelist must be allowed the palm for time, as his latest "Adventure" had been on the bookstalls for nearly a fortnight before the *coup* of the police.

28 November 1903

THE BOOKMAN

True Sherlockians

To the Editors

I should like to ask you three straight questions and to have you give me three straight answers to them.

(1) You have a good deal to say about true Sherlockians. Now don't you really think in your heart that *you* are the only true Sherlockian?

(2) Haven't you a pretty good opinion of yourself anyway?

(3) Why does everything that you write irritate me beyond endurance?

It gives us great pleasure to answer.

(1) On the whole we must frankly admit that we are probably the only true Sherlockian. It may be that Sir Arthur Conan Doyle and Mr. Gillette are in the same class, but we are not prepared to admit it until we shall have conferred with them and tested them with regard to some of the more esoteric points. By the way, though, we don't do our thinking in our heart.

(2) How could we fail to have a pretty good opinion of one who is the only true Sherlockian?

(3) We are sure that we don't know why we irritate this gentleman. He doesn't irritate us in the least. Indeed, we trust that he, and for that matter, all our readers, are going to have a very Merry Christmas and a Happy New Year.

January 1904

TIT-BITS

"Father O' Flynn"

D. W., during the festive season, has been greatly struck with the popularity of that good old favourite song, "Father O'Flynn". He alleges that wherever it is heard it invariably brings down the house. "No doubt," says D. W., "the reverend father had a wonderful way wid him, but to my mind 'the wonderful way' Sherlock Holmes has with him is far more captivating. Why should the redoubtable Sherlock not have a song all to himself? Something in the style of 'Father O'Flynn' would become immensely popular."

We quite agree, and offer a Prize of Three Guineas to the reader who sends the best Sherlock Holmes song in the "Father O'Flynn" style. Words are only wanted meantime. We may arrange a competition for musical readers to set the words to music afterwards. Send in by Tuesday, 26th inst. Envelopes marked "Holmes".

16 January 1904.

The Prize of Three Guineas recently offered for the best "Sherlock Holmes" song in the style of "Father O'Flynn" has been awarded to Mr. A. H. Hamilton, 53 Spencer Road, Wealdstone, Harrow.

Sherlock Holmes

> We've many detectives of great personality
> Famous for hunting down crime and rascality;
> But still there's none of them reached the finality
> Of Sherlock Holmes, who's the king of them all.

Chorus:

> Here's health to you, Sherlock, my boy,
> Tales of whose deeds fill our hearts with such joy;
> > Smartest clue scenter
> > And best crime preventer,
> And cutest thief tenter in all the wide world.

Don't rave of your experts in crime that's political,
Nor of your savants with minds analytical,
For I would say, without being too critical,
> Our Sherlock Holmes would make sport of them all.
All evil-doers have heard of his fame,
Shake in their shoes when one mentions his name;
Right from the flyest one down to the shyest one,
> Fear of him lies on their hearts like a pall.

Chorus.

Who but yourself could have found out so handily
All of the facts in the murder at Mandily;
Proved that the murderer must have walked bandily
> Just by the prints of his feet on the floor?
Then you just picked up a thread from his vest,
Analysed that, and it told you the rest,
Told you his weight, and the food that he ate, and
> How he had done the foul deed, and lots more.

Chorus.

Though yet you've not entered the state matrimonial,
Gladly we'd help you at that ceremonial,
See you installed in a manor baronial,
> Enjoying the fame you've so worthily earned.
Then, as the little ones grew up around,
In the home circle you'd shine, I'll be bound,
Study paternity down to eternity,
> And other joys that you've hitherto spurned.

Chorus.

13 February 1904

> THERE'S NO PLACE LIKE HOME
> AND NO HOLMES LIKE DOYLE'S.
>
> ———
>
> Only address: STRAND.

6 April 1904

TIT-BITS

The Memoirs of Oliver Wendell Holmes

PUBLISHER'S READER sends the following story, which he thinks will interest our readers:

A lady entered a bookseller's shop and looked round inquiringly:

"I want a copy of the *Memoirs of Oliver Wendell Holmes.*"

"I am sorry, madam, but we haven't it."

"Oh, yes, you have," said the lady, pleasantly. "My sister bought one here yesterday, and you had a number of them. *Memoirs of Oliver Wendell Holmes.*" She looked at him doubtfully. "Don't you know – Holmes, the man that came alive again?"

The bookseller was somewhat startled, not having heard of the genial autocrat's reappearance on the scene of his earthly experiences. He was wondering how to get the evidently demented lady politely out of his shop when she suddenly exclaimed, "There's the book now on that shelf. How odd that you should not know about your own books!"

It was the *Memoirs of Sherlock Holmes*, and the customer carried it off in triumph, serenely unconscious of her mistake.

11 June 1904

THE QUARTERLY REVIEW

The Adventures of Dr. Watson with Mr. Sherlock Holmes

Watson is indeed a creation; his loyalty to his great friend, his extreme simplicity of character, his tranquil endurance of taunt and insult, make him a rival of James Boswell, Esq., of Auchinleck. Dazzled by the brilliance of Sherlock, who doses himself with cocaine and is amateur champion of the middle-weights, or very nearly, the public overlooks the monumental qualities of Dr. Watson. He, too, had his love affair in *The Sign of Four*; but Mrs. Watson, probably, was felt to be rather in the way when heroic adventures were afoot. After Sherlock returned to life – for he certainly died, if the artist has correctly represented his struggle with Professor Moriarty – Mrs. Watson faded from this mortal scene.

The idea of Sherlock is the idea of Zadig in Voltaire's *conte*, and of d'Artagnan exploring the duel in *Le Vicomte de Bragelonne*, and of Poe's Dupin, and of Monsieur Lecoq; but Sir Arthur handles the theme with ingenuity always fresh and fertile; we may constantly count on him to mystify and amuse us. Of his debt to Poe there is no more to say than he has said. Perhaps he has not himself observed that his tale of "The Man with the Twisted Lip" is a variant of the adventure of Mr. Altamont in the "Memoirs of James Fitzjames de la Pluche". The "mistry" of that hero's "buth", by the way, seems to be revealed in his Christian names which, like the motto of the Clan Alpine, murmur, "My race is royal." Readers who remember the case of Mr. Altamont are not puzzled by the disappearance of Mr. Neville St. Clair.

Possibly the homicidal ape in "The Murders in the Rue Morgue" suggested the homicidal Andaman islander in *The Sign of Four*. This purely fictitious little monster enables us to detect the great detective and expose the superficial character of his knowledge and methods. The Andamanese are cruelly libelled, and have neither the malignant qualities, nor the heads like mops, nor the weapons, nor the customs, with which they are credited by Sherlock. He has detected the wrong savage, and injured the character of an amiable people. The *bo:jig-ngijji* is really a religious, kindly creature, has a Deluge and a Creation myth, and shaves his head, not possessing scissors. Sherlock confessedly took his knowledge of the *bo:jig-ngijji* from "a gazetteer", which is full of nonsense. "The average height is below four feet"! The average height is four feet ten inches and a half. The gazetteer says that "massacres are invariably concluded by a cannibal feast". Mr. E. H. Man, who knows the people thoroughly, says "no lengthened investigation was needed to disprove this long-credited fiction, for not a trace could be discovered of the existence of such a practice in their midst, even in far-off times".

In short, if Mr. Sherlock Holmes, instead of turning up a common work of reference, had merely glanced at the photographs of Andamanese, trim, elegant, closely-shaven men, and at a few pages in Mr. Man's account of them in the *Journal of the Anthropological Institute* for 1881, he would have sought elsewhere for his little savage villain with the blow-pipe. A Fuegian who had lived a good deal on the Amazon might have served his turn.

A man like Sherlock, who wrote a monograph on over a hundred varieties of tobacco-ash, ought not to have been gulled by a gazetteer. Sherlock's Andamanese fights with a blow-pipe and poisoned arrows. Neither poisoned arrows nor blow-pipes are used by the islanders, according to Mr. Man. These melancholy facts demonstrate that Mr. Holmes was not the paragon of Dr. Watson's fond imagination, but a very superficial fellow, who knew no more of the Mincopies (a mere nickname derived from their words for "come here") than did Mr. Herbert Spencer.

Sherlock is also as ignorant as Dickens was of a very simple matter, the ordinary British system of titles. He has a client, and he looks for that client in another "book of reference", not the light-hearted gazetteer which he consults with the pious confidence that Mrs. Gallup bestows on the *Encyclopaedia Britannica.* He discovers that the client's name is "Lord Robert Walsingham de Vere St. Simon, second son of the Duke of Balmoral" – not a plausible title at best. Yet, knowing this, and finding, in the *Morning Post*, the client's real name, both Sherlock and the egregious Watson speak of Lord Robert St. Simon throughout as "Lord St. Simon"! The unhappy "nobleman", with equal ignorance of his place in life, signs himself, "Yours faithfully, St. Simon".

Of course we expect that so clumsy a pretender to be the second son of a duke will be instantly exposed by the astute Sherlock. Not so; Sherlock "thinks it all very capital". Now would Sherlock have called the late Lord Randolph Churchill "Lord Churchill", or would he have been surprised to hear that Lord Randolph did not sign himself "Churchill"? Anthropology we do not expect from Sherlock, but he really ought to have known matters of everyday usage. The very "page boy" announces "Lord Robert St. Simon"; but Sherlock salutes the visitor as "Lord St. Simon", and the pretended nobleman calls his wife "Lady St. Simon". But do not let us be severe on the great detective for knowing no more of anthropology than of other things! Rather let us wish him "good hunting", and prepare to accompany Dr. Watson and him, when next they load their revolvers, and go forth to the achieving of great adventures.

ANDREW LANG
July 1904

"The Adventure of the Three Students"

I have often thought that Dr. Watson overrates the acuteness of his friend and hero, Sherlock Holmes. In some cases Sherlock has blundered egregiously, and been taken in, though he never knew it. Now, in the *Strand* for June, Sherlock is the victim of a college don and an undergraduate, who have "played it rather low" on the world-famed detective.

Sherlock was at Oxford or Cambridge, studying "early English charters", couched, probably, in the Latin language. Soames of St. Luke's came to him with a cock-and-bull story, which would not have taken in a Fifth Form boy. According to Soames, the tutor, who proved too hard for Holmes, he was one of the examiners for the Fortescue Scholarship – whether a University scholarship or an in-college affair does not appear, but it was for senior men. The first paper was to be Greek "unseen", "a large passage of Greek translation which the candidate has not seen". Now, it is never easy to know what candidates have *not* seen, and a chunk of Heliodorus might do, with a bit of the *Cassandra* of Lycophron, and perhaps a corrupt little piece out of Herodas, if he spells his name that way.

But Soames, guying the innocent Holmes, actually persuaded him that, by way of unseen, he was setting "half a chapter of Thucydides". Naturally every man who went in (they were not schoolboys, but senior men) had read the whole of Thucydides. To set the Halimusian for unseen would be the act of an idiot. Next, the passage was so long that, though only half a chapter of the history which the son of Olorus compiled, it covered "three long slips" of printers' proofs. No chapter, no *whole* chapter in "Thicksides" is as long as that, I think; certainly no half-chapter is. They are quite "snappy little pars.", many of them – the chapters in Thucydides.

But Sherlock sucked it all in. He believed that a bad young man, wanting to get up unseen Thucydides, would be such an inconceivable donkey as to begin copying it out in pencil. Of course, even if he had not read all Thucydides, he would merely glance at it, and see what book the extract came from. Nobody who goes in for a scholarship for senior men could make such an error. However ignorant he was, the first line would suffice for his wicked purpose. He could compare it with the beginnings of chapters, but, if he knew no more than to be in doubt, he could not have got the Fortescue Scholarship. But Soames palmed all this series of transparent hoaxes off upon Holmes – every step in the series an obvious "sell" – and so Holmes went about to catch the culprit. One of the men was in the joke with Soames; he was one of the three on the tutor's stair, and confessed to having surreptitiously copied a huge cantle of a half-chapter of Thucydides in pencil, from the proof-sheet of the examination paper, and the same with intent to deceive.

"Well, Soames, we have cleared your little problem up," said Sherlock with his usual complacency, and when he had left the tutor's rooms that grave man threw off his dignity, and waltzed with his undergraduate accomplice round the table. For not one of the incidents could have occurred. Thucydides could not, I hope, have been set for unseen in such an examination. A half-chapter of Thucydides could not be as long as three examination-papers. A dishonest man would not have needed to copy more than a line, if he copied any of it. Soames, in the circumstances, would have substituted any other paper for the first, and set new pieces of unseen; not one monstrous slice of one author. What Sherlock Holmes will say to Dr. Watson for thus exposing him I know not, and Watson would have done better to keep the whole story in reserve, as giving him a hold over Holmes, when next he was bumptious – his besetting sin. That a don and an undergraduate took in Holmes by means so simple and so audacious is rather a comfort to a less successful explorer of mysteries (historical). Literature triumphed over Science, for once in a way. *Non omnia possumus omnes*, as Partridge said; we all have our moments of weakness. If Holmes had asked Soames to show him that half-chapter in the original, Soames would have been exposed himself.

Let me not be supposed to depreciate the great qualities of Sherlock. If an adventure of his appeared every day, it would find in me a happy reader. The mistakes may be Dr. Watson's, and the unseens may have been unseens that could be set in the Fortescue Scholarship. Probably they are best selected out of things like Plato, his *Laws*, or Callimachus, or Polybius, or other authors whom few undergraduates have read exhaustively.

ANDREW LANG
July 1904

PUNCH

The Curious Incident of the Dog in the Night-Time

[H. Rider Haggard, in *The Times* of 21 July 1904, recorded how he dreamt of the death of his dog, Bob, and gave the testimony of a servant and of the two plate layers who discovered the dog's corpse.]

This is an imitative age, and Mr. Rider Haggard's success as a dreamer has naturally produced a crop of similar experiences among his fellow-novelists. One is printed below:

Sir A. Conan Doyle

Perhaps you will think with me that the following circumstances are worthy of record, if only for their scientific interest. It is principally because of this interest that, as such stories should not be told anonymously, after some hesitation I have made up my mind to publish this one over my own name, although I am well aware that by so doing I may expose myself to a certain amount of ridicule and disbelief.

On the night of Saturday, 23 July, I went to bed at 12.19 and immediately fell asleep. At 3.14 I awoke with the feeling that my favourite terrier, Joe, was trying to communicate with me. Having read Mr. Rider Haggard's recent letter in *The Times*, long though it was, I knew what to do, and, summoning my household, we at once set out for the nearest point on the South Western Railway where the line crosses water. We searched there and in other places, even as far afield as the Frensham Ponds, all day, but without success. At nightfall we returned home crestfallen and heart-heavy, only to find that Joe had been in his kennel all the time. Naturally we had not thought to look there before. This shows how unwise it would be to elevate Mr. Rider Haggard's fantastic, and, if I may express the opinion, somewhat tedious experience to the dignity of a precedent.

I will only add that I ask you to publish the annexed documents with this letter, as they constitute the written testimony at present available to the accuracy of what I state.

Undershaw, Hindhead, 26 July.

No. I

DEAR SIR, – In pursuance of your instructions I have inspected the dog found in his kennel at Undershaw.

He is in good health and has had distemper.

I believe that the cause of his presence in the kennel is that he was affixed to a strong chain.

HENRY DE WET, M.R.C.V.S.

Haslemere, 25 July.

129

No. II

I spent the whole of Sunday, 24 July, in tramping over Surrey with Sir Conan Doyle looking for a dead dog. I did not find one.

WILLIAM POTTS (Gardener)

No. III

Sir Arthur Conan Doyle has told me his dream several times with the utmost particularity and has never altered a syllable. Upon it I constructed several theories, none of which, however, could be thoroughly tested owing to the presence of the dog alive in his kennel.

SHERLOCK HOLMES
3 August 1904

TIT-BITS

Inscription for a Sherlock Holmes Monument

IN MEMORY OF
THAT SLEUTH-HOUND THAT DOGGED GREAT CRIMES, THAT TERROR OF INGENIOUS LAWBREAKERS,
SHERLOCK HOLMES
LATE OF BAKER STREET, LONDON.

A gifted soul, an intellect without flaw,
Expert in many arts – in medicine, law,
Tobacco, conversation, and disguise,
Retorts (both chemical and otherwise).

He used his strange, encyclopaedic lore
The subtle schemes of criminals to floor;
Oft *Strand*-ed, yet emerging from the fray,
A tireless ferret, to the light of day.

If puzzled, then his musings would begin
To the weird music of his violin.
Be glad, ye rogues, your cunning schemes push on,
Rejoice, ye criminals, your terror's gone!

And thou, O Scotland Yard, may'st once again
Resume thy title "Great", which thou wert fain
To drop when "Holmes" was heard on all men's lips –
A brighter sun, that put thee in eclipse.

And yet beware! they say he has a knack
Of being reported dead, then coming back!

R. PARRY
24 December 1904

THE READER

Sherlock Holmes's Lament

[Sir A. Conan Doyle has stated that he considers the British police to be the best in the world.]

Sir Arthur, in those happy days
  (Now dead) when first you made me,
Upon my word I never thought
  That you would have betrayed me.
I always used to think that you
Shared my contempt for men in blue.

Where'er the bull's-eye of the truth
  They failed to land their shots on
(I speak in metaphor), I'd smile,
  And wink at dear old Watson.
And murmur nonchalantly, "Pooh!
These foolish, bungling men in blue!"

And when their weak attempts to solve
  A problem I derided,
I thought that you despised them quite
  As fervently as I did.
We scoffed together at their clue,
Those very comic men in blue.

And now you come, and in the Press
  Deliver this corrective,
And state without a touch of shame,
  "The Force is not defective."

131

By gad, you know, it's rather hard
  Upon a poor detective.
I never thought to hear that you
Had gone and praised the men in blue.

P.G.W.
14 October 1905

Re-Porte

[The Sultan of Turkey has decorated Sir Arthur and Lady Conan Doyle.]

Abdul, the artful, trembling for his spoil,
Spreads mild seductions for detective Doyle.
Constantinople's minarets and domes
Welcome great Sherlock to his host's at Holmes.
Some deep-laid plot will come to light anon,
But we in England want to know Wat's on.

November 1907

ADVERTISEMENT

"The Adventure of Wisteria Lodge"

Mr. Sherlock Holmes presents his compliments to the reader, and begs to say he will have much pleasure in renewing a long-standing acquaintance in the *Strand Magazine* for September 1908.

8 August 1908

COLLIER'S WEEKLY

Ballade of Baker Street

I've followed many a devious way,
  I've travelled fast and travelled far;
Beyond the night, across the day,
  By many a mountain, lake, and scar.
  'Neath ilex, palm, and deodar
I've viewed the homes of Fame's *élite*;
  Ah, why does frowning Fortune bar
Those hallowed rooms in Baker Street?

There's Carlyle's house (you have to pay),
  Houses of Shakespeare, Poe, Legare;
There's Landor's at Fiesole,
  And Some One's Villa at Dinard.
Nero's and Borgias' houses jar,
  Though Baedekers their charms repeat;
They should note with a double star
Those hallowed rooms in Baker Street.

My eager quest I would not stay
  For jewelled house of Alnaschar,
Diogenes' quaint tub of grey –
  Historic Bough of old Omar –
Peterhof of the Russian Czar –
These were to me no special treat,
  Could I but reach, by cab or car,
Those hallowed rooms in Baker Street.

L'Envoi

Sherlock! My fondest wishes are
  That on a day I yet may greet,
Haply in some far avatar,
  Those hallowed rooms in Baker Street.

CAROLYN WELLS
15 August 1908

IF

If Conan Doyle Lived to be 200

December 2058　　　　　*Now Ready*
THE STRAND MAGAZINE
OVERWHELMING ATTRACTION
———
FINAL
AND
ABSOLUTELY FATAL DEATH OF
SHERLOCK HOLMES

C. L. GRAVES AND E. V. LUCAS
Isaac Pitman, 1908

Sir Arthur Conan Doyle as Sherlock Holmes

The story – possibly apocryphal – is told of Sir Arthur, the creator of Sherlock Holmes, that one day a woman wished to consult him about some thefts. "My detective powers," he is reported to have replied, "are at your service." "Well," said the woman, "frequent and mysterious thefts have been occurring at my house for a long time. Thus there disappeared last week a motor horn, a broom, a box of golf balls, a left riding boot, a dictionary, and a half-dozen tin pie plates." "I see it," said the author. "The case is perfectly clear. You keep a goat."

21 November 1910

V. THE LATER YEARS
(1910–1930)

———◆———

The Cornish Horror

Extraordinary Tragedy Puzzles the Police

Was Brenda Tregennis Murdered?

When Brenda Tregennis was found, yesterday morning, quite dead, sitting in the sitting-room of her home in a Cornish village, the police of the district realised that a tragedy had occurred, but were inclined to think that at least the sad occurrence would be capable of a simple explanation. Inquiries, in many directions, only deepen the mystery. Already people are saying that the sudden death of a healthy woman under such circumstances is no accident, and that Miss Tregennis has been foully murdered.

A Brother's Terrible Discovery

Mr. Mortimer Tregennis says:

"On Monday night I spent the evening at Tredannick Wartha, in the company of my sister, Miss Brenda Tregennis, and my two brothers, Owen and George Tregennis, who have made their home there for some time. I stayed there until ten o'clock, and when I left them, still playing cards, round the dining-room table, they were in the best of health and spirits.

"This morning I was summoned by Dr. Richards, who was responding to an urgent call from my sister's residence. I went with him, and on arrival at Tredannick Wartha we found an extraordinary state of things.

135

My two brothers and my sister were seated round the table exactly as I had left them the night before, the cards still in front of them and the candles burnt to their sockets. My sister lay back stone dead in her chair, while my two brothers, one on each side of her, sat laughing, shouting, and singing. They had evidently gone quite mad with terror.''

This is the situation exactly as Mr. Tregennis describes it, and there seems to be no further detail which explains it.

Questions that Need Answering

The arrangement of the room and the circumstances of the tragedy discount the theory of suicide.

There is no sign of violence or a struggle in the room. There are no goods mising.

Yet everything points to the fact that something terrible happened in that room, almost immediately after the departure of Mr. Mortimer Tregennis, which resulted in the death of Miss Brenda Tregennis and drove her two brothers, healthy and strong men, to instant insanity.

The questions everyone is asking are: What happened in that room after ten o'clock, and who killed Miss Tregennis?

The mystery has thrilled the whole of Cornwall, and the wildest theories are afloat. None, however, appears to afford a satisfactory explanation. The dead woman cannot speak, and the brothers, who were with her, are still suffering so much from shock as to be unable to give a coherent account.

The Tregennis Family at Redruth

All the members of the Tregennis family are well known in Redruth, writes a DAILY STRAND correspondent. They were actively engaged in the tin-mining trade here for many years, had a prosperous holding, and were generally esteemed.

Some years ago they sold out to a company, which is now running the mine, retiring from business with ample means and severing their connection with the town. Miss Brenda Tregennis, the murdered woman, had many friends in this locality, all of whom are shocked to hear of her sad end.

Inquiry shows that at the time the business was converted into a company there was some ill-feeling between members of the family, but of this there is no direct confirmation.

Extraordinary Development: Sherlock Holmes Called In

An extraordinary statement reaches us to the effect that Mr. Sherlock Holmes, who has been staying in the neighbourhood, recuperating his health, was called in to investigate these strange facts early in the day. Mr. Holmes, who is accompanied by Dr. Watson, refused to see the Press men last night. Dr. Watson, who was interviewed, did not deny that Sherlock Holmes was taking an interest in the strange crime, and hinted that a solution, startlingly dramatic, would be found in the Christmas Number of THE STRAND MAGAZINE, which is published today.

It is too late to give the solution in THE DAILY STRAND, as Sherlock Holmes's narrative in THE STRAND MAGAZINE Christmas Number only came to hand as we were going to press. We strongly advise readers who desire to examine the strange evidence by which Sherlock Holmes is able to reconstruct a ghastly crime, that might but for his shrewd observation have gone undetected, to hasten to the nearest bookstall or newsagent and see for themselves, by perusing the story, what actually happened in the grim little villa in a Cornish hamlet, on which the attention of the reading public is now being focussed.

7 December 1910

THE STRAND MAGAZINE

Sherlock Holmes Drawings
By the late Sidney Paget

The artistic creations from the pen of the late Sidney Paget are known the wide world over. In no illustrations did he show to a larger extent the genius that was undoutedly his than in his drawings for the famous Sherlock Holmes series of stories.

We have received so many inquiries for these drawings that we have decided to offer the remaining specimens at the Reduced Price of One Guinea.

This is an opportunity that will not occur again. Lovers of Sherlock Holmes – and that they number hundreds of thousands has been proved – should take advantage of this chance to secure a lasting memento of one of the most famous characters in modern fiction. Those who have files of THE STRAND MAGAZINE may inform us of the pictures they prefer; or we shall be pleased to send a parcel on approval.

All applications to: The Cliché Dept., George Newnes, Limited (Dept. S), Southampton Street, Strand, London, W.C.

April 1911

The War Service of Sherlock Holmes

The logical imaginary idea places Sherlock Holmes as chief of the Secret Service of the British Empire.

Leadership in the British Secret Service is a distinction which Holmes has earned by his achievements in the past. For all of his cases were not confined to recovering missing race horses, establishing identities, or frustrating cleverly planned bank-robberies. There were adventures of international flavour, in which world-wide interests were at stake. One of the earliest of them all involved the King of Bohemia and the adventurous Irene Adler, to whom Holmes always afterwards referred as *the* woman. The world war raging today might have come earlier had the papers outlining the terms of the Naval Treaty, purloined by Joseph Harrison, and recovered by Holmes, found their way to a certain Continental capital. Problems of espionage, of which we have been hearing so much of late, were outlined in the story "The Adventure of the Second Stain", which involved a blazing indiscretion put on paper by an exalted monarch, who, though not specifically named, was obviously he whose ears should be burning the hottest in the world today.

In addition to the tales of international aspect in which Holmes figured that have been told, there are the yet unwritten stories to which mere allusions have been made. We know that on one occasion he served the interests of the King of Scandinavia, and on another earned the gratitude of the president of the French Republic; that there was an "Adventure of the Reigning Family of Holland"; and we strongly suspect that world politics were connected with the unwritten adventure of the Grice-Patersons in the Island of Uffa, as they certainly were in the case of the Trepoff murder. In another age d'Artagnan was made to change the face of history and to restore Charles II to the throne of England by his device of kidnapping General Monk in the midst of the camp at Newcastle and taking him across the Channel to the Netherlands in a box. Sherlock Holmes is of today and we feel sure that he has long since answered the call to the colours and is serving in that high capacity for which he is so admirably fitted.

December 1914

Conan Doyle and the Railways

The unexpected often happens, though one does not expect a novelist of the calibre of Sir Arthur Conan Doyle to trip lightly into errors, railway or otherwise, for he is essentially one of the moderns and a scientific man. A few years ago there appeared in one of the magazines a series of miscellaneous tales, since collected in book form under the title of *Round the Fire Stories*, among which is a story called "The Lost Special". Perhaps it is not surprising that it did get lost, as it was routed from Liverpool, Lime Street, to London *via* St. Helen's (not St. Helen's Junction), Collins Green, Kenyon, and Manchester! However, the special got mislaid between Kenyon Junction and Barton Moss – the two intermediate stations were not asked about it, so say nothing – by the simple expedient of connecting a disused colliery branch with the main line. How this could have been done in broad daylight on such a busy section of the London and North Western Railway is quite beyond the imagination; it can only be supposed that everyone connected with the company's ways and works in those parts had suddenly fallen into a trance. To add to the difficulties, the fireman of the special, having killed the driver, took the train "running at great speed" on to the newly-connected branch – the imagination must again work overtime – which led to the mouth of a disused pit-shaft; into this the train fell and got "lost". Faith, as an Irish cleric once said, is believing things that you know to be untrue.

This, however, is an odd story, a thing by itself and the only one of its kind in the book. But it comes as a rude surprise that the creator of Sherlock Holmes, one of the most wonderful characters in the literature of our age, should fall into such odd errors whenever he touches a railway. Perhaps the egregious Dr. Watson looked after that department? An instance may be remembered in "Silver Blaze", when the party returns from Dartmoor by the South Western in a Pullman to Victoria; now, Pullmans have never been run on the West of England line and the South Western's London terminus is not Victoria. A more modern example of Mr. Holmes's weak spot may be found in "The Bruce-Partington Plans", which is included in Sir Arthur's latest book, *His Last Bow*. Here the story opens with the finding of a man's body on the line outside Aldgate station: Holmes traces the cause of the crime to a house near Gloucester Road station, situated over the Inner Circle roads; out of a window in this house the body was lowered on to the roof of a passing train, conveniently held up there. It (the body) travels all the way to Aldgate before it falls off, and only does so there because there is a combination of curve and points; the train, that same night, "is broken up and the coaches redistributed" – a most unusual thing with Circle train sets. At the inquiry no ticket is found on the dead man, so Holmes remarks to Watson: "No ticket! According to my experience it is not possible to reach the platform of a Metropolitan train without exhibiting one's ticket." Perhaps Mr. Holmes never travelled in the "rush" hours! Several points of railway interest are raised in this tale. The situation of the house in "Caulfield Gardens, Kensington", so convenient for the crime, is rather far-fetched but within the bounds of possibility, although at the spot described it would be very unusual for trains to halt regularly, as there was no signal. Such a stoppage has occurred since the electrification owing to failure of current, but the period of the tale is in the steam days. Then, again, whether the train travelled *via* Bayswater or *via* Victoria is not mentioned, though this seems immaterial; there are many curves and points, in combination or otherwise, on both routes – the junction with the Hammersmith line, King's Cross, Farringdon Street, Moorgate, Victoria, and Mansion House come to mind at once. So why the body should stay on the sloping roof of a by no means easy-riding coach during its many lurches is scarcely more probable than the fact that nobody, passenger or company's servant, noticed anything on the roof in spite of the many opportunities for looking directly down on to the train.

BASIL MERCER
April 1918

MEMORIES OF THE FUTURE

Lady Porstock's Statue of Sherlock Holmes

[Lady Porstock's recollection of the Private Member's Bill introduced during her time in Parliament, 1953–9, from her autobiography, *Memories of the Future*, written some years before.]

I need only mention one other of my public activities, which remains a legitimate boast; it was a Private Member's Bill, brought forward by myself, that procured the erection of the great statue of Sherlock Holmes in Baker Street. I pointed out that London was now the only European capital which had no statue of the kind, and the plaque on No. 221b Baker Street was a quite inadequate recognition of the famous detective's services. The question whether he had ever existed did not affect, or ought not to affect, the feelings of veneration with which we regarded him. When the bill passed, I was elected a member of the Committee which was to decide between the various designs sent in. The prevailing taste at the moment was Futuribilism, but none of the artists then in vogue seemed to have treated his subject adquately. Several of them represented the head merely as a square block of stone, on the ground that all attempts to imitate the features in sculpture were a violation of the canons of Art. Another, on the same ground, represented the figure as strictly globular. I am glad to say that it was at my instigation the Committee chose the design sent in by Wrightman, then quite un-known, but destined to become famous as one of the leaders of the neoclassical school in the 'sixties. The conception is a noble one, and if some have found fault with the pipe as out of keeping with the classical draperies in which the figure is represented, it is not for us to complain. "We must approach Art," Burstall used to say, "as a goddess demanding a sacrifice; and the victim she asks of us is the Actual."

RONALD A. KNOX
Methuen, 1923

THE SPHERE

The Latest Series of Sherlock Holmes Stories

It is cheering to find that Sir Arthur Conan Doyle can sometimes be seduced from the field of psychic research to the breezier field of literature. I remember the day when breathless schoolboys counted the hours till the new *Strand Magazine* might be on sale on the bookstalls, and hurried home with their copies for a glorious hour with Sherlock Holmes. The dingy Victorian lodging in Baker Street is Aladdin's Palace to scores of bald-headed, rheumatical grandfathers alive today, and Dr. Watson, that type of all that is Victorian and commonplace, still wields a magician's wand and opens for us the magic door that leads us to the Copper Beeches, the Noble Bachelor, the Study in Scarlet, and the Speckled Band. But everything must have an end (do not scores of half-baked sequels to successful novels teach us the lesson?), and even the creator of Sherlock Holmes must at last bid good-bye to his goldmine. Long, long since the vein ran out. It was a bonanza mine and has paid rich dividends to its deserving owner, but recent washings have revealed baser metal. Of the last thirty tales of Sherlock Holmes, two dozen at least have been unworthy of Holmes, unworthy of his creator. I don't know how Dr. Watson could have had the face to chronicle them, and indeed it is clear from the last narrative that he has put his foot down. "Holmes," he said, "my old wound is troubling me; I fear that the task of a further examination of your note-books must devolve on yourself." And Holmes reluctantly complied, with lamentable results. I feel it deeply. In the last decade, Sir Arthur has struck a score of staggering blows at my idol.

6 November 1926

In a recent number I referred to Sir Arthur Conan Doyle's latest series of Holmes stories, and I frankly admitted that, though I turn to them as keenly as ever, I read Ichabod on the page. This criticism brought me – most undeservedly – a couple of charming letters from Sir Arthur. Never did author treat his unworthy critic more serenely and more generously. I feel indeed like Queen Victoria's Eton nephew, who, on applying to her for a temporary loan to relieve financial stringency, received back something far better and more valuable than cheque or note – an autograph letter worth five times the sum suggested. Sir Arthur's letters give me some extraordinarily interesting first-hand information as to the author's judgement of his masterpiece. It is interesting to me to know that he himself has never taken Sherlock Holmes seriously, that he rates a story called "The Lion's Mane", which is the next new story to appear, as among his best, and places at the bottom of the list the old story of "The Noble Bachelor". In Sir Arthur's view, the Holmes stories have not fallen below their high level, and it is his determination to abolish the sleuth the moment that he has evidence that in the public view he is past his best. He accounts for my criticism of some of his recent stories by the fact that as we grow older we become *blasé* and stale, and our youthful favourites no longer appeal. And though *The Adventures of Sherlock Holmes, The White Company, Rodney Stone, The Tragedy of the Korosko, Brigadier Gerard*, and *Uncle Bernac* are still among my bedside essentials, I doubt not there is truth in what he says. By the same post a well-known publisher asks me to suggest to Sir Arthur that, in compiling further stories, he should not seek for titles beyond those incredibly intriguing ones to which in the older tales Dr. Watson refers when selecting an adventure from Holmes's note-books for special record. I like the idea and offer it to Sir Arthur. I offer him also my sincere thanks for his courtesy and trouble, and I shall preserve his letters among my autographs, which range from a Ramillies letter from the Duke of Marlborough to a very characteristic hotch-potch from Henry James.

THE OLD STAGER (JOHN GORE)
27 November 1926

After Thirty-Five Years

Those who were about fifteen years old when they first made the acquaintance of Sherlock Holmes, and when Dr. Watson first wrote about him, must be about fifty by now. To whom else has it been given to share life so long with so persistent, though fictitious, a contemporary? For though Watson is no more, Holmes, as can be gathered from the magazine to which he has been steadily faithful – the *Strand* – is still bee-farming in Sussex, and in his green old age, for he must be over seventy, has broken the habit of a lifetime by becoming his own biographer. His creator ought indeed to be proud of him, for Sir Arthur Conan Doyle must have done what no other author has been able, or perhaps even tried, to do. Dickens never returned to Sam Weller, though Sam might very well have come into several of his later novels. Thackeray made Pen and Laura continue into *The Newcomes* only as pale ghosts from their original stage, and the Bishop of Barchester and Mrs. Proudie, though they recur with decided effect in Trollope, had short lives at the best. When once Mrs. Proudie was dead there was no resuscitating her, and there could be no demand for her resuscitation; but the death of Holmes had to be revoked. It was a tragedy that thousands took to heart, and the author's recantation must rank as a classic. Even that was so long ago that it is doubtful whether the youth of today know the circumstances. At any rate they know it only as history, as they would know the Boer War, unlike contemporaries who remember reading of it at the time. In certain backward countries, it is said, full obituaries of the great Sherlock were published as of a real man; and those who spent any time on the Continent about twenty years ago may recollect seeing on bookstalls and in booksellers' shop what seemed to be whole libraries of apocryphal Holmes literature, not by any means translations, but the free creations of a mythological fancy, rather like the Eastern legends of Alexander the Great, preserving little association with the original beyond the name. Even the verb to "sherlock" circulated on men's lips, if not in print; and in German it once materialised visibly as *sherlockieren*; it meant to track down, to detect, to expose, to show up, as Sherlock would. The Continental Sherlocks have probably not survived to this present; but if all the false prophets who at one time or another arose in that name and covered wide areas of Europe could be reassembled, the result would be astonishing.

Holmes, Dr. Watson, and Sir Arthur Conan Doyle have of course not escaped criticism either from professional or from literary quarters; but to one and all they can unite in replying *securus judicet orbis*, Holmes, or Sherlock, as his closer intimates like to call him, is one of the very few characters of modern fiction whose names are household words. We are not so well off as our Victorian fathers were for fictional friends. They must have had at least ten for every one whom we can show. Besides Holmes, who are ours? A few certainly there are; it would be invidious to name them; but they are a small band, and their hold on the public is not as Holmes's. Yet there was never more fiction poured out, and never was there so high a standard of professional efficiency among writers of fiction. Compared with many novelists of today the older ones seem to be mere amateurs, who rambled into success without quite knowing how they got there. Possibly Holmes was exceptionally happy in the hour of his birth, or rather of his first public appearance. He was an amateur, at least at first, for fiction writing for popular illustrated magazines was only beginning when he made his *début*. It is curious that whole books have been written about the 'nineties without giving him his due. He alone of that far-off, pre-motor, pre-telephone, pre-flying, pre-wireless age survives, and is not only tolerated but welcomed by a generation that can have no conception how difficult it was to be a detective under such privations. Or is he after all only a great Philistine, and as such contemned by the highbrows? Fame is a capricious beldam; but why is Holmes the only prolonger of his own life, the only survivor of his own biographer and obituarist, the only personage privileged to be his creator's never-failing resource? We will not attempt an explanation, except the obvious one of continuity honestly deserved, and, leaving to others the task of subtler analysis, simply wish Sherlock and Sir Arthur Conan Doyle the compliments of the season.

(FOURTH LEADER)
10 December 1926

Sherlock Holmes: the Modernised Version

To the Editor

SIR, – Your delightful tribute to Sherlock Holmes declares that books on the 1890s ignore that admirable creation. One book, at least, gives him a line in history; for the chapter on "Literature since 1832", which I wrote for a new edition of Stopford Brooke's Primer, gravely mentions Arthur Conan Doyle as a writer "who has given the national mythology a new figure in Sherlock Holmes". What, so far as I know, has escaped notice is the debt that the author unconsciously owes to an earlier master. Prince Florizel of Bohemia and Colonel Geraldine almost begin to be

Sherlock Holmes and Dr. Watson, and they certainly move in the London of mystery and dark adventure proper to Sherlockian drama. Is not "The Adventure of the Hansom Cab" true Sherlock in title and substance? And who is the terrible President of the Suicide Club but Professor Moriarty, that unhappy afterthought, who ruined the later Sherlock Holmes stories by sheer vacuity and abstraction of person, when Holmes, Watson, and the rooms in Baker Street had saved them by hundreds of homely, human touches? It is impossible not to regret that Stevenson left the detective story untouched. He began, and stopped. "I arranged this afternoon with a celebrated detective," says Colonel Geraldine; and then we hear no more.

Sherlock Holmes proved too much for his creator. He grew naturally from *A Study in Scarlet* and *The Sign of Four* to the perfected figure of the first two series. After that he became less admirable, and in the end his creator ruined him. He actually made him grow old – as if it is not clear to every reader that Sherlock Holmes is a fairy, one of the static figures of literature, remaining himself, ageless and unchanged, in a whirling stream of adventure. Micawber, Pickwick, and Sam Weller are similarly static figures. The crime of modernising Sherlock is all the worse because he plainly belongs to a definite period. Read through the whole set of stories, and you find yourself in a veritable but vanished London, a silent London of hansom cabs, a dark London of gas lamps, a London without electric glare, without motor cars, without tubes, without wireless, and even without telephones. To drag an aged Sherlock Holmes into the modern jazz world is as bad as banishing Micawber to Australia. Really, some authors don't deserve their own creations.

Yours faithfully,
GEORGE SAMPSON

Reform Club, Pall Mall, S.W.1.

13 December 1926

JOHN O' LONDON'S WEEKLY

Holmes in Baker Street

A Plea for Brighter Statues

I hope to see the day when there shall be a statue of Sherlock Holmes in Baker Street, as there is a statue of Peter Pan in Kensington Gardens.

This sagacious remark by Mr. G. K. Chesterton in a recent article has been greeted as a Chestertonian joke of the authentic vintage. I wonder why. It seems to me a perfectly sane suggestion, made in all seriousness, not by a man standing on his head, but by one who has observed that the statuary characteristic of British cities and the eminent parties thereby commemorated are, for the most part, just about as interesting and inspiring as a slag-heap. I am altogether with Mr. Chesterton, and I would go a good deal farther.

To rid ourselves of dull statuary and replace it with something that will make us smile and reflect pleasantly where we see it is only a small part of the campaign, but it is well worth pressing. And why not follow Mr. Chesterton with his suggestion that we should put up in our public places statues of those great figures of fiction, who are just as important influences in our national consciousness as the work and memory of any inventor? I suggest they are more important; they have given us great joy and made us happy – in spite of the inventors.

COLOPHON
12 February 1927

Holmes, Watson and the Lefroy Murder Case

To the Editor

SIR – The *Weekly Illustrated Graphic*, dealing with the celebrated crime of Lefroy murdering Mr. Gold on the Brighton Railway, in the year 1881, makes mention of the "Station Master at Three Bridges telling that *dull detective, Mr. Holmes*, to keep a sharp eye on Lefroy as he is sure that he, Lefroy, knows something about it". There was also a witness by the name of *Watson* in the case.

I have (unfortunately) not read all the Memoirs of Sir A. Conan Doyle. I wonder if any of your readers know if he refers to it in any way; if not, I think it a remarkable literary coincidence.

EDWIN COLES
26 February 1927

Silver Blaze

To the Editor

SIR, – Your recent controversy on the subject of inexactitudes appearing in well-known sea stories brings to mind the fact that mistakes are not only confined to this form of fiction. Even quite famous authors are apt to make slips in their books. Conan Doyle's story, in *The Memoirs of Sherlock Holmes*, "Silver Blaze" always strikes me as being quite impossible in that part where the horse Silver Blaze runs in the Wessex Plate. The horse is well known with its white forehead and mottled off foreleg, and starts as favourite. But in the race it runs as an unmarked bay, having been in the hands of a "horse-faker", and even its owner doesn't recognise it.

IVOR THOMAS

West Didsbury, Manchester.

15 September 1928

THE SUNDAY DISPATCH

Sherlock Holmes of Baker Street

It is amazing how credulous people are. Last week I was asked to show a young French boy of fifteen the "sights" of London; and heaven knows, there are enough "sights" in London. But he had one ambition, touristically, and one only. That was to visit the house of Mr. Sherlock Holmes in Baker Street; and, if it would not be carrying presumption too far, to catch a glimpse of the great man on his way to unravel some national problem.

Here was the germ of a joke, I thought, so we solemnly took a taxi-cab to Baker Street. I tapped on the window and stopped it outside a gloomy, narrow house. The French boy gazed in touching rapture at the grubby front door. He showed no inclination to move, and after shivering for about ten minutes (it was unbelievably cold in London last week) I suggested the National Gallery. He shook his head.

"I will stay here," said the ardent Sherlock-fan, "on the chance of seeing either Monsieur Holmes or even *le docteur* Watson. I could never forgive myself, nor would my family forgive me, if I left without seeing them."

My teeth were chattering with the cold. "I am sorry," I said, "but Mr. Holmes retired three months ago and is now running a bee farm in Sussex. The taxi-driver here has just told me so, and he seems a most reliable man." My young friend was desolated and proceeded to look ten years older. He sighed repeatedly and resignedly. However, I thought my troubles were over. But no.

Huskily he requested that we should go to the waxworks, so as to see the numberless victims of Mr. Holmes in waxen effigy. So to Tussaud's we went. To the Chamber of Horrors we went. The bloodthirsty boy enjoyed it, but I became steadily colder, and emerged glassy-eyed and numb. I can't bear gruesomeness. And I spent the next day in bed, dumbly meditating an outspoken letter to Sir Arthur Conany Doyle.

LADY ELEANOR SMITH

16 December 1928

147

THE TIMES

Sherlock Holmes in Constantinople

To the Editor

Sir, – One of the greatest tests of authorship is the ability to create from the shadows of the mind characters which become as real to the imagination as one's next-door neighbour. There must still be thousands of people in the world who not only think but *know* that Sherlock Holmes was a real person of flesh and blood. There must be many instances of this belief.

In 1920 it was decided to complete the occupation of Constantinople in a military sense. Acting on sure information, certain "nationalist" elements, which might have organised resistance, were rounded up in the early hours of the morning, and later in the day the occupation of the Turkish War Office and Admiralty was effected without incident. The Turkish populace, however, insisted that the great English detective Sherlock Holmes must have been behind the scenes, informing the High Command with his keen intellect and directing the measures which led to the removal of the recalcitrants and the consequent peaceful completion of the military occupation.

I am, Sir, your obedient servant,
FREDERICK HAMER

20 Kenilworth Court, S.W.15.

10 July 1930

THE OBSERVER

Competition No. 225. Sherlock Holmes Stories

We offer a Prize of Three Guineas for a selection of the Best Eight Sherlock Holmes Stories, the result to be decided by the votes of competitors.

13ʳJuly 1930

Judged by the votes of competitors, the favourites among the Sherlock Holmes stories are, in order:

1. "The Speckled Band"
2. *The Hound of the Baskervilles*
3. *The Sign of Four*
4. *A Study in Scarlet*

5. "The Red-Headed League"
6. "A Scandal in Bohemia"
7. "The Naval Treaty"
8. "The Man with the Twisted Lip"

closely followed by "Silver Blaze" and "The Copper Beeches". The vote for the first five was almost unanimous, "The Speckled Band" being a long way ahead. The lists submitted embraced nearly all the published stories, including even such late ones as "The Lion's Mane" (of which the author himself thought highly) and "The Sussex Vampire".

It may be of interest to give Sir Conan Doyle's own list of favourites, as published in the *Strand Magazine*:

"The Speckled Band"
"The Red-Headed League"
"The Dancing Men"
"The Final Problem"
"A Scandal in Bohemia"
"The Empty House"
"The Five Orange Pips"
"The Second Stain"
"The Devil's Foot"
"The Priory School"
"The Musgrave Ritual"
"The Reigate Squires"

No reader gave the complete eight in his list, and one imperfect student did not manage to get one. A large number had six correct, and we divide the prize between the two who named seven of the favourites: Miss Estelle Urban Smith, 2 Thurleigh Mansions, Thurleigh Road, S.W.12, and "G. W. Rhiwhina".

27 July 1930

THE GRAPHIC

The Conan Doyle Claims

Although we may misbelieve mediums and
With doubt and suspicion or minds may be filled,
Sherlock Holmes, we must grant, reappeared in the *Strand*
A number of times after having been killed.

26 July 1930

VI. SHERLOCKIAN STUDIES (1930–1937)

————◆————

THE SATURDAY REVIEW OF LITERATURE

Sherlock Holmes in America

The Reader's Guide

S.C. writes from Chicago: "I suppose the phrase that leaps to the mind of millions of people when they hear the name Sherlock Holmes is, 'Quick, Watson, the needle!' It is curious, and true, that this line does not occur in any of the Doyle stories about Holmes, neither does it occur in the Gillette play – unless my researches have been uncommonly faulty. Where in the world did it start?"

There was at least one among the millions to whose mind it did not leap. This was the late Sir Arthur Conan Doyle, whom I immediately consulted. He said he never heard the phrase, and that it "sounds amusing". Mr. Stanley Morrison, author of *John Bell* (Cambridge University Press), who can give you chapter and verse on anything about Sherlock Holmes, says it comes from a burlesque of the Gillette play, popular in England at the height of the Holmes furore; the needle introduced was built on the lines of a bicycle pump, only considerably larger. It is sweet to start a Holmes fan upon his dear topic; Christopher Morley should know something of this, being of this company. S.C. is clearly one; notice he has been conducting "researches". The most enlivening of these in recent years – indeed the most enlivening that have ever been conducted – may be found together with a number of other excellent amusements in Ronald Knox's *Essays in Satire* (Dutton). Here the problem of whether Holmes ever did come back from that bout with Moriarty over the cliff and write the later stories is resolved with the utmost sobriety and after the methods of "Higher Criticism".

Holmes and Watson are safe to stay with us for at least another American generation; so I learned at the Lincoln School of Teachers College not long ago. The children were presenting famous characters in hastily improvised costume; each was allowed to speak one short sentence, cross the stage, and leave the company to guess who he was. Two ten-year-old boys in dressing-gowns took their seats across from each other at a table, each with a pipe in his mouth. The audience looked a bit puzzled till one spoke. "Elementary, Watson!" said he, and the school cried out the dear detective's name as one child.

May Lamberton Becker

26 July 1930

JOHN O' LONDON'S WEEKLY

The Dates in "The Red-Headed League"

To the Editor

Sir, – I must have read "The Adventure of the Red-Headed League" at least a score of times, but it was not until re-reading it in this week's (26 July) *John O' London's* that I noticed an error so obvious as to be rather remarkable in a writer so generally accurate as the late Sir Arthur Conan Doyle.

The date on which the advertisement appeared in the *Morning Chroncile* was 27 April 1890 – "just two months ago," comments Watson. This would lead one to suppose that Mr. Jabez Wilson's visit to Sherlock Holmes took place about the end of June. As a matter of fact (according to the opening sentence of the story), it was "autumn", and the exact date is later given as 9 October on the notice announcing the dissolution of the League which led Mr. Wilson to go to Baker Street. Since he informs Holmes that he had worked for eight weeks in the office in Pope's Court, it is obvious that the original advertisement must have appeared about the beginning of August – not on 27 April, as Watson announces.

It is curious how even the most careful of writers occasionally go astray over matters of detail in this way. I have noticed many instances of this in my own reading and I am sure that other readers of your paper must have had the same experience.

A. N. Scott

185 Drake Street, Rochdale, Lancs.

16 August 1930

The Index System of Sherlock Holmes

To the Editor

SIR, – The letter in your issue of 16 August, which points out a curious error in Conan Doyle's "Adventure of the Red-Headed League", prompts me to write to you regarding a point which I noticed in reading "The Adventure of the Sussex Vampire". In this story, as most of your readers will probably remember, Holmes asks Watson to hand down Volume "V", and turning it over to look for Vampires comes across "Voyage of the *Gloria Scott*" and Victor Lynch. Now surely a man who wished to be able to refer to such things quickly would have indexed them under "G" and "L" respectively?

Another point in the same story is that Holmes received a letter from a firm of lawyers and replied as if to an individual.

H. G. WOTHERSPOON

Gibson Street, Glasgow.

6 September 1930

Dr. Watson's Wound

To the Editor

SIR, – May I add to my letter which you were good enough to publish in your issue of 16 August the record of a still more curious error which has just been pointed out to me in the Sherlock Holmes series.

In *A Study in Scarlet* (Chapter I), Dr. Watson tell us:

> I was removed from my Brigade and attached to the Berkshires, with whom I served at the fatal battle of Maiwand. There I was struck on the *shoulder* by a Jezail bullet which shattered the bone and grazed the subclavian artery.

In *The Sign of Four* (Chapter I), Watson writes:

> I . . . sat nursing my wounded *leg*. I had had a Jezail bullet through it some time before, and though it did not prevent me from walking, it ached wearily at every change of the weather.

The italics are mine. Apparently, Conan Doyle, when he wrote the second story, forgot the reference in the earlier one. Singularly enough, by the time he came to *The Hound of the Baskervilles*, he seems to have forgotten the reference in *The Sign of Four*, for we read (Chapter XIV):

> Never have I see a man run as Holmes ran that night. I am reckoned

fleet of foot, but he outpaced me as much as I outpaced the little professional.

A. N. Scott

185 Drake Street, Rochdale, Lancs.

13 September 1930

Dr. Watson and Professor Moriarty

To the Editor

Sir, – I have been much interested in the correspondence concerning errors made by Conan Doyle, but none seems to have noticed a slip of the kind that Sherlock Holmes himself would have shuddered at.

In "The Final Problem" Holmes makes a surprise call on Dr. Watson and confesses that he is afraid of air guns. Holmes says: "You have probably never heard of Professor Moriarty?" Dr. Watson replies: "Never." In this story Holmes and Moriarty are killed. Holmes was later resurrected by Conan Doyle, but Moriarty was for ever dead.

In *The Valley of Fear* Moriarty is also introduced, and although this story was written after "The Final Problem", the adventure with which it deals must obviously be taken as having occurred before the adventure of "The Final Problem". At the end of it Holmes says he must have time in order to get level with Moriarty. Yet early in the story Dr. Watson has heard all about Moriarty. Holmes says: "You have heard me speak of Professor Moriarty?" and Watson replies: "The famous scientific criminal, as famous among crooks as—" and so on.

Until "The Final Problem", in which Moriarty was killed, Watson had never heard of him; in *The Valley of Fear* he had.

There is another oversight on the part of Conan Doyle. In "The Resident Patient" (*Memoirs*) appears an account of how Holmes breaks in upon Watson's thoughts with the remark, "You are right, Watson. It does seem a very preposterous way of settling a dispute." This account of Holmes's thought-reading abilities also appears, word for word, in "The Cardboard Box" (*His Last Bow*).

Alfred C. O. Whitehall

24 The Vale, Philippsville, Northampton.

20 September 1930

Sherlock Holmes and the Railways

To the Editor

Sir, – When Holmes accompanied by Watson is running away from Professor Moriarty they take the Continental boat train. Moriarty

153

appears on the platform just as the train starts, and Holmes rightly conjectures that he will engage a special train for the pursuit.

Conan Doyle makes that boat train run *via* Canterbury! There it stops, and Holmes and Watson get out. It has hardly gone on (only a few minutes) when the "special" follows, dashing through the station! But I think I am right in saying that it would have taken eight minutes before, by the "block" working, the line could have been signalled clear.

Again, in the story of "The Five Orange Pips", Doyle makes a man, between eight and nine o'clock at night, cross Waterloo Bridge *to take a train to Horsham*. The direct route was, of course, from either Victoria or London Bridge, and not from Waterloo. One could, I know, have gone from Waterloo, *via* Guildford, a roundabout route, but even then, at the time the story was published, the last train had gone long ago, and the journey that night was impossible.

VICTOR L. WHITECHURCH

Stone Vicarage, Aylesbury, Bucks.

20 September 1930

A Reply to Canon Whitechurch

To the Editor

SIR, – To admirers of Conan Doyle's Sherlock Holmes stories it is at least satisfying to know that so soon after his death, his works have been definitely established among the classics – if the comments that have recently appeared in your Letter-Box are any indication. Whatever the detractors of Doyle may say, it is surely a tribute to his work that so much time is being spent in studying it, if only for the purpose of finding faults.

Unfortunately even commentators sometimes go astray. For instance, a correspondent pointed out last week that it would not have been practical for the man mentioned in "The Five Orange Pips" to leave Waterloo between eight and nine o'clock at night for Horsham. Although I have not a late nineteenth-century time-table to hand, a man could, judging from the present possibilities, take a train at that time *via* Raynes Park to Dorking and thence a "local" to Horsham.

Again, the same correspondent says that a special train could not dash through a station only a few minutes after a previous one had left, as it would have taken eight minutes before the line could have been signalled clear. Surely a writer of detective stories is allowed some licence? Are we to insist upon the lapse of an additional five minutes in order to conform with correct railway practice at the expense of a close chase? I think not.

F.C.G.

Horsham.

4 October 1930

Sherlock Holmes and the Cocaine Habit

To the Editor

SIR, – It is often asked why it was that Conan Doyle, himself a doctor, and therefore alive to the dangers of drug-addiction, should have "boosted" cocaine as a powerful aid to intellect and imagination. But he was really entirely blameless when he made cocaine familiar to his increasing public.

He never excited any longing for cocaine as Scott and Dickens raise a gusto for food and wine. And he never made the kind of mistake which a lady novelist recently made over her detective hero, a gentlemanly *flâneur* with a good following and a liking for old pubs. As I had more than a sneaking fondness for the fellow and his catholic tastes, I followed him with note-book and pencil during a whole day's trail through a delectable, inn-strewn countryside; he had thirty-seven beers, fourteen sherries, at least half-a-dozen whiskies, and some noble liquor at dinner which I could not get near enough to recognise.

The Sherlock Holmes stories really contain a history of the medical profession's changing attitude to cocaine. The drug came into medicine about the time when Doyle began to write, and as it was widely used as a local anæsthetic in eye work he would study its properties during his dreary efforts to set himself up as an oculist. Cocaine was considered rather a wonderful drug when it was first introduced, and it was largely used by the medical profession to wean patients from the dark potion beloved of Coleridge, De Quincey, deans, scholars, learned doctors, and other great figures and makers of the past. But cocaine was found to be a more potent destroyer than the drugs for which it was substituted, and it gradually grew into disrepute except as a local anæsthetic.

Conan Doyle never lost touch with medicine, and consequently the time came in a later story when Dr. Watson proudly recorded that he had weaned Holmes from cocaine.

MEDICINÆ BACCALAUREUS

Glasgow

8 November 1930

"The Sign of Four"

To the Editor

SIR, – Conan Doyle, in naming one of the characters in *The Sign of Four* Mahomet Singh, tripped badly. Mahomet is, of course, a Mahometan name, while Singh is Hindu. The two cannot be yoked together.

F. R. H. CHAPMAN (Major)

Authors' Club.

29 November 1930

THE TIMES LITERARY SUPPLEMENT

Sherlockholmitos

To the Editor

SIR, – One curious piece of evidence seems to have escaped the notice of all students of Sherlockholmitos. In *The Valley of Fear* Holmes convinces a more than usually imbecile C.I.D. man that Moriarty really is a criminal by pointing out that his expenditure is great and his official stipend small. He has, says Holmes, no relation but a brother, a railway porter in a country station in the West. In "The Final Problem", his brother, Colonel James Moriarty, is described as trying to clear his late brother's reputation.

Has any scholar explored the evidence supplied by the way in which people are represented as dressing in the various stories? Do colonels wear gaiters with a frock coat? The description of Colonel Ross in "Silver Blaze" suggests a gas inspector. Do colonels wear long light beards? Colonel Valentine Walter, in "The Bruce-Partington Plans", does. There is a vast sphere of learned research open to any well-equipped student in this matter.

PETER GREEN,
Canon of Manchester

The Cathedral, Manchester.

3 November 1932

THE TIMES

Points from Letters about Sherlock Holmes

To the Editor

In my 1923 diary is an entry: "Told Walter Haigh Branfoot over the teacups on Enford Rectory lawn how I used to hold my breath in 1892 when passing Arthur Conan Doyle's brass plate. He surprised me by saying he supplied Conan Doyle with the story of *The Hound of the Baskervilles* and some others."

Branfoot was known to hundreds of Bluecoat boys as a classic and his intimates among them can testify. He was at Lincoln College, Oxford, 1872–1876. He also supplied Stanley Weyman with the theme of *The Castle Inn* and some others.

A. S. BRYANT

Upway Rectory, Weymouth.

3 November 1932

Conan Doyle himself acknowledged indebtedness to Fletcher Robinson for the story of *The Hound of the Baskervilles*, which was based upon a Dartmoor legend of a spectral dog. No doubt a number of interesting affinities might be traced between Conan Doyle's stories and those of other writers; Fr. Knox has already indicated this line of research, and your reviewer in *The Times Literary Supplement* last week proposes a connection between *A Study in Scarlet* and Stevenson's *Dynamiter*. I would suggest that "The Man with the Twisted Lip" owes its inception to Thackeray's tale of Mr. Altamont (a name with a strong Holmesian flavour) in his *Yellowplush Papers*.

T. S. BLAKENEY

67 St. George's Road, S.W.1.

5 November 1932

THE SUNDAY TIMES

The Finances of Baker Street

To the Editor

SIR, – Without claiming the erudition of Mr. Desmond MacCarthy and the eminent writers whose researches he analyses ("Sherlockismus", 30 October 1932), I was always under the impression that Holmes had private means.

Watson, of course, never made any secret of his income. With soldierly bluntness, he more than once referred to his limited means in the early days, and as time passed he took an honest pride in his increasing practice. Holmes, on the other hand, from the beginning, had the detached attitude to expenditure which marks the quietly moneyed man.

Mr. MacCarthy mentions the cost of the Baker Street ménage, and puts it at £5 weekly. I am of opinion that this figure must have been exceeded very often. There was always a meal and a fine fire for every caller at 221b. Very often the fire was in full blast before breakfast, and the habit Holmes had of sitting at his deductions through the night shows how careless he was about coal. No man brought up to earn his living would have acted thus. He would have done his deductions in bed.

Cabmen had good reason for knowing the generosity of Holmes. He was continually flinging half-sovereigns or sovereigns, whichever came to his hand first, and there is no record of his ever having borrowed from his friend, as a needy detective might well have done.

There is much other evidence to show ample resources. He had his helpers in all quarters, and could call upon them at a moment's notice. All these people must have had a regular retainer from him. His newspaper and book bill was very heavy. All the papers were delivered regularly, and his library of scientific and criminal works must have been the finest in Europe. Similarly, he would often go to fashionable concerts, an expensive item even in those days.

We must aim at the truth, of course, but I cannot help feeling that the detachment and impartiality of Holmes are impaired by the suggestion that he was at any time pressed for money. He has always seemed to me the ideal independent gentleman as well as a great detective.

A. G. THORNTON

Waddon, Surrey.

6 November 1932

Mr. Holmes's Financial Position

To the Editor

SIR, – The able discussion by your correspondent, Mr. Thornton, of Sherlock Holmes's financial position sheds interesting light on one of the most perplexing problems of the Holmes cycle. In "The Dying Detective" Watson describes Holmes as "the very worst tenant in London". "On the other hand," he continues, "his payments were princely. I have no doubt that the house might have been purchased at the price Holmes paid for his rooms during the years I was with him."

The problem is to reconcile this account with the express statement of young Stamford in the *Study in Scarlet* that "Holmes was bemoaning himself this morning because he could not get someone to go halves with him in some nice rooms which he had found and which were too much for his purse", followed a few pages later by Watson's remark that "so moderate did the terms [at Baker Street] seem when divided between us that the bargain was concluded on the spot".

My own explanation, which I put forward tentatively, is that the first account is nearer to the facts. Holmes, as Mr. Thornton has demonstrated, undoubtedly could afford "princely payments". He felt he needed the intellectual stimulus of companionship; but, knowing that he would be unlikely to find a partner who could afford to bear half of the heavy domestic expenditure in which his peculiar way of life tended to involve him, he arranged the proportioning of the terms beforehand, and, to avoid Watson's gentlemanly scruples, gave him (and also young Stamford) the impression that costs were to be shared equally.

This hypothesis might appear hazardous, were it not strikingly confirmed by a passage in the "Norwood Builder" which gives an account of a very similar instance of Holmes's generosity. Here Watson has sold his practice for a considerable sum to a Dr. Verner, and does not discover till long after that the greater part of the money was supplied by Holmes himself, of whom Dr. Verner was a distant relative. (We know that Holmes's great-uncle was Vernet, the French painter, so that Dr. Verner probably belongs to an Anglicised branch of this family.) No doubt in the case of the Baker Street rooms Watson later discovered Holmes's delicate deception and so was able with justification to write the passage in "The Dying Detective".

ANTHONY GOLDSCHMIDT

Oxford.

20 November 1932

THE MORNING POST

"Sherlock Holmes Street"

J. Joseph Renaud, the French novelist and dramatic author, to test the popularity of Conan Doyle's stories, recently sent a letter to a friend living in Baker Street. It was addressed as follows:

> Miss Compton,
>   The same street as Sherlock Holmes,
>   London.

The letter was delivered by the first post the following morning. The conclusion drawn is that Sherlock Holmes is still fresh in the memory of the English and that the English postal authorities are both erudite and conscientious.

Paris.

3 February 1933

The Sherlock Holmes Society

The first dinner of the Society was held on the evening of Derby Day, Wednesday, 6 June 1934, at Canuto's Restaurant in Baker Street. The following members were present: Dr. H. R. L. Sheppard, C.H. (in the Chair), Mr. Ivor Back, F.R.C.S., Mr. E. M. Behrens, Mr. H. W. Bell, Mr. Anthony Berkeley, Miss Winifred Blazey, Mr. Denis Browne, F.R.C.S., Mr. C M. Giveen, Mr. R. I. Gunn, Mr. Gerald Hopkins, Miss Ianthe Jerrold, Mr. Gerald Kelly, R.A., Miss Gladys Mitchell, Mr. F. V. Morley, Mr. Stanley Morrison, Mr. E. R. Punshon, Mr. S. C. Roberts, Miss Dorothy Sayers, Miss Helen Simpson, Mr. Dominick Spring-Rice, Captain A. E. W. Thomas, D.S.O., M.C., Mr. Richard Heron Ward, Mr. K. Hobson, and Mr. A. G. Macdonell (Hon. Secretary). A genial note of welcome was struck by placing in front of each member a copy of Mr. Roberts's masterly study of Dr. Watson.

Two members arrived, it is understood, in a hansom cab, and two at least drank Beaune because it was Dr. Watson's choice on a notable occasion. At the close of dinner a happy inspiration of Mr. Kelly's led to the appearance of a dish with a large metal cover, the removal of which by the Chairman, temporarily inveigled into the role of "Tadpole" Phelps, disclosed a facsimile of the Naval Treaty. This was followed by the presentation to the Chairman of copper beech leaves and orange pips by Miss Simpson and of an ear-flapped travelling-cap by Mr. Spring-Rice. These unexpected and ingenious touches of local colour put the company in the best of humour, and served as an admirable introduction to the business of the evening.

The proceedings were opened by Mr. Macdonell, who won unanimous approval for his proposal that the Society should elect Dr. Sheppard its President in recognition of his services in forcibly resuscitating Sherlock Holmes. (Later in the evening the President described the exact nature of the pressure which he and two friends applied to Sir A. Conan Doyle for this purpose during an I Zingari tour.) Mr. Macdonell then referred to various messages of greeting which he had received from, among others, Mr. Vincent Starrett and Mr. Desmond MacCarthy, and read extracts from a letter written by Mr. T. S. Blakeney from a town in Southern India, which must, as several members eagerly exclaimed, have been Pondicherry.

Mr. Ivor Back was then asked to speak on Dr. Watson's medical qualifications, and responded by reading a letter which he had recently received from him. It appears that the doctor is now eighty-two years of age, but still has a few patients, one of whom, suffering from the loss of a big toe, he proposed to send to Mr. Back for examination. Advancing years, however, have shaken Dr. Watson's confidence in his professional powers, and he frankly admitted to his correspondent that he felt that he was now an even greater danger to the public than when he recommended strychnine in large doses as a sedative.

Mr. Morley then rose to read a cryptic telegram of greeting to the Society from the Gasogene of the Baker Street Irregulars. He explained that the latter are a body of enthusiasts established in New York, and that the Gasogene is their chief officer, the other two being the Tantalus and the Commissionaire. The Society's interest in its American counterpart was increased by the extracts which Mr. Morley read from the Irregulars' highly original constitution, while his eloquent plea for a memorial plaque in Baker Street, or, if this should rekindle the fires of controversy, in Montague Street, obviously appealed strongly to his fellow-members' sense of fitness.

A reference by Mr. Morley to the unsolved problem of how two, or possibly three, Moriarty brothers each came to bear the name of James gave Mr. Gerald Kelly his cue for a brilliant diatribe on the subject of Moriarty's Greuze. He challenged Holmes's argument that the acquisition of a picture by this artist presupposed an income far in excess of a professorial stipend: the Vernet blood in his veins may well have caused Holmes to set a misplaced value on Greuze's work. Alternatively, why should not "La Jeune Fille à l'Agneau" have been a liability inherited by Moriarty from his father, whose unimaginative choice of names for his sons revealed him as a man of indifferent taste? Or again, might not Holmes himself have planted the work on his arch-enemy with the deliberate aim of undermining his morale?

Mr. Roberts and Mr. Spring-Rice continued the discussion, the latter drawing attention to the curious incident of the train which left Winchester and arrived at Victoria after the race for the Wessex Cup. Mr. Bell propounded an ingenious theory that, notwithstanding Holmes's descent from country squires, his familiarity with London dated from early days; the evidence being that the thoroughfare which he identified as Robert Street in 1886 had for a number of years previously been renamed Robsart Street.

Miss Sayers then proceeded to improve upon Mr. Morley's proposal by asking why, if mere creatures of the imagination, like Peter Pan, are to be commemorated with statues, this honour should be withheld from national figures such as Sherlock Holmes and Dr. Watson. Nay more, let members consider the claims of Mrs. Hudson, that paragon of

161

landladies, whom Baker Street Irregulars could not dismay nor thoughts of vanished tidiness betray. Does not she, the Happy Warrior of below-stairs, whom every kitchen-maid should wish to be, deserve a statue if anyone does?

So far Miss Sayers was on safe ground, but her next excursion landed her in a heated controversy. An incautious reference to Cambridge as Holmes's University brought Mr. Macdonell to his feet with the indignant rejoinder that anyone who meant to study the exact sciences must have chosen Edinburgh. Miss Sayers replied with spirit, citing chapter and verse in support of her view, but Mr. Macdonell remained unconvinced. Meanwhile the champions of Oxford discreetly bowed their heads before the storm.

Discussion of two questions of future policy concluded this first and highly successful meeting of the Society. One was concerned with the form of government, and on this point Mr. Macdonell advocated an autocratic Soviet, of preferably one person, to deal with such questions as the number and election of members, and disarmed criticism by proposing himself as the Soviet. That this proposal was entirely to the taste of his fellow-members was evident from the way in which they endorsed Mr. Back's thanks to the Honorary Secretary for his previous labours on their behalf.

The remaining question was that of future meetings of the Society. It was agreed that not more than two dinners should be held each year, and that the choice of Derby Night for one of them could not be improved upon. Mr. Back's plea for the anniversaries of Holmes's and Watson's birthdays would have gained more support but for the total lack of evidence as to when these anniversaries fell. Ultimately it was decided that the second dinner should be held in November. This, it was generally conceded, would give the Society the best chance of autumnal wind.

R. Ivar Gunn
11 August 1934

THE SUNDAY MAIL

"The Man with the Twisted Lip"

Sherlock Holmes's admirers will remember the "Man with the Twisted Lip". He was a beggar who sold matches all day outside the Bank of England, at five o'clock changed his rags and greasepaint for formal City clothes, and travelled first-class to a well-appointed suburban villa where they believed him to be "something in the City". Thirty years

162

after Doyle wrote this story, a London detective has shown that the idea is by no means incredible. During an investigation, he had to disguise himself as a match-seller, and to his amazement took £8 in a week without the slightest effort.

ONE IN THE KNOW
19 August 1934

THE BRITISH MEDICAL JOURNAL

The Origins of Sherlock Holmes

To the Editor

SIR, – When a student at Liverpool in the late 'nineties I read a paper on Sherlock Holmes to the Students' Debating Society. The chairman on that occasion was George Hamilton, assistant honorary surgeon to Mitchell Banks, and he took the opportunity thus afforded to tell us of his own acquaintance with Doyle, when both were students at Edinburgh. He told us that *at that time* Conan Doyle, deeply interested in Poe's detective works, but recognising that they were "caviare to the general", told Hamilton that he had the idea of writing detective fiction according to the system of Poe, but greatly simplified and brought down to the level of ordinary people.

W. J. YOUNG

Harston, Cambridge.

25 August 1934

THE SUNDAY TIMES

Sherlock Holmes at Cambridge

To the Editor

SIR, – I submit that Sherlock Holmes was almost certainly a member of Magdalene College, Cambridge. His behaviour is hardly consistent with membership of a large college, and his only two friends, Trevor and Musgrave, were thoroughly representative of the sporting and aristocratic undergraduates of Magdalene in the 'seventies.

Moreover, while the presence of a bulldog inside Trinity was no doubt always unthinkable, the discipline at Magdalene was not as keen as I hear it is today.

There is a difficulty in the fact that in the three adventures of Holmes at Cambridge, Watson appears not to know that he was on familiar

163

ground. But the identity of the guilty student which was discovered in Holmes's busy year, 1895, at "one of our great University towns" was traced by a pellet of the peculiar mixture which Watts used to fill the long-jump pit at Fenners. I believe this was a secret composition of his own, which he only allowed to be used elsewhere for the University sports at Queens', and which was not available at Oxford.

It is clear from the story of the three students that Holmes recognised the nature of the pellet as soon as he saw it, and it is probable that, besides his boxing and fencing, Holmes did some running and jumping while he was an undergraduate.

Why Holmes did not mention the fact of his familiarity with Cambridge to Watson is not apparent. But undergraduates who have terminated their career after two years are not always anxious to mention the fact, and Holmes, who was certainly an addict of cocaine at a very early age, may very well have met with little encouragement from the college authorities.

H. MacNaghten

Lyminster, Sussex.

9 September 1934

THE RAILWAY MAGAZINE

The Railway Journeys of Mr. Sherlock Holmes

To the Editor

Sir, – In his charming article in your May number, Mr. Alan Rannie, referring to what he so justly describes as the great epic of *The Hound of the Baskervilles*, says he likes to think that the platform from which Holmes said good-bye to Watson and Sir Henry was No. 1 at Paddington. There can at any rate be no doubt that the station was Paddington, because on page 96 of the original edition, Holmes says, "We shall meet at the 10.30 train from Paddington." Of course, the date of the story (1889), and when it was written (1901), were long before the date of the Limited. Probably Sir Arthur Conan Doyle was thinking of the Cornishman, which, of course, was the principal West of England express at the time he was writing. Am I not correct, though, in thinking that in 1901 the down Cornishman left Paddington somewhat later, round about eleven o'clock? If my recollection is correct, the Cornishman only commenced to run in the 'nineties, so the principal West of England express in 1889 would presumably have been the "Flying Dutchman". Did this leave Paddington then at 10.30? And at what point was the train running when Dr. Mortimer showed Sir Henry his first sight of the moor?

In my young days I lived at Truro and travelled fairly frequently between there and London, and setting my youthful imagination to work as to where this spot was, I came to the conclusion that it was going up Dainton Bank. The first sight of the moor, I believe, is on approaching the bridge over the Teign on the London side of Newton Abbot, and looking up the valley towards Hay Tor, but I submit that the passage which Mr. Rannie quotes is a description of a purely country scene to which the view over part of Newton Abbot and the junction of the Bovey Tracey line would hardly apply. There are continuous views of the moor as the train climbs Rattery, but we must assume from the book that Sir Henry wanted to get the first "wild" view of Dartmoor that he could. The book goes on, "Baskerville sat for a long time, his eyes fixed upon it", but I think this proves my point, because, having once got his first view from Dainton, he would naturally sit all the way to Plymouth by the right-hand carriage window facing the engine. Therefore, I plump for Dainton.

A. G. R. Hickes, B.A.
June 1935

THE ABBEY ROAD JOURNAL

Sherlock Holmes at Abbey House

Circumstance has involved us in a mystery. A mystery deep and dark enough to satisfy any juvenile sleuth under ninety, and with elements as baffling as anything in the long literature of self-torment which is called detective fiction. The mystery which concerns us belongs to epic enigmas of a higher flight. It ranks with the unquenchable queries of history, literature, and the day before yesterday. It is a problem to align with the permanent guesses of mankind. Savants will investigate it and journalists resuscitate it as surely as they periodically inquire if Mary of Scots killed Darnley, or ponder the mystery of Edwin Drood, the whereabouts of Cromwell's vanished head, of what happened to Colonel Fawcett. It may even be enshrined in schoolboy howlers.

The winged Mercury, father of streamlining, broke the news of our mystery. Appearing in the thin disguise of a Post Office messenger, he parked his bicycle on our kerb, interrupted his whistling to give us an anticipatory grin, and whisked out a letter.

"You're 221 Baker Street," he reminded us. "Sign, please."

We signed, remained calm . . . and collected. We took up a paper knife, had a sharp struggle with the instinct that got Paul Pry into his trouble, then put the knife down. We had no legitimate excuse for slitting the envelope and could not extemporise a passable reason for opening it accidentally.

Two hundred and twenty-one! As appreciative students of Baker Street literature the number is written into our affections more clearly than Calais on the heart of an English Queen, or on the suitcase of one returning from his first Continental trip. According to the local postal authorities, 221 is also written over the doorway of Abbey House. Renumbering and re-christening in 1930 altered our postal address from the more prosaic 43/45 Upper Baker Street and we became 221 Baker Street. Since when we have basked in the Holmes oriflamme, and foreign visitors have gazed reverently at our first floor windows, there to glimpse imaginatively the lean and saturnine figure of an immortal before departing to view Rima and the Albert Memorial. Yet their devout attention, like the delivery of this letter, only plunges us deeper into our mystery. Where was 221 Baker Street?

Our familiarity with the detective's way of life, and with the interior of the collaborator's dwelling, does not blind us to Watson's amazing reticence regarding its exterior. There is a strange dearth of clues from which its actual site can be identified. Readers have consequently entertained their own ideas of its situation and there can be few houses in Baker Street which have not had their lingering spectators. The problem has not altogether yielded to scholarship for the experts merely agree to differ.

Anxious to solve this problem without cross words, we realise that for such amateur enthusiasts as ourselves to make a suggestion towards this identification may smack of rushing in where experts fear to tread. But we are fortified by the thought of posterity and the advice of our old Professor who took us in Mental Hygiene, before taking a vacant chair at Broadmoor.

"To the dry bones, gentlemen," he urged us, through that ever challenging inkstained beard. "Nobody can write a thesis worth a publisher's remainder, without getting his facts first-hand from original sources. Test everything yourself . . . " And to original sources we hurried.

With gentle firmness we recommend students of the Watsonian text to seek marrow in the dry bones and get back to the original sources. Meaning, further back than they have hitherto stopped. For our modest but epoch-making pointer is simply to say that the experts have canvassed the wrong street. All their theories are based on the general belief that the earliest reference to the Baker Street rooms occurs in *A Study in Scarlet*. This is the first Sherlock Holmes story and at the beginning of its second chapter Dr. Watson records: "We met next day as he had arranged and inspected the rooms at No. 221b Baker Street, of which he had spoken at our meeting."

Our gift to scholarship is emphatically to disagree that this is either the first or the most reliable indication of the detective's residence. Another document, we claim, is the most original of original sources. The solution to the problem which – until we took up the trail – has baffled some of the best brains outside Scotland Yard, the Paris Sûreté, and the Chancellories of Europe, lies overlooked in the most obvious place of all. That is, in the notebook of its creator!

The author's rough jotting records the idea of *A Study in Scarlet*, and his first detective adventure. The Sherrinford Holmes of this memorandum later became Sherlock, as the world knows; and the Ormond Sacker became Dr. Watson. And they lived at 221b *Upper* Baker Street!

According to this genesis, therefore, the famous establishment did not lie in Baker Street itself. Its situation is fixed within a much smaller radius; to wit, in that stretch of less than two hundred yards on our side of Marylebone Circus, the same Upper Baker Street in which Abbey House was first established.

Anyone who knows our methods may now ask: then on which side, exactly where, or opposite what, lay the elusive rooms? We refuse to be flattered by this confidence in our powers of deduction. To reveal exactly where the residence stood (and perhaps stands) would be taking all the joy of life from those who find in polite controversy what others find in bridge or, alternatively, in a friendly game of cards. Our task has been to start the hare, not run with the hounds. We now sit back to watch the unleashed pedants spring forward with the bound of a Haskerville.

For the last illustration of deduction, we turn to the letter itself and apply the three methods of envelope detection familiar to readers of our monograph on the subject. The fourth method, which is simply to open the confounded thing, is equivalent to allowing oneself three cheats at Patience.

It is by simple, logical steps that we perceive the writer to be a Swede. In any case, the sender's name and address written on the back of the envelope were definitely Swedish.

Should the unknown correspondent read this, may we add a word of advice to explain why he has not yet received a reply from Mr. Holmes. He will find, if he turns again to the story of the "Musgrave Ritual", that the great detective had a playful habit of transfixing his unanswered correspondence by a jack-knife to the centre of his wooden mantelpiece. A still older Englsh custom is to miss the mantel and hit the burning grate.

F. WALKER
Autumn 1935

THE DAILY TELEGRAPH

The Residence of Sherlock Holmes

To the Editor

Can your readers acquaint me with the supposed number of Mr. Sherlock Holmes's residence in Baker Street?

J. S. POPE

33 Netherhall Gardens, N.W.3.

17 July 1937

221b Baker Street

To the Editor

SIR, – In response to your correspondent's question regarding Mr. Sherlock Holmes's residence, this is given in one of the books as 221b Baker Street.

I take this information from an old diary which I was keeping when, as a boy, I made a fruitless search along Baker Street in the hope of finding that number.

Yours faithfully,
F. G. NUTTALL

Bury, Lancs.

21 July 1937

Fretherne House

To the Editor

SIR, – That part of Baker Street between Paddington Street and the Marylebone Road used to be called York Place. I went to a preparatory school at Fretherne House, which was then No. 19.

By a careful study of the run of the numbers in Baker Street we boys calculated that No. 221b should be the house immediately opposite the school. Holmes was such a real personality to small boys in those days

168

that I think we always half expected the great man to step out one day!

Yours, &c.,

JOHN R. POLAND (Commander)

Sevenoaks.

24 July 1937

JOHN O' LONDON'S WEEKLY

"Murder in the Cathedral"

To the Editor

I noticed when reading Mr. T. S. Eliot's play that the following passage is almost identical with a passage in Conan Doyle's Sherlock Holmes story, "The Musgrave Ritual". Can you tell me what the connection is between the two?

THOMAS: Whose was it?
TEMPTER: His who is gone.
THOMAS: Who shall have it?
TEMPTER: He who will come.
THOMAS: What shall be the month?
TEMPTER: The last from the first . . . etc.

D.J.H.

Middlesborough.

We are informed that Mr. Eliot makes no secret of the fact that occasionally in order to obtain a special effect certain passages from his works are taken from the writings of other authors, and that the passage in question was actually adapted by him from the Conan Doyle story.

6 August 1937

COUNTRY LIFE

Sherlock Mews

It was with an unspeakable thrill that I read, one day last week, a small piece of news in an early edition of an evening paper. The editor did not, apparently, share my enthusiasm, since the paragraph had wholly vanished from a later edition; but I trust that a few early readers were as delighted as I was. The news was this: that certain streets in London were to be re-christened, and that York Mews South – if I remember correctly, leading out of Baker Street – was to be born again under the name of Sherlock Mews. I hope that it is superfluous to add that

Sherlock Holmes lived at 221b Baker Street.

Doubtless I am about to betray ignorance, but this is often a wise thing to do, since various erudite correspondents come down on one like a hundred of bricks with interesting information. The man who gives a false clue in a crossword puzzle is, I am told, snowed under with letters. Therefore I will take the risk and say that I do not know of any other street that has been called after a famous character in fiction. The most obscure persons in real life have this honour paid them, but not those who are, to thousands and thousands of people, infinitely more real and alive. At any rate, if this is the beginning of a new era, no better beginning could have been made. Here is one of the few characters in literature, perhaps the only one in modern literature, to whom an allusion can be made in any company without fear of a blank stare. Not even a judge has ever asked, with their always whimsical assumption of innocence: "Who is Sherlock Holmes?"

As regards Holmes I am, if I may so describe myself, a fundamentalist, a person of childish beliefs, who does not hold with scholarly but blasphemous inquiries into the chronology of the stories. To me *A Study in Scarlet* comes first: it is, as it were, the first chapter of Genesis. With an invincible faith, I refuse to believe that which I know perfectly well, namely that the adventures of the *Gloria Scott* and the Musgrave Ritual must in fact have been earlier because they belonged to Holmes's undergraduate days. Being thus simple and orthodox, I have little sympathy with those researches that would identify No. 221b with any particular house in Baker Street. Therefore I cannot say whether Holmes and Watson passed along this particular mews on their way to trap Colonel Sebastian Moran in the empty house opposite 221b, but I like to think that they did. Dr. Watson does tell us that, through Holmes's extraordinary knowledge of London byways, they traversed "a network of mews and stables the very existence of which I had never known", and that brings me to an important point. There must be other mews near Baker Street to be re-christened, and the matter must not be allowed to end here. Sherlock cannot be commemorated and Holmes forgotten. Poor Watson, too, must not be left out; and what of Mrs. Hudson, who ministered to them for so many years, put up with Holmes's pistol practice, and even risked her life by going on hands and knees to move the image which was to be the target of Colonel Moran and his deadly air-gun?

Fortunately, there is an example ready to the hands of the christening powers. In the little cluster of streets by Charing Cross and the Adelphi the names of John Villiers, Duke of Buckingham, are commemorated one by one. There are John Street, Duke Street, Villiers Street, and

Buckingham Street (where David Copperfield endured the tyranny of Mrs. Crupp), and I have always been told, on rather vague authority, that there is, or was, Of Alley, though I have never found it. Surely, then, Sherlock and Holmes, Hudson and Mycroft, could all be mews, and poor old Watson could at least be fobbed off with an alley. That would satisfy me to begin with, but I confess that I should like to go further; a whole range of new streets rises before my prophetic eye, called after the various detective officers who suffered so much at the great man's hands – Gregson and Lestrade, Athelney Jones, Hopkins and Macdonald. Has not Moriarty Mansions a noble and opulent sound? The neighbourhood of Baker Street might, under proper direction, take on the character of a mythology.

If once this movement can be successfully set on foot, there is no knowing where it will end. We know that when Pickwick first burst on the world all manner of objects, from cabs to tobacco-jars, were called after it, though the name of only one of them, the Penny Pickwick, still faintly suggests a cigar. But has there ever been a Pickwick Avenue? In the small village where I live a group of some half-dozen houses bears the name of Weller Place, but there is no reason to think that they were called after Mr. Weller of the Belle Sauvage, or his son. Mr. Pickwick lodged in Goswell Street, and its name is now, I believe, Goswell Road. Since once a change has been made, let there be another and a greater change, and let it be Pickwick Street. Urged on by this fervour of re-christening I should be almost tempted to call Old Street after Mr. Guppy, Newman Street after Mr. Turveydrop, and Windsor Terrace after Mr. Micawber; but perhaps I am being carried away.

At any rate even if old streets cannot be generally renamed, the principle of Sherlock Mews might well be applied to the brand-new ones which are springing up everywhere. A few years ago some genius discovered that all possible permutations and combinations of stripes had been exhausted in the devising of club ties; so he had the happy notion of dotting crowns and roses, elephants, corkscrews and other symbolical objects upon a plain background; a whole new race of ties came into being, and there is still an inexhaustible supply. Today, suburbs are already full of Sylvan Avenues; the name hunger is acute; here is the way out. Woodlands and Glensides and Hillcrests have had their day.

BERNARD DARWIN
16 October 1937

A Case for Sherlock Holmes

Baker Street is not what it was in the days of gas lamps and hansom cabs, and the postman with a letter in his bag for Sherlock Holmes may well be puzzled. The Post Office London Directory gives no help in finding the rooms that Holmes shared with the amiable Dr. Watson at "221b Baker Street"; although it shows that the gap between premises numbered 219 to 225 is filled by Abbey House.

This is the headquarters of the Abbey Road Building Society, and several business concerns also have their offices there. So the postman who recently found himself carrying a letter with a foreign postmark for "Mr. Sherlock Holmes" at the old address seems to have concluded that an ageless detective might have relinquished his bee-farming in Sussex to start a new career as a company director. At any rate, he picked upon Abbey House and delivered the letter at the offices of British Home Stores, Limited, on the third floor. Whether this was a neat official joke or the result of some mysterious processes of reasoning would have formed a pleasing subject for a professional discourse by Holmes.

It was found that the letter came from an elderly woman in a small town in Denmark who respectfully asked for a little charitable assistance for herself and her husband in the hard times which have come upon them through business misfortunes. These two pensioners sought the detective's help in starting a shop, which would give them a better livelihood, and the writer concluded: "I am quite sure we shall have the pleasure of hearing from you."

Such a letter, had he been there to receive it, would probably have appealed to the generous impulses of the wizard of Baker Street. Had it come at some quiet interval in those adventurous lives he might even have bundled off Dr. Watson (without his revolver) in the next steamer to investigate the merits of the case upon the spot.

18 October 1937

Sending for Sherlock Holmes

To the Editor

May I thank you, I am sure on behalf of innumerable readers, for the item of news in THE TIMES of 18 October headed "Case for Sherlock Holmes". I am reminded by it of an incident in my own experience. Some years ago my home in Oxfordshire was burgled during the

172

temporary absence of my family, and the village policeman, having failed to track down the intruders, said to me, with a deep sigh: "What a pity Sherlock Holmes is dead."

JOHN SHERBORNE

12 Nairn Road, Talbot Avenue, Bournemouth.

20 October 1937

The Post Office's Dilemma

A letter addressed to "Mr. Sherlock Holmes, 221b Baker Street" was recently delivered by the postal authorities at the premises which now fill the gap between Nos. 219 and 225. It proved, when opened, to be a respectful request for financial assistance from an elderly couple in Denmark; and it would be intriguing to know how the Post Office, who were responsible for returning the missive to its senders, explained their reasons for doing so. None of the customary formulae would have met the occasion. "Try No. 122" would have been sheer moral cowardice on the part of what the *Post Office Guide* calls the "officer deputed for the purpose". Nor could this hapless functionary take refuge – without committing a falsehood – in some such curt, inhuman intimation as "Not known at this address"; for there is hardly an address in London at which Holmes is not a household word. "Gone away" is no good, for the detective was never there, but to say that he was never there – especially just after the L.C.C. has named two thoroughfares in the locality Sherlock Mews and Watson Mews – is to court endless misgivings and invoke far-reaching doubts. Finally, "Died some years ago" can hardly be said of an immortal.

The more closely we examine the problem, the sorrier we become for the deputed officer. His duty as well as his instincts bid him spare as far as possible the feelings of the indigent and imploring Danes. They must be persuaded, gently but firmly, that their hopes of a loan from 221b are vain; yet there would be a grave risk in telling them the truth, and indeed it might not be at all easy to convince them that it was the truth. After all, they presumably considered with some care the question of approaching the eminent detective. They believe in his existence, they have hopes of his generosity, they know his address. To tell them that there never was any such person is to upset their whole scale of values, confuse them unutterably, and threaten the very foundations of their sanity. Besides, *was* there never any such person? The Danes, embittered and suspicious, could collect an impressive pile of monographs all written on the assumption that there was; their authors are respectable and learned Englishmen, and the Danes will hardly believe that men of

173

their stamp devoted their energies to solving such problems as those represented by the date of Watson's second marriage, and by Holmes's standing as an apiarist, if both Holmes and Watson were mere figments of a novelist's imagination. They might, of course, be referred to the parallel and even more striking case of their own compatriot, Hamlet, who has probably had more written about him than any other character in history, whether real or imaginary; but the analogy breaks down because Elsinore still stands, and 221b does not.

The whole affair is delicate and distressing – not quite so shocking perhaps as "the dreadful business of the Abernetty family", nor so dire as "the repulsive story of the red leech and the terrible death of Crosby, the banker", but quite as tantalising as either: for – as in these two cases – we shall never hear the end of the story, never learn just how the Post Office conveyed to the Danes the sad realities of their illusion and how the Danes stood up under the shock. These things – unlike the case of the Matilda Briggs, which was "not the name of a young woman, Watson; it was a ship which is associated with the giant rat of Sumatra" – are most emphatically not "a story for which the world is not yet prepared".

(FOURTH LEADER)
25 October 1937

THE EVENING NEWS

The Traditional Home of Sherlock Holmes

Next time you pass along Baker Street, take a glance at No. 111. It is a house famous throughout the United States of America as the home of Sherlock Holmes and Dr. Watson, and yet it was missed by the postman who recently delivered a letter to"Mr. Sherlock Holmes" at Abbey House.

The elderly Danish lady who wrote the letter had addressed it to the non-existent "221b"; but had the postman taken it to No. 111 it would at least have joined the bulk of the Sherlock Holmes correspondence which still comes in from abroad, some of it from genuine would-be clients of the famous detective.

Few Londoners know the house as the focal point of a living legend, and yet members of the Sherlock Holmes Society have come all the way from America to gaze at it; and those who can't come in person write reams of letters to the occupants asking them to count the stairs to see if Watson was right when he said seventeen, and begging for photographs.

WALTER SHEPHERD
13 November 1937

VII. THE GREAT DETECTIVE
(1938–1950)

———◆———

Sherlock Holmes in the Limelight

At the moment I seem pursued (merely conversationally, I should explain) by that fellow Sherlock Holmes, and his satellite, Watson. The whole affair started a few weeks ago when a contributor to this page referred to Watson as probably the most stupid character in fiction and went on to express surprise that Conan Doyle "should have believed it possible for any man to qualify as a doctor and remain as witless and as unobservant as Dr. Watson".

Immediately a student of such matters drew my attention to the origin of Sherlock Holmes. He said he believed that Holmes's technique was largely inspired by and modelled on the uncanny deductive methods of Dr. Joseph Bell, a professor at Edinburgh University when Doyle was a medical student there, and that Doyle was probably writing with his tongue in his cheek when he made the laborious Watson a doctor.

Then up spake a Scot, for whose opinions I have the soundest respect, to say this was not so and point out that though it was hard to see why the cleverness of a physician in real life should have led Sir Arthur Conan Doyle to emphasise the stupidity of one in fiction, nevertheless the original Holmes was, indeed, one of the leading doctors in the Scottish capital – Charles Bell, not Joseph Bell; the two were related. Watson's part was merely to act as a foil for that hero's cleverness.

And only this week I heard Professor Hamilton Thompson subject the exploits of Holmes, with Pickwickian geniality, to the acid test of historical criticism for the delight of an audience at Leeds University.

This constant cropping up of Holmes has led me now to believe with the Professor that while Watson has quite probably gone to Paradise by way of Kensal Green, Holmes still survives; and that on the brow of the cliffs between Seaford and Beachy Head, in the precincts of a lonely cottage, a tall, veiled figure, still strong and active, moves sedulously among the bee-hives. Octogenarian though he must be, Holmes's physical toughness was one of his strongest suits, and it is difficult not to believe that there might not be still some further exploit before him. But who is to provide it? Whom would you choose?

Talk turned on these lines after supper, and a mild argument ensued, one school holding that Holmes was out of date and that the technique of detective fiction has progressed since his last exploit, and the other that Doyle's hero is not a back number and that his methods of deduction make him, from a logical point of view, far the most satisfactory detective in fiction we have.

I remained neutral, being somewhat attached to the methods of Father Brown.

G.L.
28 February 1938

Sherlock Holmes and Father Brown

To the Woman's Page

MADAM, – If Sherlock Holmes is an "immortal", and I for one believe he is, then his methods of detection can never be out of date. Certain advances may have been made in the technique of detection, as, for example, in chemistry, in blood tests, in the efficiency of the microscope, and in radio telegraphy. The aeroplane and the high-powered car are other technical advances. But the arts of induction (by which the search for clues is narrowed) and deduction remain constant. There is a lesson here for humanity in general. No amount of external progress can avail us anything unless the mind of man applies proper methods by which to assimilate it into the general body of human knowledge.

A nebulous "psychologist" like Father Brown is not in the same street as Holmes, who, I venture to say, will always live in Baker Street, and is not to be found on the Sussex coast, as you, in your "Musings", have imagined him in his old age.

There is only one thing I have against Holmes. He used the hypodermic syringe too much.

One other thing about Holmes that often causes me to daydream is this, and it is one that should interest the readers of this page. Why did Holmes never marry? Could any of your female readers imagine themselves married to him? He is certainly a man's man.

Yours, etc.

MORIARTY

1 March 1938

THE SATURDAY REVIEW OF LITERATURE

Sherlock Holmes and the "Norah Creina"

To Old Q

The *Gloria Scott*, the *Lone Star*, the *Sea Unicorn* of Dundee play a part in the stories of Sherlock Holmes; and Dr. Watson mentions other ships incidentally in Holmes's cases: the *Sophy Anderson*, for example, and "the shocking affair of the Dutch steamship *Friesland*, which so nearly cost us both our lives". "The Resident Patient" in *The Memoirs of Sherlock Holmes* (1893) ends thus:

> From that night nothing has been seen of the three murderers by the police, and it is surmised at Scotland Yard that they were among the passengers of the ill-fated steamer *Norah Creina*, which was lost some years ago with all hands upon the Portuguese coast, some leagues to the north of Oporto.

I always regretted the loss of that ship – such a pretty Irish name! – but I have been glad to discover that Dr. Watson was in error, for, only a year before, the *Norah Creina* carried Mr. Todd safely into Honolulu: see R. L. Stevenson's *The Wrecker*, which appeared serially in *Scribner's Magazine* in 1891 and as a book in 1892. Possibly the change from the Pacific to the Atlantic proved, ultimately, too severe a one for the gallant barque.

ALAN LANG STROUT

Lubbock, Texas.

8 April 1939

JOHN O' LONDON'S WEEKLY

The Habits of Moorland Ponies

To the Editor

SIR, – Even the most painstaking of authors are not immune from slips. I should like to draw the attention of your readers to a curious error in one of the best Sherlock Holmes stories, *The Hound of the Baskervilles*, a film version of which has just been released. Sir Conan Doyle speaks of a moorland pony wandering into a bog and being sucked into a slimy grave while still alive. This is a thing which never happens. A moorland pony, whether going singly or in a drove, never becomes bogged.

Moorland ponies have an uncanny and unerring knowledge of the proximity of bogs, and therefore give them a wide berth. On approaching a bog, even by night or in the thickest fog, Dartmoor ponies will turn at a sharp angle to avoid it, and never by any chance do they overrun themselves.

B. Crocker

Bedford.

17 November 1939

The Dartmoor Ponies

To the Editor

Sir, – I can assure your correspondent that he is wrong when he states that Dartmoor ponies are never lost in the bogs on Dartmoor. Uncanny as the instinct of these animals may be, they are certainly not infallible, for hundreds perish every year in the "quakers". I could direct Mr. Crocker to a bog known locally as the "Ponies' Graveyard".

Norman Lee

B.E.F., France.

29 December 1939

THE TIMES

In Memory of Sherlock Holmes

Fifty years ago to-day there perished, locked in each other's arms in the swirling torrent of the Reichenbach Falls, the most dangerous enemy of society and the foremost champion of the law. Some say – and Sir Arthur Conan Doyle was among them – that in reality only Professor Moriarty perished on that day. Tales began to circulate – and Dr. Watson, it must be regretfully admitted, stooped to spreading them – of an itinerant bookseller who was in truth none other than the great Holmes, and of an apocrypha of later, successful detective cases. Such stories are not uncommon when princes or heroes die. Edward II was said to have appeared at the Papal Palace at Avignon, garbed as a monk, in just such a fashion, but history is satisfied that he lies in Gloucester Cathedral. The Poles have their false Demetrius, the Portuguese their false Sebastian, the French their escaped and grown-up Louis XVII. We know this folklore well, and the longing and affection it embodies. So likely did our ancestors hold it that the unwitnessed death of any prominent person would be denied that they took care, as after the murder of Henry VI, to display the body in the streets.

Habeas Corpus did not run at the Reichenbach Falls. After going so grandly to his Valhalla, Sherlock Holmes became a body that could not be produced, and the task of the impostors and rumour-mongers was all the easier. But the whole world, which has a sound instinct in these matters, judged where the truth lay, and knew that Holmes was truly and gloriously dead, dead and immortal with the tremendous conclusion of the *Memoirs*. If Conan Doyle, and with him the not very independently minded Dr. Watson, chose to think otherwise, the idiosyncrasy was understandable as the habitual professional optimism of medical men making light of a small thing like a tumble over a waterfall; and on death and the hereafter Conan Doyle, though not Watson, was well known to hold unusual views. Holmes was a hero and he had a hero's end; and, as often happens with heroes, he had it as a crowning mercy only just in time.

Eighteen ninety-one was none too soon for Holmes and Moriarty to depart. Especially for Professor Moriarty. It was all very well to be the master-mind directing a vast network of criminals in the 'eighties. The profession was not then so public, so developed, or so overcrowded as it has since become. How many master-minds there have been since, and how many more there would have been but for the premature close of the late Edgar Wallace's career! The rivalry of younger men is something which ageing stars find it hard to relish, and Holmes was too great a national figure to have ended as a disgruntled bee-keeper, expressing a grudging scepticism at the tales of the next generation of detectives, the hosts of new figures, some of them Inspectors from the Yard, but most of them young men with highly amateur status, who now solve mysteries of a complexity and improbability undreamed of in Holmes's simpler Victorian day. Nothing ever came to the rooms in Baker Street whose solution was so wildly bizarre as many of the tasks of M. Hercule Poirot.

The glory round the head of Holmes (and of Moriarty, the first to endear Irish professors of mathematics to the great British public) is that they are Homeric figures. They belong to the early heroic age of the detective story. Their valour and cunning shine all the brighter, just as that of Homer's heroes does, from the crudeness and simplicity of the setting and the weapons. How jejune today seems the Professor's habit of dislodging a few bricks or tiles to brain Holmes as he walked the London streets. Master-minds have learnt more wholesale methods

179

since. (But 221b Baker Street remains unscathed.) How nonplussed would be all the criminals and those who catch them in the serried volumes of the present great age of detective fiction, if asked to commit their murders and catch their murderers without the telephone, or the electric light, or the high-powered car, or the wireless. Neither party could begin. But Moriarty could commit crime on a grand scale, and Holmes could run him to earth, with no weapons but the special trains of the South Eastern & Chatham Railway, the four-wheelers of the London streets, and the street urchins to run with messages. The poverty of the armament does but serve to display the strength of the warriors; and they remain for all time secure and unapproachable in a fame that a hectic half-century finds quite undimmed.

(FOURTH LEADER)
4 March 1941

Moriarty and Plato

To the Editor

SIR, – Your leading article on Holmes and Moriarty is an excellent piece of piety, but it does not quite dispose of the matter.

Some four or five years ago I read in a London newspaper that Professor Moriarty, who had led a life of crime in America, had been blown up by his own explosives in his own car. The Press generally lost a grand opportunity here. Secondly, there is a school of thought which holds Moriarty to have been a figment of Holmes, who used him in order to give the slip to the boring Watson. Lastly, has anyone noticed that Watson's concluding words about Holmes are almost precisely what Plato said of Socrates at the end of the *Phaedo?*

Yours &c.,
ONE OF THE NINETIES
5 March 1941

AMERICAN NOTES AND QUERIES

Sherlock and Oliver Wendell Holmes

The charming picture of the late Oliver Wendell Holmes (as disclosed in the recently published *Holmes–Pollock Letters*) "sweetening"his philosophic studies at ninety-two by dipping again into Sherlock Holmes recalls that Conan Doyle surnamed his detective for the jurist's father

O. W. Holmes, Sr., whom he greatly admired. The first Sherlock Holmes story appeared in 1887 and several more volumes were written and published well before the real-life Holmes died in 1894. Is there any evidence to show whether the elder Holmes knew that the detective was named for him; or ever read the tales at all?

HOWARD HAYCRAFT
May 1941

To the best of my knowledge there is no direct evidence that Conan Doyle surnamed his immortal detective after the American poet and physician. My own categorical statement to that effect, first made in an article entitled "Enter Mr. Sherlok Holmes" (*Atlantic Monthly*, July 1932), and later included in *The Private Life of Sherlock Holmes* (New York, 1933), is a bold assumption – or deduction – based on a line in Sir Arthur's volume of bookly reminiscence, *Through the Magic Door* (London, 1907), in which, speaking of Oliver Wendell Holmes, he writes: "Never have I so known and loved a man whom I had never seen." The inference seemed clear to me at the time, and I still believe it to be justified. As far as I know, this claim of mine was the first suggestion anywhere that Doyle had named his detective after the American he most revered. All other similar assertions that I have seen have been subsequent to it, and have been, I believe, directly or indirectly, based on the statement in my book. If any earlier evidence exists, I shall be delighted to hear of it.

In the circumstances, it is at least conceivable that Oliver Wendell Holmes never dreamed that he had lent his name to the world's foremost private detective. Whether or not he ever read the stories I am unable to say. Doyle visited America in the late Autumn of 1894, the year of Holmes's death, but failed to meet his favourite American. I have no evidence to suggest that the two men ever corresponded. If they did, the evidence must be found in the writings of Holmes the poet or Holmes the jurist; it is not in any published statement by Conan Doyle that I have seen.

While I am confessing, perhaps I should add that the story concerning Sherlock's given name – i.e., that Doyle once made thirty runs against a bowler named Sherlock and thereafter had a kindly feeling for the name – also appeared for the first time (in accessible form) in my *Private Life*. I found the statement years ago in an English newspaper interview with Doyle; but I could not now say where or when the item appeared. It is possible, I suppose, that the story is apocryphal; my memory, however, is entirely trustworthy as to its newspaper appearance. But it *is* a little odd, I think, that in his autobiography, *Memories and Adventures*, Conan Doyle has no clear word to say about the origin of either name.

VINCENT STARRETT
June 1941

THE SATURDAY REVIEW OF LITERATURE

Dr. Watson's Mother-in-Law

To the Editor

SIR, – Recently re-reading *The Adventures of Sherlock Holmes* the following contradictory statements in two stories caught my attention. Perhaps some of your readers – and Sherlock Holmes's – can explain the discrepancies.

In *The Sign of the Four* Mary Morstan, the woman Dr. Watson married, makes the following statement: "The facts are these. My father was an officer in an Indian regiment who sent me home when I was quite a child. My mother was dead and I had no relatives in England."

Says Dr. Watson in "The Five Orange Pips": "My wife was on a visit to her mother's and for a few days I was a dweller once more in our old quarters at Baker Street."

MARY STEWART

Los Angeles.

29 November 1941

Dr. Watson and Mr. Doyle

To the Editor

SIR, – Mary Stewart must not blame Dr. Watson for the contradictory statements about Mrs. Watson's mother in the American texts of *The Sign of the Four* and 'The Five Orange Pips". The fault lies at the door of one Mr. Doyle, who had something to do, for better or worse, with the editing of the good doctor's writings.

"The Five Orange Pips", as originally published in the *Strand Magazine*, did actually contain a reference to the orphaned Mrs. Watson's being on a visit to her "mother's". Dr. Watson, of course, called Mr. Doyle's attention to this slip of editing, and the passage was corrected, when *The Adventures* were published in book form in England, to read "on a visit to her *aunt's*". The John Murray (English) omnibus volume also follows this text. But Mr. Doyle forgot to inform the American publishers of the change, and both the collected *Adventures* and the Doubleday omnibus perpetuate the error down to this day – as they do many others of a like nature.

EDGAR W. SMITH
13 December 1941

THE LONDON QUARTERLY AND HOLBORN REVIEW

A Salute to Sherlock Holmes

Since the days of Sherlock Holmes the technique of criminology has advanced by leaps and bounds. On the whole, modern crime novels are better constructed, but Sherlock's supremacy remains undimmed. Though we have bigger and better murders to-day, Conan Doyle has the imperishable glory of the pioneer. Later detectives stand on Holmes's shoulders. No story has been written since that has excited and astonished readers as *The Sign of Four* and *The Hound of the Baskervilles* excited them. In sheer magic of personality Holmes and his faithful henchmen have no rivals. Conan Doyle had the wit to focus the spotlight upon the personality of the detective. In later stories the emphasis tends to fall upon the process or mechanism of detection. However brilliant Sherlock Holmes's solutions, the man is even more fascinating than his methods. The long series of tales are bound together by the personality of Holmes. In this way Conan Doyle adroitly achieved serial continuity, and at the same time forged a link between the *Strand* and its readers.

Dr. Moulton, the pious and learned founder of the Leys School, used to boast that he could pass an examination on "Holmesology". This sort of mock-serious study used to be common. In my own family, Holmes was an institution. We got up the texts as if they had been for Higher Certificate. We set papers and staged viva-voce exams, challenging one another to finish quotations, give contexts or identify characters: what reasons are there for believing Holmes to be a Cambridge man? What colour were his eyes? What year was he born? Who was "chevvied about at school and hit over the shins with a wicket"? Was Watson's bullet-wound in the shoulder or leg? What grounds are there for suspecting that Watson was a bigamist?

Desmond MacCarthy tells us that when he learned from the pages of that fatal *Strand* that Sherlock Holmes was no more, he rushed before chapel to the rooms of a college friend, and announced, "Sherlock Holmes is dead; he has fallen down a chasm with Dr. Moriarty." "Never," he goes on, "shall I forget the look of dismay on the face of my friend."

Years were to elapse before we knew that Holmes was still alive. He

183

wasn't dead, and never had been. For a time Conan Doyle did not know the glorious truth. For three long years even Watson did not know it. And when, leaving his researches into the coal-tar derivatives at the laboratory in Montpellier, Holmes returned to London to solve the mystery of the death of the Hon. Ronald Adair, faithful readers of the *Strand* rejoiced and thought of Psalm cxxvi.

Holmes's fame is literally world-wide. His name is synonymous with detection. We do not say of a man with an itch for investigation, "You're a regular Thorndyke, a regular French, a regular Poirot"; but, "You're a regular Sherlock Holmes."

Among the boarders in a Madrid lodging-house was an officer of the city C.I.D. Whenever he came in to meals he was greeted with shouts of, "Here comes Sherlock Holmes." In Egypt the Holmes stories were translated into Arabic and issued to the local police as a text-book.

Like other schoolboys of my day, I burned incense to Sherlock Holmes. On my first visit to London (1898) I persuaded my people to stay in Baker Street. Our rooms were actually quite close to 221b. Alas! nothing extraordinary happened. Holmes and Watson must have been away from home. I had hoped to spot Holmes issuing forth in one of his disguises, Mrs. Hudson gingerly opening the front door to a squad of the Baker Street irregulars, clients in various degrees of agitation stumbling up the steps. Nothing happened. No revolver shots, no plain-clothes men lurking in doorways!

Not many years ago, I passed Sherlock Holmes's old rooms. To my disgust there was no memorial plaque or tablet on the wall. Yet plaques are everywhere. In Rodney Street, Liverpool, a plaque adorns the birthplace of Mr. Gladstone. In Bloomsbury certain sons of Belial have put up a plaque on Karl Marx's house. Yet 221b Baker Street remains unplaqued.

Even foreigners can teach us better. A company of Fremch schoolboys came to London on a sightseeing tour. Asked by the conductor what they wanted to see first, they shouted joyously. "The lodgings of Sherlock Holmes in Baker Street." Holmes and Watson made it the most famous street in London. Who wants to bother with Roman walls, feudal towers, sham-Gothic Houses of Parliament, or a cathedral with a roof like an umbrella, when they might tread in Sherlock Holmes's steps in Baker Street? Lady Porstock's scheme for erecting a statue of Sherlock Holmes came to nothing. A railway-engine, wearing the immortal name, and running in and out of Baker Street station, is our only memorial of a man compared with whom the statesmen, soldiers, judges, and divines of his time are shadowy pygmies.

Wonder has been expressed that the executors of Holmes and Watson did not make a museum of 221b Baker Street. Thomas Hardy's sitting-room and study, preserved exactly as the novelist left them, can be seen in Dorchester. Few people are interested in Hardy, whereas Sherlock Holmes and Dr. Watson are household words with the million. Can we not picture rapt multitudes gazing upon Holmes's revolvers, his pipes, slippers, dressing-gown, deer-stalker caps, his caped ulster, his chemical apparatus, the easy chair and sofa on which he would curl up to spend the night in thought, the loaded hunting-crop (his favourite weapon) – and of course the unbelievable Strad. Glass cases would contain his trophies and souvenirs – the poisoned darts of Tonga, the emerald tie-pin (a gift of Queen Victoria), the famous air-gun made by von Herder the blind German mechanic, the snuff box of old gold with a great amethyst in the lid (a token from the King of Bohemia), the diamond ring (a graceful offering from the Royal House of Holland – a case of such extreme delicacy that Holmes concealed it even from Watson); autograph letters from His Holiness the Pope, the President of the French Republic, and other potentates; his cross of the Legion of Honour; the watch-chain with the pendant sovereign given him by Irene Adler; the photograph of Irene, who once outwitted Holmes and was always, to the great misogynist, *the* woman.

In one case would be Watson's books and his two pictures; in the other those read and owned by Sherlock Holmes; in a third an impressive row of works written by the detective himself. Portraits of distinguished criminals would adorn the walls, Dr. Moriarty in the place of honour. By the side of the fireplace would hang the Persian slipper (the tobacco-receptacle); sticking in the mantel-shelf would be the jack-knife transfixing the correspondence. The coal-scuttle would be furnished with its complement of cigars. The patriotic V.R.s and other monograms on the wall would be illuminated by electric light. In the centre of the room, sitting in a chair, is the wonderful wax model of Holmes, the masterpiece of M. Oscar Meunier of Grenoble, that served as decoy to Colonel Moran. On their old shelf there would repose the row of formidable scrapbooks and books of references, which so many of Holmes's fellow-citizens would have been glad to burn.

Such a museum, opened in war-time under the auspices of the Red Cross Society, would produce millions.

Sherlock Holmes's enthusiasm for a good understanding between Great Britain and the U.S.A. would have gained Mr. Churchill's warm approval. "It is always a pleasure to meet an American, Mr. Moulton, for I am one of those who believe that the folly of a monarch and the blundering of a minister in far gone years, will not prevent our children from being some day citizens of the same world-wide country, under a flag which shall be a quartering of the Union Jack with the Stars and Stripes."

Could there be a more timely note on which to end this salute to that strange genius whom Dr. Watson called "the best and the wisest man I have ever known"?

F. BROMPTON HARVEY
April 1944

THE LONDON MYSTERY MAGAZINE

221b Baker Street, N.W.1.

DEAR READER,
You will have noticed that we are writing to you from the address of Sherlock Holmes, Esq. We hope that we shall prove to be tenants worthy of our great predecessor and make this magazine the best in its class of mystery-crime-detection. The accent is heavily on mystery – the mysterious in life, literature, history, science, and art. Like King Lear, we would

> . . . take upon us the mystery of things,
> As if we were God's spies!

We shall present the best authors and the best artists in the best way we can, and we hope that the result will find a permanent place on your bookshelves.

This is our aim – to publish a storehouse of fact and fiction providing entertainment and food for thought for the connoisseur in this popular field.

We are a London-based enterprise, but hope to reach kindred spirits throughout the world.

EDITOR
June 1949

THE STAR

Sherlock Holmes and 221b Baker Street

Sherlock Holmes and No. 221b Baker Street, his address in Sir Arthur Conan Doyle's stories, figured in a Chancery Division action to-day.

Mr. Denis Percy Stewart Conan Doyle, executor of the late Sir Arthur Conan Doyle, sought an interim injunction against the London Mystery

Magazine, Limited, of Lincoln's Inn Fields. He wanted the injunction to restrain them from using the name Sherlock Holmes and the address 221b Baker Street, without making it clear that their business and magazine had no connection with Sir Arthur Conan Doyle and his works.

Mr Justice Wynn-Parry refused to grant the injunction. He said that there was no such address as 221b Baker Street. That number was contained in a block owned by a building society and the firm had arranged with them to use that address. If there had been such a character in real life as Sherlock Holmes, and if he had carried on his "interesting profession" at 221b Baker Street, Mr. Doyle would have had some right to protection.

18 October 1949

THE SUNDAY TIMES

The Baker Street Irregulars, of New York

On a foggy and drizzling evening in January 1950, at a club in New York City, fifty men drank a standing toast. It was in regret and homage to their own boyhoods; it was occasioned by the soon approaching demise of the *Strand Magazine*. Some thirty of the convives were members of the Baker Street Irregulars, a club whose membership is limited to sixty – the number of the Sherlock Holmes stories. The others were delegates from "scionist" societies, viz. satellite chapters from other faubourgs or cities, of which there are about thirty.

Surely it is a unique tribute to an author whose name, officially, is never mentioned. The traditional *mystique* is that Holmes and Watson are so much more real than their creator that except by privilege from the Chair (known as the Gasogene) the Agent is never mentioned by name.

Whatever decision the British electorate may reach at the forthcoming polls, nothing can ever change the world-wide magic and renown of Holmes and Watson. They are fixed in parallax; dioscuri of modern fiction; stylised as the lion and the unicorn. I know even less about economics than Lord Beveridge, but I suspect that Holmes and Watson are the largest and most luscious of Britain's Invisible Exports.

And (since you insist) the Baker Street Irregulars, of New York, now enjoying their sixteenth year of lively homage, actually began with four schoolboys in Baltimore about the year 1902. They called themselves then, and still do, The Sign of the Four. One is the senior professor of Greek at Harvard; one is a physicist of the Naval Research Laboratory

187

in Washington, and knows more than anyone needs to about undersea explosions; one is a renowned physician in Baltimore; and the last is your reporter.

The fundamental doctrine of the B.S.I., when they set aside for an evening the irrelevant trivialities of their own lives, is that the Holmes-Watson saga (officially denominated by Mr. Elmer Davis "The sacred writings") is more actual, and more timely, than anything that happens to ourselves or happened to its mortal mouthpiece. The greatest art is the annihilation of art.

With profound insight the B.S.I. have adopted as their colours the three shades of Holmes's dressing-gown. It faded, as all mortal energies do: from royal purple to blemished blue; from heliotroped blue to mouse. Mouse, by the way, was the colour of the settees in Simpson's famous Chess Divan, as reported in R.L.S.'s *New Arabian Nights*, from which A.C.D. unconsciously borrowed so much.

So the B.S.I. published for three years a quarterly journal (whose motto was "When was so much written by so many for so few?"), but if you can get from your bookseller (Argus Bookshop, Mohegan Lake, N.Y.) those three volumes you will have the best winter evening reading of a lifetime. Myself, I would rather have them than a first Bristol Cream of Wordsworth and Coleridge's *Lyrical Ballads*.

Wordsworth and S.T.C. were also greatly anxious about affairs in 1798. But now we need to know, as Holmes asked Watson, "What do you know of the black Formosa corruption?" How I would have loved to ask Madame Generalissima Chiang that question, just before she took off by plane lately – she is, obviously, the Irene Adler of South-East Asia.

Or when Holmes spent the great hiatus (1891–94) in Tibet, wasn't he making arrangements sixty years ahead for what's getting ready now? Or the reptilian Moriarty, oscillating his cobra brow over the dynamics of an asteroid, was doubtless precursing uranium and hydrogen bombs, all fission spent. What could the great untold storty of the Politician, the Lighthouse, and the Trained Cormorant have suggested but the career of Sir Stafford Cripps?

These are the hints the B.S.I. follow through. Why did passengers on the G.W.R. *have* to take lunch at Swindon? Exactly how (and with what type scalpel) do you nick the tendons of a horse? What was the precise layout of the rooms in Baker Street? Was Sherlock illiterate, I mean could he read? Why did Watson always have to read aloud to him all letters and telegrams? Why did Holmes never eat fish, but always game, beef, and boiled eggs? Why did he never drink tea? Why was he such a poor marksman? These are the *paraleipses* or *paralipomena* to which we devote the most innocent diversion of our lives.

Myself, I do not wholly agree with the tradition that A.C.D. should never be formally mentioned. I loved him long before his heirs and assigns and agents were born, and I find in his writings the most delicious asymptotes to the Holmes-Watson codex. As I have often said, how ridiculous he was only Knighted – he should have been Sainted.

My Christmas carol of last year was this:

> What opiate can best abate
> Anxiety and toil?
> Not aspirins, nor treble gins,
> Nor love, nor mineral oil –
> My only drug is a good long slug
> Of Tincture of Conan Doyle.

CHRISTOPHER MORLEY
29 January 1950

The Refreshment Rooms at Swindon

To the Editor

SIR, – Christopher Morley propounds as one of the questions that puzzled the Baker Street Irregulars: "Why did passengers on the G.W.R. *have* to take lunch at Swindon?"

Looking by chance through C. Hamilton Ellis's *The Trains We Loved* I came across what perhaps supplies the answer. Writing in reference to competitive timings on the old G.W.R and L.&S.W.R., he says: "At Swindon, however, the Great Western was then (*circa* 1876) bound by contract to hold all trains for ten minutes to afford passengers an opportunity for patronising the extremely bad refreshment rooms . . .'

L. C. GATES

Lincoln. *5 February 1950*

The Baker Street Saga

To the Editor

SIR, – Mr. Christopher Morley's charming article cannot fail to stir those like myself whose spiritual home has always been 221b Baker Street. I found especially engaging the suggestion that some of the "untold" Holmes–Watson stories glance at the shape of things to come, and in particular that the story of the "Trained Cormorant" foreshadowed the career of Sir Stafford Cripps. Having lifted a

189

corner of this curtain I hope Mr. Morley will go on and tell us what politician of what party is prefigured in some of the other "untold" stories: e.g. the "Adventure of the Tired Captain", and the "Repulsive Affair of the Red Leech"?

Mr. Morley asks: "Was Holmes illiterate? I mean, could he read?" and points out how often Holmes delegates the reading of notes and letters to Watson. Personally I think this was a pure affectation. He needed no help from Watson in deciphering the letter written in alternate words by the Cunninghams in the "Reigate Squires". As to books, although Watson describes his friend's knowledge of literature in disparaging terms, Holmes had read (and Watson had not) Winwood Reade's *Martyrdom of Man*.

Mr. Morley rightly stresses Holmes's addiction to game (he is fantastically voracious of woodcock) and eggs. But "boiled" eggs? In those spacious days Mrs. Hudson generally combined her eggs with ham, and this almost necessarily implies an absence of shell.

And was Holmes a "poor marksman"? He emptied five barrels of his revolver "into" the flanks of the Hound of the Baskervilles and therefore presumably hit them. Mr. Morley may say that having regard to the size of the hound it would have been as difficult to miss him as a haystack at point-blank range. But the same cannot be said of the "patriotic V. R." traced with the punctures of revolver bullets, with which Holmes decorated the walls of his Baker Street rooms.

The oldest puzzle of all (raised as far back as 1911 by Monsignor Knox, "the father of English Watsonology") was why an Afghan bullet which hit Watson in the shoulder caused him, for the rest of his life, to limp. Can the "Baker Street Irregulars" supply the answer? And have they any views as to whether Watson was a dipsomaniac, married twice, married three times?

The evidence for the first two of these propositions is impressive; but I entertain some doubts about the third.

CYRIL ASQUITH

Royal Courts of Justice.   *5 February 1950*

Dr. Watson's Limp

To the Editor

SIR, – Even without records from the Ministry of Health, it does not require the researches of the Baker Street Irregulars to clear up the little matter of Dr. Watson's limp.

Dr. Watson took part in the battle of Maiwand in the Afghan

campaign in 1880, and was struck in the shoulder by a Jezail bullet which shattered the bone and grazed the subclavian artery. So much is plainly stated in the *Study in Scarlet*. But, even here, there is some hint of further injury, since his orderly, Murray, had to use a packhorse to get him to safety. This further injury was in fact to the leg, and though it did not prevent Watson from walking, it ached wearily at every change of the weather (*Sign of Four*), and made him limp impatiently about the room at what he thought was Holmes's charlatanism.

E. O. D. Stanford

12 February 1950

Twickenham

Sherlock Holmes Commemorative Stamps

To the Editor

SIR, – I have been too bashful to say how happy the Baker Street Irregulars (of New York) have been in your readers' response to an innocent letter of nostalgia. Even though the letters, whether from Lord Justice Asquith or Mr. Desmond MacCarthy*, or others of equal spirit, showed that your Sherlockian students are still balking at some fences that our esoterics cleared long ago.

My only claim at this moment, on your scant Scandinavian pulp, is that one of our scionist groups (The Musgrave Ritualists, of Uptown, N.Y.) appealed to the British G.P.O. to suggest a possible centennial issue of postage stamps for the year 1954, to mark the one hundredth birthday of Sherlock Holmes. The year 1854 has been oecumenically assigned (by what Chaucer called the "eyrisshe beastes", viz. signs of the zodiac) as Holmes's birth year (6 January).

But H.M. Postmaster-General writes that he "regrets the infeasibility of issuing commemorative Sherlock Holmes stamps in 1954, on the ground that only events of national, international, or Post Office importance are marked in this way".

Is this really final? If so, we can still inculcate the U.S. Post Office, which is always wild for new stamps; but we feel the great Holmes-and-Watson stamp should come from your side.

CHRISTOPHER MORLEY

New York

*"Watsoniana", 12 February 1950. Desmond MacCarthy commented on the spate of letters about Sherlock Holmes and explained his theory about the date of Watson's marriage, which he had put forward in 1928.

VIII. THE SHERLOCK HOLMES EXHIBITION (1950–1951)

———— ❖ ————

THE TIMES

A Sherlock Holmes Exhibition

Councillors of St. Marylebone have rejected a suggestion by the Borough Library Committee for a Sherlock Holmes exhibition in the public library as a contribution to the Festival of Britain. Councillor Tom Vernon (Lab.) said: "It would be more constructive to show the world the great progress this borough has made in clearing away the noxious slums of one hundred years ago." Alderman F. W. Dean (Con.), leader of the Council, said for once he agreed with the other side; St. Marylebone had "many things to show off about without Sherlock Holmes". The public libraries are to prepare another scheme.

27 October 1950

The Proposed Sherlock Holmes Exhibition

To the Editor

Sɪʀ, – It is doubtful whether Mr. Sherlock Holmes will have seen the paragraph in Tʜᴇ Tɪᴍᴇs to-day [27 October] recording the singular decision of the councillors of St. Marylebone to oppose the proposal for an exhibition of *materiae* of my old friend and mentor for the benefit of visitors to the Festival of Britain. Engrossed as he is in bee-keeping in Sussex, he is unlikely to rally to his own defence, and you will perhaps allow me, as a humble chronicler of some of his cases and

192

as a former resident in the borough, to express indignation at this decision.

There is much housing in the Metropolis but there is but one Mr. Sherlock Holmes, and I venture to assert that visitors from across the Atlantic (who cannot as yet have forgotten my old friend's remarkable work in clearing up the dark mystery of the Valley of Fear and the grotesque affair of the Study in Scarlet) would find such an exhibition of interest. Why the councillors of St. Marylebone, in their anxiety to display their work on the clearing of slums, should deny honour to my old friend I find it hard to understand. Perhaps this is time's revenge for the exposure by Mr. Sherlock Holmes of the evil machinations of the Norwood Builder. Whatever the reason, I trust that second and better thoughts may prevail, and in the meantime subscribe myself.

Your humble but indignant servant,
John H. Watson, M. D.,
late of the Indian Army
28 October 1950

A Letter from Mr. Arthur Wontner

To the Editor

Sir, – I rejoice to see that my old friend Dr. Watson has deplored in your columns the decision of the councillors of St. Marylebone to deny honour in the Festival year to Mr. Sherlock Holmes. I feel it my duty to say, Sir, that as Mr. Holmes was unwilling to impersonate himself on the screen (being a *métier* with which he was unfamiliar), I had the honour of doing so on five separate occasions, and I can testify without fear of contradiction to the enthusiasm with which Mr. Holmes is received when an account is given of his many most interesting experiences. I think it is especially noticeable that, in the United States of America, from the Atlantic to the Pacific, his name is well known, his distinction is unchallenged, and indeed many societies exist to do him honour. If we are to welcome next year citizens of that great country, may I, as a friend of Mr. Holmes, support Dr. Watson in what he says in your columns and respectfully urge the councillors of St. Marylebone to reconsider their decision?

I am, Sir, yours faithfully,
Arthur Wontner

Garrick Club, W. C. 2.

31 October 1950

A *Sherlock Holmes Centenary Exhibition*

To the Editor

Sir, – I am delighted to see that Dr. Watson has been roused from a long silence to express in your columns his indignation at the decision of the councillors of St. Marylebone to turn down the proposal to hold a Sherlock Holmes exhibition in 221b Baker Street, in 1952. I would like to remind Councillor Vernon, who spoke so slightingly of Sherlock Holmes, that that year will be his centenary. The intrinsic evidence afforded in "The Musgrave Ritual" and elsewhere goes to show that he was born in 1852, and he will be, to some of us at any rate, the most interesting centenarian of all time. Titian might, it is true, have competed, but he had the misfortune to die of the plague at the age of ninety nine and there is some doubt about the authenticity of Methuselah.

For all one knows to the contrary, Sherlock Holmes is still tending his bees in Sussex; and what more graceful compliment could be paid to him than to ask him to come up and perform the opening ceremony? I venture to suggest a life-size statue of "Silver Blaze" as the *pièce de résistance* and I am prepared to wager that such a show would prove to be an attraction second to none in London.

I have the honour to be, Sir, your obedient servant,

Ivor Back

8 Connaught Place, W.2.

31 October 1950

Dr. Watson's Army Career

To the Editor

Sir, – While my own memory remains as good as ever, that of my brother's biographer appears to be failing. He was never in the Indian Army, but in the British Army Medical Department, attached to the Northumberland Fusiliers and temporarily seconded to the Berkshires.

Yours, &c.,

Mycroft Holmes

The Diogenes Club, Pall Mall, S.W.1.

31 October 1950

Dr. Watson's Christian Name

To the Editor

SIR, – When I called on Dr. Watson for his help in the search for my husband (you will remember the unparalleled horror of the dénouement in the Case of the Man with the Twisted Lip) I distinctly heard his wife address him as "James". It is, therefore, with no little perturbation and distress that I read in to-day's issue [28 October] of *The Times* a letter purporting to have been written by the good doctor and signed by the obviously fictitious name of "John".

Yours very sincerely,
KATE WHITNEY
31 October 1950

Sherlock Holmes and Madame Tussaud's

To the Editor

SIR, – As I am still a ratepayer in the borough of St. Marylebone, may I suggest that the obvious place for an exhibition devoted to the achievements of my former lodger, Mr. Sherlock Holmes, is Madame Tussaud's, whose premises are situated only a few yards from my house and are also, of course, in the borough of St. Marylebone. They could take this opportunity of rectifying a long-standing omission by placing models of Mr. Holmes and Dr. Watson upstairs, and of many of the criminals whom Mr. Holmes arrested downstairs. For many years I have been a regular visitor to Madame Tussaud's, but I have never yet noticed Professor Moriarty, Dr. Grimesby Roylott, "Mr. Stapleton", or any of the others in that famous basement. American visitors would naturally be pleased to see Abe Slaney too.

Naturally, gruesome relics will be required. Dr. Watson has several which Mr. Holmes gave him (including Mr. Culverton Smith's black and white ivory box), and I expect Mr. Holmes still has that large tin box full of papers and souvenirs. Perhaps the present Duke of Holdernesse could be prevailed upon to lend his set of cow-like horses' shoes, and I will lend the wax bust of Mr. Holmes which Monsieur Oscar Meunier made and Colonel Moran spoilt with his air-gun bullet. Please forgive an uneducated person writing to so important a newspaper as *The Times*.

Yours truly,
MRS. HUDSON
221b Baker Street, W.1.   *1 November 1950*

The Sherlock Holmes Exhibition

A sense of relief will be spread in surprisingly wide circles by the news that Tuesday night's meeting of the Library Committee of St. Marylebone confirmed its proposal to hold a Sherlock Holmes exhibition during the Festival of Britain next year.

1 November 1950

Mr. Sherlock Holmes

To the Editor

Sir, – To-day I visited Mr. Sherlock Holmes and conveyed to him the welcome news that St. Marylebone will hold an exhibition in his honour during the Festival of Britain. I could see he was deeply moved by this tribute, as also by the correspondence in which your readers have so warmly supported my plea. Several of those letters raise the subject of commemorative material to be placed on exhibition. Alas, but little remains, for a mysterious and disastrous fire at my old friend's Sussex home some years ago (the details of which are not yet ready to be given to the world) destroyed the greater part of the relics of his cases. St. Marylebone, I fear, will have to manage without his help.

May I trespass a little further on your indulgence to reply to two of your correspondents? Mycroft Holmes is, of course, technically correct in stating that I was not in the Indian Army, though I did in fact so describe myself on the battered tin dispatch-box which until recently lay in the vaults of Cox's Bank in Pall Mall. But it was the custom in 1878, when I was wounded at Maiwand, for those in whatever regiment in Indian they served to describe themselves as "of the Indian Army", a point of which Mycroft in his omniscience will be well aware. As for Mrs. Whitney, I am surprised that, in spite of her close friendship, she is apparently unaware that my dear first wife used "James" as a pet name for him who remains,

Yours faithfully,
JOHN H. WATSON, M.D.
2 November 1950

Sherlock Holmes and Scotland Yard

To the Editor

Sir, – Long years of retirement have failed to break the professional habit of careful examination of the personal columns of THE TIMES newspaper and a necessarily hastier perusal of its other contents. Thus I have learned with no little surprise of the proposal to stage an exhibition perpetuating the performances of my old acquaintance, Mr. Sherlock Holmes. Surely in this correspondence to-day's [1 November] letter from Mrs. Hudson, his worthy landlady, places the abilities of Mr. Holmes in their right perspective. A place of amusement, such as Madame Tussaud's, is surely the proper setting for a record of Holmes's amateur achievements. It would be ungenerous of me to deny that on occasion the gifted guesswork of Mr. Holmes has jumped a stage in the final solution of a crime. It may not be inappropriate to remind your readers, however, of the fable of the tortoise and the hare, and the true student of criminology will continue to regard as the only true source the so-called "Black Museum" of that institution on the Victoria Embankment which for so many years I had the honour to serve.

I am, Sir, your obedient servant,

G. LESTRADE,

ex-Inspector, Metropolitan Police

Laburnum Road, Tooting, S.W.

2 November 1950

The Wax Portrait Bust of Sherlock Holmes

To the Editor

SIR, – I read Mrs. Hudson's letter with great interest, and I think I am in a position to give you information which has an important bearing upon her suggestion. Your readers may not know that at the time I made the wax bust of Mr. Holmes I was in the employ of Madame Tussaud & Sons, Limited. Holmes gave me many sittings so that I could obtain a perfect likeness and, like so many people with whom he came into contact, I was entranced by his powers as a conversationalist. As we are all aware, his knowledge of the occult, and particularly the practice of the black arts, was phenomenal. Quite naturally, we discussed at considerable length the use of wax figures in image magic, and it did not come as a surprise to me to learn that he was disinclined to dismiss their effectiveness in certain circumstances. On the contrary, he held very strong beliefs on the subject, and when I had completed the wax bust to his entire satisfaction he asked me to ensure that at no time should a wax portrait of himself be placed on display. Although Holmes has now retired and is devoting his life to the study of bees, I am quite certain that he would still oppose any suggestion that he, Dr. Watson, or indeed

197

any of the men he brought to justice should be perpetuated by waxen images which he held in such distrust.

I have the honour to remain, Sir, yours faithfully,

Oscar Meunier,

late of Grenoble

Curthwaite Gardens, Enfield.

4 November 1950

THE NEW STATESMAN

Competition No. 1, 081. Set by Arachne MacLeod

Proposals to hold a Sherlock Holmes Exhibition as part of Marylebone's celebrations for the Festival of Britain have produced a great many letters to *The Times* from characters in the Holmes stories. But there has been no word direct from Holmes himself. The usual prizes are offered for the opening 250 words of a new Holmes story entitled: "The Case of the Missing Detective".

11 November 1950

A refresher course of the master's work was, after all, of little help in judging: the entries that kept most faithfully to the style of the original had no room to deploy the plot, and were less lively than those which tried to distil the essence of a Holmes situation, by speeding up the tempo. In passing, many curious titbits were offered about the recent history of the protagonists. Watson has gone through several wives, Holmes may be rearing Colorado beetles in Rutland, Moriarty makes a brief appearance disguised as Holmes, and J. G. H. advances the awful theory that Moriarty *is* Holmes.

Arachne MacLeod

[Five entries were published, of which one is given here.]

The Case of the Missing Detective

For the greater part of his most remarkable adventure, my friend's whereabouts were a mystery even to himself. The public knew that an atom scientist had disappeared. I knew that Holmes also had gone off, taking no luggage and leaving no address. It was many months before he returned. I must now try to give a coherent account of the events which gave rise to those curious and apparently unrelated phenomena which confused the world during his long absence; the brief appearance of a cloaked figure on top of the Dome of Discovery;

the empty pipe found at Harwell; the so-called whale in the Solent; the queer affair of the Washington Postman; the loss of New York's only hansom, and its recovery from the depths of Lake Success; the violin obbligato in the Premier's broadcast; the stranger in Mac-Arthur's uniform; the riots in dockland, the sailor in the Vatican, and the hourly cabinet meetings of Black Weekend; the banning of the *Manchester Guardian* by the Government and vice versa; the moujik in the deer-stalker cap, the blinding flash in the Urals, and the climax – the Kremlin offer which by averting the Third World War automatically began the Fourth.

FERGIE

2 December 1950

THE YORKSHIRE POST

A Sherlock Holmes Tableau for Madame Tussaud's

Mr. Ivor Brown, writing on Tussaud's exhibition in his new book on London, suggests emphatically that Sherlock Holmes and Dr. Watson, those most distinguished residents of Marylebone, should be given a place in the literary section. Considering the proximity of Tussaud's to the detective's Baker Street rooms, one can hardly believe that the suggestion will be overlooked.

19 February 1951

WINTER IN LONDON

I suggest that one of the duller historical tableaux be replaced by a set-piece of the local genius, honouring the detective maestro of Baker Street. Sherlock Holmes and Dr. John Watson could be shown, in their habit as they lived, at No. 221b. Mrs. Hudson would be seen removing dishes in the background, while Billy the page-boy introduces a trembling member of the distressful clientele, seeking the favour of Holmesian intervention. She would be a late Victorian lady of title, distinguished but distraught, white, shaky, and oppressed by one of those menaces, snake, hound, or human, which Holmes could so lucidly explain and so effectively expose and destroy. Holmes would have a pistol in one hand – for he has just been practising his marksmanship on the wall – a drug-taker's syringe in the other, a violin handy, a pipe in mouth, and his dressing-gown for robe. Watson would be deeply perusing the *British Medical Journal*.

IVOR BROWN
Collins, 1951

THE SUNDAY TIMES

Sherlock Holmes and the Litmus-Paper Test

To the Editor

SIR, – St. Marylebone Borough Council is arranging a Sherlock Holmes Exhibition as a contribution to the Festival of Britain. The exhibition will include a section dealing with some of the scientific aspects of Holmes's work, and we are anxious to illustrate, if possible, what appears to have been one of his more important investigations. Unfortunately, Watson was not himself particularly interested in chemistry, and we have failed to reconstruct the experiment from the meagre data provided. The relevant passage (from "The Naval Treaty", dated by Bell as 1888) is as follows:

> A large curved retort was boiling furiously in the bluish flame of a bunsen burner, and the distilled drops were condensing into a two-litre measure. . . . He dipped into this bottle or that, drawing out a few drops of each with his glass pipette, and finally brought a test-tube containing a solution over to the table. In his right hand he had a slip of litmus-paper.
> "You come at a crisis, Watson," said he. "If this paper remains blue, all is well. If it turns red, it means a man's life." He dipped it into the test-tube, and it flushed at once into a dull, dirty crimson. . . . He turned to his desk and scribbled off several telegrams. . . . "A very commonplace little murder," said he.

We should be grateful if any reader could suggest what precisely this experiment can have been; any solution should be chemically sound, and of such a nature that it would enable Holmes to deduce that a murder had been committed.

GEOFFREY B. STEPHENS,
Borough Librarian

St. Marylebone, N.W.1.

1 April 1951

The Litmus-Paper Test Explained

A Scotland Yard expert and a London University Professor today gave me a possible explanation of a chemical experiment made by Sherlock Holmes which has been puzzling the organisers of Marylebone Borough Council's Holmes Exhibition.

Prof. Harrie Massey, of University College, said the experiment was an elementary chemical one. Holmes was examining some substance to find whether it was acid or alkali. He distilled a sample from the retort, then he treated it in various ways by applying reagents and finally made the acid or alkali test with litmus-paper.

The Yard expert suggested Holmes might have been investigating a case of murder by poison. He could have been analysing the blood or stomach contents of the victim to show whether they corresponded with the contents of an incriminating bottle.

3 April 1951

THE SUNDAY TIMES

A Case of Methyl Cyanide Poisoning

To the Editor

SIR, – I well remember Sherlock telling me that in 1888 he had had the only case then on record of poisoning by methyl cyanide. This substance was not a scheduled poison in the Pharmacy Act of 1868, nor is it today. Nevertheless, it was effective in this case, which was an ordinary affair of a workman in a chemical factory who abstracted the poison to do away with a wife he could no longer tolerate. The man put a large dose of acetonitrile in a cup of tea and somehow induced her to drink it quickly. A director of the manufacturing firm, who had been up at Cambridge with my brother, asked for his help when the husband was suspected. The police allowed Sherlock to examine the viscera.

My brother soon identified the poison. His final confirmatory test is as well described by Watson as could be expected. Sherlock used a retort for the hydrolysis of the nitrite and for the distillation of the product, as there was no water supply in the sitting-room and no sink. He used dilute sulphuric acid for the hydrolysis, but the two-litre measure was *faute de mieux*. Since he was using a retort, there was some possibility of the sulphuric acid splashing over, and he accordingly tested a separate portion of the distillate for sulphate; but his technique of dipping a pipette into the hydrochloric acid and barium chloride reagent bottles was not ideal. When he knew that the distillate was free from sulphuric acid he relied on litmus to show the presence of acetic acid. The small amount of acid he obtained turned the litmus to a dull, dirty crimson. This provided the confirmation of his chain of deductions and he was able to proceed with the apprehension of the criminal.

MYCROFT HOLMES

Diogenes Club, S.W.1.

8 April 1950

The Chemical Capabilities of Sherlock Holmes

To the Editor

SIR, – My attention has been directed to Mycroft's unnecessarily detailed account of a case Holmes never considered worthy of describing to me. I cannot accept the implied criticism of Holmes's methods.

It is absurd to suppose that the author of the Holmes haemoglobin reaction, and one whose name will always be associated with research into the coal-tar derivatives and analysis of acetones, would be faulty in his elementary technique. As Mycroft must well know, what has happened here is that the printer or (just possibly) my own notes carelessly omitted the "s" of pipettes.

Holmes would certainly not risk contaminating his reagents in this way when so often – as in this case – "it means a man's life".

J. H. WATSON

Queen Anne Street, W.1.

15 April 1951

The Adventure of the Red Litmus-Paper

To the Editor

SIR, – With reference to the "The Adventure of the Red Litmus-Paper" (Mr. Sherlock Holmes's experiment in the Naval Treaty Case).

Forty years ago we discussed this notorious experiment during the lunch interval in Professor's Dixon's laboratory at Cambridge. (Dixon, from internal evidence, was "the most distinguished pharmacologist" to whom A. E. W. Mason makes acknowledgement in the preface to the collected Hanaud stories.)

We were driven to the conclusion either that the Master had discovered some oriental drug unknown to science that could be detected by acidity of the distillate (a proposition abhorrent to any good addict of detection) or that he was pulling Watson's leg.

The suggestion that Dr. Watson invented the incident is made unlikely by a corroborative detail. Holmes sent off several telegrams. We know that the month was July, and those telegrams no doubt referred to his bets on the coming Goodwood meeting. Holmes probably kept these activities quiet from Watson – especially after the "Silver Blaze" affair, for which he was lucky not to have been warned off the Turf for life!

F. W. Watkyn-Thomas

United University Club.

15 April 1951

(A number of readers have written asking, apparently seriously, whether "Mycroft Holmes" could be still alive, or whether we had ourselves been too credulous in printing last week's letter signed by him. – Editor, The Sunday Times.)

From the Vice-Chancellor of the University of Cambridge

To the Editor

Sir, – I am not competent to argue with Mr. Mycroft Holmes about hydrolysis, but I am sorry to note that his memory has played him false about his brother's University.

Many specious arguments have been advanced to suggest that Sherlock Holmes was a Cambridge man. In an Introduction to a volume of Sherlock Holmes stories which will, I hope, be published in the Summer, I have endeavoured to show on what slender foundations these arguments are built.

S. C. Roberts

Pembroke College

22 April 1951

ST. MARYLEBONE COLLECTION

Merridew, of Abominable Memory

To the Editor of the *Sunday Times*

Sir, – There are several points which lead one to doubt whether the case which Mycroft Holmes remembers his brother Sherlock telling him to have occurred in 1888 was indeed the one mentioned in the "Naval

203

Treaty". Mr. Baring-Gould dates the "Naval Treaty" as 1889. There is reason to believe that the case (which Mr. Watkyn-Thomas describes as "The Adventure of the Red Litmus-Paper") refers to "Merridew of abominable memory" (see "The Adventure of the Empty House").

The startling facts are that this was *not* a case of poisoning; it was *not* solved by *litmus*-paper, and was *not* indeed "a very commonplace little murder". Holmes had good reasons for withholding the details from Watson at the time – though doubtless even now a full account lies in the old tin box in Cox's vault.

Since it was a case of unique medico-legal interest, Sherlock Holmes was good enough to send me details in a private communication. Briefly, Merridew, who was a doctor, murdered his brother by imprisoning him in a room and starving him to death. The doctor pretended to be treating his brother for a chronic wasting disease and signed the death certificate accordingly. The post-mortem examination revealed neither disease nor evidence of poisoning. Holmes suspected the diabolical method of enforced starvation, and proceeded by a number of stages to prove it. The end point of his confirmatory evidence depended on the detection of acetone in certain body fluids. The analysis of the acetones was, of course, one of his special subjects. He succeeded in distilling out a sufficient quantity of acetone to enable him to test for it by his own methods. Now, if the facts are examined, it was only Watson who assumed that the paper used was litmus-paper. Holmes only called it "this paper". It was, in fact, a test-paper which Holmes himself had prepared by soaking a strip of white filter paper in sodium nitro-prusside solution. After adding a little sodium hydroxide solution to the distillate in the test-tube, the paper was dipped in and turned a "dull, dirty crimson". This indicated to Holmes the presence of acetone, one of the by-products of metabolism during starvation.

JOHN EVELYN THORNDYKE, M.D., F.R.C.P.
St. Margaret's Hospital, S.E.4

THE TIMES

Sherlock Holmes Exhibits

If any owner of a Stradivarius cares to lend it to the Sherlock Holmes Exhibition to be held during the Festival of Britain, his possession will be made unique by its return to him with a letter certifying that it has had the honour of contributing verisimilitude to the re-created lodgings of Mr. Holmes in Baker Street.

204

The Borough Librarian has prepared a list of objects still needed for the furnishing of 221b Baker Street. Applicants for a copy receive a dossier drawn up with something of the systematic thought that Holmes himself was wont to devote to a complex problem. If after studying the list an applicant feels that he has something suitable to offer, and if he "is genuinely satisfied in his own mind that it is of the period 1887–1905 and is sufficiently in keeping with the whole atmosphere of the room at 221b Baker Street as created in the Sherlock Holmes stories", there are a numbered label for attachment to the article and a form of receipt, which will be signed by the Borough Librarian and returned to the applicant.

Each article is named in a relevant extract from the story in which it figures. The organisers still need a purple dressing-gown, Holmes's long grey travelling-cloak, three pipes – briar, cherrywood, and a black clay – and a Persian slipper in the toe of which Holmes used to stuff his tobacco. A more exacting request is for a gold snuff-box with a great amethyst in the lid – that "little souvenir from the King of Bohemia in return for my assistance in the case of the Irene Adler Papers".

13 April 1951

ST. MARYLEBONE COLLECTION

A Dark-Lantern

To the Borough Librarian

DEAR SIR, – I should be very pleased to receive a copy of your list of objects still needed for the furnishing of 221b Baker Street. In the mean time I am sending you separately my dark-lantern which, according to a report in *The Times* for 13 April, is wanted by you.

According to family tradition this lantern was left by Sherlock Holmes with my great-grandfather H. A. M. Roelants, Esq., printer of Schiedam. My great-grandfather was so like our King William III that the public actually mistook him for the King during a royal visit to Schiedam in 1870. This case of identity was the beginning of a personal friendship between the King and Mr. Roelants (*vide: H. A. M. Roelants* by Frans Netscher, privately printed by Roelants, Schiedam, 1902).

As you will remember, Watson quotes Holmes in "A Case of Identity" as saying: "It [a brilliant] was from the reigning family of Holland, though the matter in which I served them was of such delicacy . . . etc." So it is not surprising that Holmes should have stayed (in 1887 or '88) at a personal friend's of the King. Anyhow, family tradition attributes my dark-lantern to Holmes.

I shall be very pleased to have your opinion.

I am, Sir, your obedient servant,
K. K. VAN HOFFEN

Groenekan, Utrecht, Holland

14 April 1951

DEAR MR VAN HOFFEN, – I am delighted to hear that you are sending for display at the Exhibition, the dark-lantern which in 1888 was left by Holmes with your great-grandfather, Mr H.A.M. Roelants. We had quite failed to trace the whereabouts of this lantern and it is a great relief to me to know that, through your kindness, it is now on its way to England.

I shall notify you on its arrival and in the meantime I am sending the list of articles we are still requiring. The list is by no means complete and it is purely representative of the type of material we are needing for the Exhibition.

Your interest in the Exhibition and your very helpful co-operation are greatly appreciated.

BOROUGH LIBRARIAN

The Grey Travelling-Cloak

To the Borough Librarian

DEAR SIR, – I am alarmed to see in *The Times* of 13 April 1951 that Holmes's long grey travelling-cloak has not yet turned up, and this is merely to remind the Public Librarian that I still am fortunate enough to retain Holmes's Inverness cloak, and would be honoured to place it at his disposal; so that it might even possibly find its way back (temporarily) to 221b Baker Street. I am perfectly certain that Holmes used this cloak on many of his journeys, in fact my father says he bought it in 1900.

Yours truly,
DOUGLAS M. ANDERSON

Hyam, Minchinhampton, Gloucester.

21 April 1951

DEAR MR ANDERSON, Thank you very much for your letter of 21st April confirming your kind offer to lend a long grey travelling-cloak for the purposes of the Exhibition.

I would, of course, be very pleased to take advantage of your offer and

I should be glad if you would be kind enough, when sending the cloak, to let me known its insurance value.

BOROUGH LIBRARIAN

"The Adventures of Picklock Holes"

To the Executors of the late Mr. Sherlock Holmes

DEAR SIR, – I hear that you are having an exhibition in honour of my dear friend.

In that scurrilous paper *Punch*, for 12 August 1893, appeared a thinly disguised lampoon against the world-renowned detective. No steps were taken by us at the time. We considered it better to let this outrageous libel lie in this almost unknown and little-read rag, than to give it the publicity of a libel action. One result of this forbearance was that the lampoon was repeated in subsequent numbers. After this, however, a strain of decency appears to have invaded the editorial offices and these libels ceased. After this lapse of time, I think little harm can be done by drawing attention to these calumnies.

If you wish to exhibit these and have any difficulty in obtaining copies of this paper (most of which were, I believe, burnt by the common hangman), I would be glad to let you have my bound copy on loan for the exhibition.

Recent publicity which I find wearisome at my advanced age forces me to conceal my present whereabouts, but the above address will always find me.

I remain, dear Sir, your humble servant,
J. WATSON, M.D.

Hill House, Cromer, Norfolk.

24 April 1951

DEAR SIR, – We have received a letter from Dr Watson drawing our attention to "The Adventures of Picklock Holes" which appeared in *Punch*, August 1893. This series had not come to our notice before and it was with considerable interest (and distaste) that we read the articles.

It is hoped that there will be room to display at the Exhibition this early and crude travesty of the methods of Sherlock Holmes. We shall not, however, have to trouble Dr. Watson to send his copies of the magazine as a full set of *Punch* is in our possession.

We should be glad if you would be good enough to convey to Dr. Watson our thanks for his information.

BOROUGH LIBRARIAN

Miss Violet Smith's Bicycle

To the Marquis of Donegall

DEAR LORD DONEGALL, – Referring to your letter of 20 April, in which you inform me of your present researches into the whereabouts of the cycle belonging to Miss Violet Smith of "The Solitary Cyclist", Sherlock Holmes's case, I am pleased to be able to tell you that on looking back through our files for 1895 and 1896 we have been able to trace a Humber bicycle which we delivered to Miss Smith's father at Charlington Hall.

As you recall in your letter, Miss Smith married and having no further use for the vehicle sold it back to us.

Many years later, when it became apparent that our earliest products would be of historical interest, it was placed among other examples of this firm's craftmanship.

It was not, however, until your letter called attention to the fact, that Raleigh Industries, Limited, realised the very special value of this bicycle, in view of its association with the immortal detective, Mr. Sherlock Holmes.

Yours faithfully,
GEORGE H. B. WILSON,
Managing Director

Raleigh Industries, Limited, Nottingham.

THE NEWS CHRONICLE

The Lesser Known Cases of Mr. Sherlock Holmes

To the Editor

SIR, – The organisers of the Sherlock Holmes Exhibition in Marylebone are, I hear, looking for the cast of the footprint of the Hound of the Baskervilles.

May I hope that they will also procure the trained cormorant, so curiously associated with a politician and a lighthouse, the repulsive red leech which (presumably) was responsible for the death of Crosby the Banker, the giant rat of Sumatra, and the strange worm – said to be unknown to science – which was found in a matchbox after it had presumably driven Isadora Persano, the well-known journalist and duellist, stark staring mad.

GAVIN BREND

Haverstock Hill, N. W. 3 *7 May 1951*

THE DAILY TELEGRAPH

The Official Opening of the Sherlock Holmes Exhibition

Mr. Sherlock Holmes was not present yesterday at the formal opening of the Festival of Britain exhibition in his honour arranged by the Borough of St. Marylebone. Engrossed as he is in bee-keeping in Sussex (according to the most reliable information on which to base any hypothesis), he was unable to see the magnificent collection of Holmsiana gathered from all parts of the world. It has been placed on show at a cost of £3,500 to the ratepayers of St. Marylebone.

Mrs. Hudson, still understood to reside in the borough, was unable at the last moment to put in an appearance. Doubtless she was unable to obtain a hansom to convey her to No. 221b Baker Street. An elementary explanation for the absence of Dr. Watson is that either he is sulking after one of his periodic tiffs with the master; or finds little time to spare after meeting all the demands this new-fangled health service makes on a long-established general practitioner of repute.

Taking part in the opening ceremony were the Mayor of St. Marylebone, Councillor Charles H. Press, members of the Public Libraries Committee, and the son and daughter of the late Sir Arthur Conan Doyle. Mr. Denis Conan Doyle and Group Officer Jean Conan Doyle, W.R.A.F. Miss Conan Doyle said the exhibition should go down as "The Strange Case of Marylebone Borough Council" because it was so unusual for a council to have such an imaginative idea.

22 May 1951

EXHIBITION LEAFLET

Sherlock Holmes and the Festival of Britain

The Festival of Britain so nearly coincides with the centenary of the birth of Sherlock Holmes that it is fitting at this time to pay tribute to the memory of this great and well-loved Englishman. One of the most incisive intellects of his age, he gained an international reputation which can rarely have been equalled in any sphere; yet such was his distaste for personal publicity that few men of his eminence can have left so few records. All that is known of his life and work we owe to his friend and biographer, Dr. John H. Watson, whose loyalty and devotion seem only to have been exceeded by his haziness in matters of detail. Dr. Watson, however, was a busy general practitioner with many calls upon his time, and humanity owes him a considerable debt of gratitude for such information as he nevertheless found time to place on record. Our greatest debt is, of course, to his colleague and contemporary Dr. (later Sir) Arthur Conan Doyle, who so brilliantly edited Watson's notes and presented them to a wider audience.

The St. Marylebone Borough Council, sensible of the honour bestowed upon the district by the fact that Holmes chose to live and work in Baker Street, is holding this Exhibition to show visitors, many of whom cherish his memory dearly, that Holmes is not forgotten in his former haunts. Despite the limited amount of information available, it has been possible to reconstruct the room in which Holmes lived and practised, to display a selection of the extensive literature which he has inspired, and to illustrate some of the scientific problems which arise in the records of his cases. By these and by many other exhibits it is hoped to commemorate this great man who became a legend even in his own lifetime.

ST. MARYLEBONE COLLECTION

To the Secretary of the Sherlock Holmes Society,
Abbey House, Baker Street, W.1

DEAR SIR, – What a splendid idea the Holmes Exhibition is. You and the Marylebone Borough Council – and too I presume the Abbey Building Society – are to be heartily congratulated.

Like many others of course, I knew Holmes personally and admired him from his first arrival in London until his retirement to the Sussex Downs a few years ago.

Indeed to many of us Holmes has never retired. We have only to stretch out our hand to the bookcase, and his tall figure reappears together with the hansoms and gaslight of Baker Street, with Watson standing at the very window where perhaps you, Sir, are standing now.

Truly – as Watson said – a remarkable man.

I hope you get crowds there and that the enthusiasm justifies all the trouble.

Yours faithfully,
T. POTTLE

Clovelly Road, Bideford, Devon.

23 May 1951

Baker Street Revisited

By Sherlock Holmes in an Interview with Henry Longhurst

I should be obliged if, through the medium of your admirable journal, I might express my appreciation of the St. Marylebone Borough Council's assistance to me in laying open to the public, in common with owners of other premises of historic interest, the chambers so long occupied by Dr. John H. Watson and myself in Baker Street.

The rooms, together with my papers, had as usual, through the supervision of my brother Mycroft and the immediate care of Mrs. Hudson, been preserved unchanged during my retirement. Only an unwonted tidiness betrayed my own long absence. How long this absence had indeed lasted was brought home to me on hearing a newspaper photographer inquire which of the items were "real" – that is, had in fact belonged to me!

The familiar interior, together with the yellow fog swirling outside our windows – almost obscuring the plaque to the actress, Sarah Siddons, on the wall opposite, which Watson failed to notice in thirty years – the street cries, the clip-clop of the horses' hooves, and the itinerant musician still repeating the same discordant song almost as though on a gramophone record, all sent my mind racing back to what has been called "a world where it is always 1895".

Those were, we are now assured, the bad old days. That they were more violent days I was reminded as my eye fell again on the harpoon in the corner (I wonder whether Allardyce's would have a whole pig for me to practise upon nowadays?), the knuckle-dusters and handcuffs, Colonel Moran's bullet-mark beside the door, to say nothing of the V.R. I so lightheartedly shot in the wall, and all the miscellaneous firearms, including not only Von Herder's celebrated air-gun, but also the superb gold-damascened Adams muzzle-loading revolver presented by the Duke of Montrose, for my services in a matter which His Grace may yet permit Watson to lay one day before the public.

I have been particularly happy to receive messages of goodwill from the Baker Street Irregulars in the United States and, as their patron, I return greetings both to them and to such scion societies as the Musgrave Ritualists of New York, the Dancing Men of Providence, the Speckled Band of Boston, and the Hounds of the Baskerville in Chicago.

It is always a joy to me to meet an American, as I told Mr. Francis

Hay Moulton, and I continue to believe, sir, that the folly of a monarch and the blundering of a Minister in fargone years will not prevent our children from being some day citizens of the same world-wide country.

As certain members of the public have during the past week addressed problems to me at Baker Street, may I add that advancing years – I will not say advanced, for I am only seven years senior to Dean Inge, who preached such an excellent sermon at Oxford only two Sundays ago – advancing years keep me in retirement in Sussex where, as President of the British Bee-keepers' Association, I apply to apiarian problems the same great powers which I so long turned to the detection of crime.

Though I did, it is true, emerge from seclusion during the recent hostilities to assist the department now known as MI5, this was only on occasions when Mycroft had convinced me that continued failure on their part would imperil the entire outcome of the war. In peacetime my retirement remains complete.

I do not, of course, rate as an exception the not unexpected visit of an agitated successor of Lestrade's in connection with the, to him, mysterious episode in Westminster Abbey – partly because I was able in any case to set him upon the track without leaving my villa and partly because, as I more than once told Lestrade himself, I care only to be associated with those cases which present some little difficulty in their solution.

27 May 1951

NEWNES PRACTICAL MECHANICS

Sherlock Holmes — Scientific Detective:
An Account of the Recent Re-Opening of No. 221b Baker Street

By the Marquis of Donegall and Dr. John H. Watson, M.D.

Dr. Watson has been nettled – I think, not without cause – by various statements which have appeared in the Press, owing to the limelight suddenly thrown on the old premises, which he and Mr. Sherlock Holmes occupied at 221b Baker Street, London.

The St. Marylebone Borough Council has rightly seen fit to open it to the public, after so long a period of time, in the interests of the Festival of Britain, at Abbey House, very near Baker Street Station.

The re-opening of the rooms which Holmes and Watson decided to abandon *in statu quo* does not, however, excuse accusations against Watson that he knew nothing of flora and fauna, had obviously never looked at a map of Dartmoor before reporting *The Hound of the Basker-villes*, and did not even know that a goose had no grit-bag when engaged on the case of "The Blue Carbuncle". Watson never said that it had. It was the crop that was in question.

In any case, as Watson pointed out on our way to the old chambers that he and Holmes occupied for so long, he found his brain too slow on occasion to catch up with the deductive reactions of Holmes.

As we come into the room there are, on the left, scientific charts on the wall. It was in the case of "The Masserine Stone" that Watson refers to certain scientific charts on the wall. "They were," Watson tells me, "geological charts from some of which Holmes derived his knowledge of clays and other geological matters, from which he made his famous deductions about mud on the boots of his clients."

Continuing, we have a portrait painted by Vernet, great-uncle of Sherlock Holmes; his grandmother was Vernet's sister. Holmes was seldom voluble about his relatives. But Watson recalled that he said of his brother: "One has to be discreet when one talks of high matters of state. You are right in thinking that Mycroft is under the British Government. You would also be right in a sense if you said that, occasionally, he is the British Government."

Next comes the "V.R." in Holmes's bullets reported in the case of "The Musgrave Ritual". On the sideboard, of course, there is the gasogene, which is a very early form of soda-water syphon, mentioned in the case of "The Masserine Stone". There is also the spirit case, referred to in "A Scandal in Bohemia", and Holmes's service revolver. The service revolver comes into the earlier part of *A Study in Scarlet*, just before the arrest is made. The famous deer-stalking cap, which was never so-called, and the long grey travelling-coat that Holmes wore in "The Boscombe Valley Mystery" hang near the door. Watson tells me that it was *his* cap, anyway, and that Holmes was always borrowing it.

Then we come to Dr. Watson's top hat, which has a dent in it because he kept his stethoscope in it. Dr. Watson, having come back into practice, bought a "modern" stethoscope which is exhibited with the hat. On the other hand, on the breakfast table is his old wooden stethoscope which made the dent, characteristic of medical practitioners of the period, in his top hat.

Coming round the room, we find next the portrait of General Gordon, killed at Khartoum, as mentioned in the case of "The Cardboard Box".

Directly under the picture of General Gordon we saw the bullet-hole made by Col. Sebastian Moran's murderous air-gun in the case of "The Empty House". Not very far from the hole made by Moran's bullet we have the harpoon with which Holmes practised in the case of "Black

Peter"; the settee littered with the original newspapers, and a bookcase on top of which lie the boxing-gloves that come in repeatedly as illustrating, according to Dr. Watson, Holmes's proficiency in boxing. The bookcase has the small medical shelf that Watson mentioned in *The Hound of the Baskervilles*; on the next shelf *Crockford's Clerical Directory*, 1897, and the *Medical Register* for 1896; on the bottom shelf the famous scrapbook and the great index books referred to in "The Sussex Vampire".

Still going on towards the right Dr. Watson and I came to the mantelpiece, and there we found, on the top shelf, the small ivory box with its deadly mechanism from the case of "The Dying Detective". On the right-hand side, at the top, the hypodermic syringe and the bottle of cocaine. Right in the centre of the mantelpiece, the jack-knife still transfixes the unanswered correspondence.

The Persian slipper containing the shag tobacco hangs vertically by the side of the fireplace. Holmes's night binoculars, used in *The Hound of the Baskervilles*, are also on the mantelpiece with his pipe.

It was well known that in Baker Street they had gas and oil lamps as there are many references to them, and it was to be presumed that they had gas-brackets over the mantelpiece, as, indeed, we found them.

Moving again round the corner we get Holmes's table of "stinks". Over the "stinks" table is the cane rack of "The Red-Headed League", where it is recorded that Holmes takes down his heavy hunting crop. There is Holmes's violin – a Stradivarius – and the code of "The Dancing Men", pinned up on the wall. "Holmes was bending for a long time over a low-powered microscope."

On Holmes's desk the cabinet photograph of Irene Adler left for him in "A Scandal in Bohemia". On this occasion that Watson and I visited the old rooms, we found the lamp-with-the-shutter on Holmes's desk, with the revolving office chair in red leather in front of it. The velvet-covered chair at the right of the bust is mentioned in *The Sign of Four*.

Inspecting the breakfast table we discovered the burglars' kit in the butter-dish. (Butter-dishes were larger in those days!) It consists of a bunch of skeleton keys and some mysterious tools. The cigars were, as left, in the coal-scuttle and the famous pair of handcuffs used in various cases was on the writing table.

Now the air-gun for dealing death to Holmes at the hands of Colonel Sebastian Moran. "Holmes picked up the powerful air-gun from the floor and was examining its mechanism. 'An admirable, and unique weapon,' said he. 'Noiseless and of tremendous power.' " This came in the case of "The Empty House". The air-rifle of Colonel Sebastian

Moran was of a complicated type and prone to go out of order. The butt-section is an air-reservoir which can be pumped up by means of a small-diameter air-pump to a pressure of 50 lb. A large spring-controlled poppet-valve with a protecting steel shank contains the air in the reservoir. The outer barrel is smooth-bored and takes a small charge of shot pellets for use against small game. A breechloading device for the use of the spherical ball in the larger barrel is incorporated. The weapon has to be cocked against a very powerful mainspring by a detachable cocking-lever and is discharged by pressing on a small stud on the left-hand side with the thumb. Small fixed sights are fitted. The weapon considered as a rifle is as efficient as a revolver of equivalent calibre and is much quieter. As a shot-gun its performance is poor beyond twenty yards' range.

But as a rifle, a range of over 150 yards is well within its capacity. Ten to twelve shots can be fired without loss of efficiency or repumping; but as pressure declines, some variability in penetration occurs.

At the end of our visit Dr. Watson, whose wound from the second Afghan War still continues to trouble him at times, handed me some remarkable photographs of the "Solitary Cyclist" and of Mrs. Hudson moving the dummy of Sherlock Holmes.

"Nobody knows," said Dr. Watson, "who took the picture of Miss Violet Smith. He or she must have been concealed behind the yew hedge which I described. It came anonymously into my possession quite recently and has obviously been copied with modern apparatus.

"The photograph of Mrs. Hudson was taken by Billy, our page-boy, who kept quiet about it because he had been ordered to go home. He is now managing director of a large firm of photographic suppliers and desires to remain nameless!" That Billy was in advance of his time as a photographer is obvious; hence his present position.

THE DAILY TELEGRAPH

Dr. Watson's Stethoscope

To the Editor

SIR, – It seems ungracious to make any criticism of the magnificent reconstruction of Sherlock Holmes's room in Baker Street, as reproduced in the photograph in the DAILY TELEGRAPH.

I had always understood, however, that Dr. Watson used an earlier type of stethoscope, which consisted of a short rigid tube with the usual nozzle at one end and a flat disc as an earpiece. Doctors were in the habit of carrying them in their hats, and as these caused a slight bulge it was always an elementary matter to pick out doctors from other wearers of silk hats.

Yours, &c.,
W. J. Cairns

London, W.8.

24 May 1951

Dr. Watson and Modern Medicine

To the Editor

Sir, – I cannot agree with Mr. W. J. Cairns that the stethoscope exhibited in the Sherlock Holmes Exhibition is of the wrong type and too modern for Dr. Watson to have used it.

This pattern of binaural stethoscope was firmly established in use by 1902–3. It could be and was carried in a doctor's top hat as well as the old wooden pattern, and could produce the same bulge.

No doubt Dr. Watson was brought up on and used the old wooden pattern when he was first in practice, but he was a painstaking and careful doctor (in spite of Holmes's strictures) who kept himself abreast of modern medicine. His statement that even when his Jezail bullet was throbbing in his wounded limb he sat studying the latest treatise on surgery proves this.

We can feel assured that early in this century he adopted the modern stethoscope.

Yours faithfully,
W. H. C. Romanis

Harley Street, W.1.

26 May 1951

The Medical Capabilities of Dr. Watson

To the Editor

Sir, – While I would hesitate to join issue with Mr. W. H. C. Romanis, who gives a view of Dr. Watson from the vantage-point of Harley Street, I feel that the medical profession as a whole would fight shy of accepting as a "painstaking and careful doctor" one who was so conspicuously bamboozled by Holmes, as in the case of "The Dying Detective".

It will be recalled that, for reasons of his own, the Great Man was malingering when Dr. Watson, on the urgent plea of Mrs. Hudson, was summoned to attend him. Not only was Watson taken in by vaseline, belladonna and beeswax, at a range of twelve feet, but he was unable to say that he had even heard of the black Formosa corruption or Tapanuli fever.

As an Army doctor, Watson must have been very popular with such soldiers in his unit as were anxious to "dodge the column".

Yours, &c.,

W. R. MICHELL, Cmdr. (S) R.N.

Haslemere.

29 May 1951

Dr. Watson's Knowledge of Medicine

To the Editor

SIR, – It is impossible to accept Mr. Romanis's assertion that Watson kept himself abreast of modern medicine. We have Watson's own somewhat shameful confession that by the late 'nineties he was so much out of touch with his profession that the name of Dr. Leslie Armstrong was unknown to him.

Inability to distinguish clearly between a wound in the shoulder and one in the leg in his own person may force one to disagree with Mr. Romanis's contention that Watson was a painstaking and careful doctor.

Yours, &c.,

T. A. A. BROADBENT

Blackheath

29 May 1951

THE CONTINENTAL DAILY MAIL

Ngaio Marsh and the Baker Street Plaque

Ngaio Marsh, brilliant New Zealand detective novelist, whose new book, *Opening Night*, marks the twenty-first birthday of Great Britain's Crime Club, whose detective "Handsome" Alleyn has definitely inherited the caped cloak of Sherlock Holmes, is pleased about the exhibition and reconstruction of his famous sitting-room at 221b Baker Street.

Miss Marsh (whose name in Maori means "Sun upon the Water" or "Little Bug", whichever way you like it) once had a wrangle with me about the exact spot in Baker Street that actually held Sherlock Holmes, Dr. Watson, Mrs. Hudson (the landlady), the violin, the Persian slipper with tobacco, and all. Ngaio claims there is a plate in Baker Street to commemorate Sherlock Holmes. She said that I, who lived in Baker Street, was very, very ignorant not to have seen it.

NANCY SPAIN
30 May 1951

THE SOUTHERN DAILY ECHO

The Portrait of Irene Adler

For Sherlock Holmes she was *the* woman. Watson, himself something of a ladies' man, had to admit that his friend's attitude to the fair sex was rather inhuman. The detective took good care that the gentler emotions should not interfere with his powers of ratiocination. But he made an exception in Irene Adler's case.

Yet it seems that the photograph of this quick-witted beauty, which Holmes chose as his reward in preference to the King of Bohemia's proffered tie-pin, is absent from the reconstructed room in Baker Street which now houses the Sherlock Holmes Exhibition. We cannot say positively that it is not there, but we have looked in vain for any reference to it in the many detailed reports which have appeared lately in the Press.

The Case of the Missing Photograph is indeed a strange one. Is it possible that Irene Adler took a leaf out of her Baker Street opponent's note-book and recovered the picture by turning amateur burglar? More probably Holmes, growing sentimental in his extreme old age, refused to part with it, even for a few months. Our own theory is that it remains in its silver frame in the study of his Sussex farmhouse.

(LEADER)
4 June 1951

ST. MARYLEBONE COLLECTION

A Letter to Miss Irene Adler

DEAR MADAM, – The Public Libraries Committee of the Borough of St. Marylebone thank Miss Irene Adler for her communication regarding the photograph which Mr. Sherlock Holmes claimed as a reward from the King of Bohemia and beg to inform her that this photograph is displayed in a prominent position on the desk in Holmes's sitting-room.

In view of this fact and as space is rather limited, the Committee must regretfully decline the loan of a second photograph while expressing their appreciation of so kind an offer.

BOROUGH LIBRARIAN

Public Library, St. Marylebone, N. W. 1.

THE SOUTHERN DAILY ECHO

A Letter from Mr. Sherlock Holmes

To the Editor

SIR, – Since my withdrawal to my little Sussex home, where I have given myself up entirely to the soothing life of Nature for which I had so often yearned during the long years spent amid the gloom of London, my privacy has been invaded several times. I resisted the importunities of MI5, but when Mr. Churchill himself appealed to me I felt bound to look into the Case of the Missing D-Day Plans, which proved to be very elementary.

Shunning publicity as I do, I have been caused considerable annoyance by the absurd articles which have filled the public prints lately concerning an exhibition now being held at my old lodgings in Baker Street.

I have, of course, no intention of wasting time on such tomfoolery, but in the interests of truth, I'm obliged to point out, my dear sir, that the photograph of Irene Norton, *née* Adler, given to me by Wilhelm Gottsreich Sigismond von Ormstein, King of Bohemia, remains in its silver frame on my desk at Baker Street where I left it nearly fifty years ago.

The writer of your leaderette of 4 June must be as unobservant as my old friend, the worthy but muddle-headed Watson.

SHERLOCK HOLMES

Fulworth, Sussex.

13 June 1951

Sherlock Holmes and Irene Adler

To the Editor

SIR, – The fact that Holmes agreed to lend the photograph may be taken as some indication of his high regard for *the* woman. The omission of any reference to the photograph in Press reports was, I believe, due to a desire on the part of all concerned to respect Holmes's feelings.

However, I feel sure my friend would wish me to correct any erroneous impression that he had refused, as your leader suggests, to allow Miss Adler to share in the honour bestowed upon him by the exhibitors.

STANLEY MACKENZIE

Bassett Road, W.10.   *19 June 1951*

THE RADIO TIMES

A Broadcast from Baker Street

28 June 1951

A visit to the rooms of the famous private consulting detective at 221b Baker Street, with scenes from his life and cases dramatised from Dr. Watson's notes edited by Sir Arthur Conan Doyle.

The guide at 221b Baker Street is Wynford Vaughan Thomas.
Sherlock Holmes played by Laidman Browne.
Dr. Watson played by Ivan Samson.

(HOME SERVICE)
22 June 1951

THE DAILY TELEGRAPH

Baker Street Visitors

In Baker Street the Sherlock Holmes Exhibition is having a great success. Since it opened on 21 May, 18,630 have paid a shilling to probe into the private life of the great detective.

In the atmosphere of his chambers the reality of his existence is overpowering. Two comments that have been heard are: "What will he say when he comes back?" and: "How very interesting! My son was at school with him."

PETERBOROUGH
13 July 1951

THE DAILY MAIL

The Smoking Habits of Mr. Sherlock Holmes

I notice that Mr. Bruce Angrave's sketch for the catalogue of the

Sherlock Holmes Exhibition shows Holmes, in deer-stalker hat and apparently hot on the scent, puffing at a large calabash pipe.

This, I submit, is wrong. There is no evidence that Holmes smoked his pipe away from 221b Baker Street. Pipe-smoking to him was a ritualistic aid to concentration, not to the chase, on which a cigar sufficed. Witness his reply to Watson's query in "The Adventure of the Red-Headed League" as to the next move. Said Holmes: "To smoke. This is quite a three-pipe problem."

TANFIELD
1 August 1951

A Sherlock Holmes Thesis

It is impossible to keep Sherlock Holmes out of this column. The ultimate tribute to his immortality has just been paid. A student of Arizona University, taking his degree in literature, has put in "Sherlock Holmes" as his thesis. Mr. C. T. Thorne, curator of the Baker Street Holmes Exhibition, tells me that the young man's father has written to him seeking his aid in collecting material.

TANFIELD
6 August 1951

EMPIRE NEWS

Sherlock Holmes at 61 Baker Street

To fans of Sherlock Holmes there is one great unsolved mystery – just where in Baker Street did the great detective lodge? For months past they have employed every trick of amateur detection from psychology to a painstaking analysis of Holmes's walks with Dr. Watson to arrive at an answer.

My friend Sebastian Lamb, a writer on legal subjects, tells me there can be no doubt that Holmes lived at 61. How is he so sure? Because Sir Arthur Conan Doyle told him so himself. "We were walking down Baker Street together," he says, "and Sir Arthur pointed to No. 61 saying, 'That is where Holmes lived.' "

PETER NELSON
12 August 1951

THE SPECTATOR

Sherlock Holmes's University

The question of Sherlock Holmes's University, on which no clear light has yet been shed, is manifestly a matter of the first importance, and when the Vice-Chancellor of Cambridge – who I see is the President of a new Sherlock Holmes Society of London – sets himself (as he does in an Introduction to a World's Classics edition of selected Sherlock Holmes stories, published this week) to disprove the suggestion that Holmes was at Cambridge, then one of two conclusions must be reached – either that Cambridge would wish to disclaim Holmes, which is incredible, or that the Vice-Chancellor is (as all who know him would expect) being scrupulously honest. He points out that no Cambridge man would talk, as Holmes does in one story, of running down to Cambridge. I am not so sure; an old Cambridge man, talking to a non-Cambridge man, might quite well fall into railway parlance, in which everything is down from, or up to, London. The Vice-Chancellor seems to accept Miss Dorothy Sayers's contention (though not her conclusions based on it) that since Holmes lived out of college his first year, and that was a distinctive Cambridge custom in those days, Holmes must have been at Cambridge. But was it a distinctively Cambridge custom? I should say it was a college, not a University, custom. Plenty of Cambridge colleges had many first-year men living in, and many second- and third-year men living out. Evidence that Holmes was at Cambridge may be inconclusive, but the evidence that he was not is at least as much so. A Fellowship thesis on the whole subject is plainly needed.

JANUS
Spectator

THE EVENING STANDARD

Sherlock Holmes and his University

To the Editor

SIR, – The reasons why Sherlock Holmes could not have been a Cambridge man – put forward by Mr. S. C. Roberts, Vice-Chancellor of the University – do not seem to me altogether convincing.

It is perhaps presumptious to join issue with so redoubtable an authority on the Holmes tradition, but I distinctly remember the college "court" at Clare College, when I was an undergraduate there in 1910, being referred to affectionately as the "quad".

As to the tying up of dogs in the college porches, I am more cognisant of the methods in relation to the Proctor's bulldog variety. But I am not aware that there was any rule against Victor Trevor keeping a dog in the porter's lodge, if that obliging member of the staff had been diplomatically approached.

In any case, Dr. Conan Doyle was an Edinburgh man and may possibly have based his conceptions of Oxford and Cambridge customs on his more familiar Alma Mater.

WILF. H. GRONOW

Crane's Park, Surbiton.

16 August 1951

Cambridge Manners

To the Editor

SIR, – Another reason why Sherlock Holmes could not have been a Cambridge man – his attitude towards Watson was most offensive. He was condescending. A superior manner is unknown on the banks of the Cam.

H. W. WESTBROOK

Flood Street, Chelsea.

20 August 1951

THE NEW YORKER

Sherlock Holmes in Russia

To the Editors

GENTLEMEN, – I was much interested to see in Mollie Panter-Downes's article on Sherlock Holmes, which you printed not long ago, a reference to a Soviet edition of "The Six Napoleons", published in Moscow in 1945. It should not be thought, however, that Russian admiration for the Master dates only from these relatively recent and unregenerate days. As a small boy in the Imperial Russia of 1904, I had the thrill of reading my first Sherlock Holmes adventure – that of the "Piostraya Lenta", which I encountered later in France as "La Bande Mouchetée", and still later in America as "The Speckled Band".

It is possible that true Holmesians will be interested to hear of the strange case of the Russian transliteration of the name of Holmes. Since

223

there is no letter "H" in the Russian alphabet, it is a rule, when one is using Russian characters, that foreign names beginning with "H" are written with a "G". Thus, Hamlet is written (and pronounced) Gamlet, the *Iliad* is the work of Gomer, and Prussia was ruled by the Gogenzollerns. Not so for Holmes, however. Some unknown, or at least completely forgotten, genius – the first translator of the Sherlock Holmes stories, no doubt – decided that nothing would do for the Master's name but the letter "X", which in Russian has the "ch" value of the Scotch "loch" or of the German "*Nacht*". This unique spelling, as far as I know, has been adhered to ever since. And so while the common herd of Hamiltons, Hodges, and Hoovers remain forever Gamiltons, Godges, and Goovers in Russian pages, Holmes has the distinction of being the only Xolmes.

Yours very truly,
A. W. ALEXANDER

San Francisco.

18 August 1951

ST. MARYLEBONE COLLECTION

The Sherlock Holmes Exhibition Catalogue

To Mr. Sherlock Holmes, or Agent

DEAR MR. HOLMES, – Since I visited your exhibition and lodgings in June (it appeared that I had missed you only by a moment) I have read and heard much of a catalogue to the exhibition. On that occasion I saw no trace of a catalogue (perhaps I have not your remarkable powers of observation) and assumed, somewhat sadly, that none had been issued. If one does in fact exist and is available I should be most grateful if you, or your good friend the doctor, or your agent, would send me a copy – I shall of course forward to you the requisite fee and your expenses at once. And if in addition you could give me some clue as to where I may obtain some information about the newly formed Sherlock Holmes Society of London, it would be a great service to me.

Pray forgive me for my inconvenient intrusion, and believe that I remain, your most obedient servant,

R. PETER MOORE
(No relation of the Colonel you met at Reichenbach)
Highcliffe Road, Sheffield.

20 August 1951

DEAR SIR, – At the time of your recent visit to 221b, Mr. Holmes had apparently been called away suddenly on an urgent case. I regret he has not yet returned and I can not disclose his present whereabouts.

In his absence, however, I am sending, as you requested, a copy of the catalogue of the Sherlock Holmes Exhibition, for which an invoice is enclosed.

I hope that the brochure relating to the Sherlock Holmes Society of London will provide the information you desire.

BOROUGH LIBRARIAN

Public Library, St. Marylebone.   *23 August 1951*

Mr. Moore and the Exhibition Catalogue

To the Borough Librarian

DEAR SIR, – Thank you for your letter of the 23rd inst. I am sorry that Mr. Holmes has not yet returned – I fear that Mrs. Hudson will have to warm up the coffee! I am grateful to you for sending me the catalogue to his exhibition, and for the brochure about his Society.

As he has not been in this part of the world since he solved the little problem of the disappearance of the Duke of Holdernesse's son from The Priory School near Chesterfield, I have not seen him for a very considerable time, but when he comes in, please convey to him my kindest regards.

I enclose herewith his fee for solving the Case of the Absent Catalogue.

Yours faithfully,
R. PETER MOORE

Highcliffe Road, Sheffield.   *25 August 1951*

George Edalji at 221b Baker Street

To the Organiser of the Sherlock Holmes Exhibition

DEAR SIR, – When at 221b a few weeks ago with my sister (who has been thrice), I was told you would like to see me.

I could come again on Saturday, 2 or 9 September; if you will kindly let me know if either date will suit you, and if about 10.45 will do.

Excuse writing as I am nearly blind.

Yours truly,
G. E. T. Edalji

P.S. I should have written Saturday, 1 or 8 September – G. E. T. E.
Argyle Street, W. C. 1.   *26 August 1951*

In Search of Orson Welles

[From the French]

My Dear Sherlock Holmes, – In the first place, it is needless to ask if I have heard of your exploits! . . . You well know the answer. I am therefore seeking your help with a trifling matter. I have asked everywhere in France, at all the film companies that are based here, but to no avail. Perhaps you will be able to help me. I need an address, that of Orson Welles. It seems that he is in England at the moment, which is why I immediately thought of you. For me, it is impossible. You, however, will probably be able to find it without even asking.

Philippe Dupont

Rue La Fontaine, Paris.

18 September 1951

Dear Sir, – In the absence of Mr. Sherlock Holmes, I have made enquiries regarding your request for the address of Mr. Orson Welles.

Mr. Welles is at present staying at Aldford House, Park Lane, London, W.1.

I do hope this information will be of service to you.

Borough Librarian

Public Library, St. Marylebone, N.W.1.

3 October 1951

THE GLASGOW HERALD

The End of the Sherlock Holmes Exhibition

Exhibitions are getting ready to close their doors all over town; tomorrow Sherlock Holmes, who, disembodied but intensely real, has been at home in Baker Street since 22 May, will receive his last visitors. It is proper on these occasions to compile exhibition statistics; the peculiar glories of No. 221b shall not be neglected. Well over 50,000 people – the round figure was passed on Monday, and was marked with customary celebrations – have come to pay homage to the great man; all sorts of distinguished, even royal persons have gazed upon the mementoes of the extraordinary adventures, pored over the documentation piled up by learned Holmesian societies, and paused, in reverent silence, in the Sanctum Sanctorum, the Den itself. Holmes and Watson have never been in, some urgent business has always called them out just after breakfast; since May they have each taken one bite out of 214 crumpets, left behind half-eaten as evidence of hasty departure; 107 pots of tea have been brewed for them and left to get cold; the never-ceasing noise outside of hansom cabs, street cries, newsboys has used up 53 gramophone records. After to-morrow official hands – not even those of Mrs. Hudson – will at last clear the breakfast things away, will tidy the Den, pack up the violin, the dressing-gown, the test-tubes, the slipper-full of shag, and all the rest of the furniture for dispersal; it will indeed be his last bow. But – it is consoling to reflect – there was always one more adventure after that.

22 September 1951

IX. THE CENTENARY YEARS (1951–1954)

---◆---

My Dear Holmes

A Study in Sherlock by Gavin Brend

Public interest in Sherlock Holmes has never been greater. What other character in fiction could hope to get his letters printed in *The Times?* Who else would have a London exhibition devoted to him? Merely because he lived there Baker Street is known all over the English-speaking world (though no one can identify his house).

When was Holmes born? Which was his University? How many times was Dr. Watson married? Why did the two Moriarty brothers have the same christian name? These are some of the puzzles considered in this book, which makes an immediate appeal to every Holmes enthusiast old and young.

George Allen & Unwin.

The Correspondence Relating to Gavin Brend's
Study of Sherlock Holmes

(Devised by John A. Lincoln and edited by James Edward Holroyd)

Sir Stanley Unwin to Dr. Watson

DEAR DR. WATSON, – Despite the excellent accounts which you have given us of the works of Sherlock Holmes, there have been hitherto many gaps in our knowledge of him – and, if I may say so, of yourself! We are, therefore, publishing a book by Mr. Gavin Brend, entitled *My Dear Holmes: A Study in Sherlock*, which will, we hope, supply the answer to some, at least, of the questions which have troubled experts for many years.

I am sending you the proofs of the book with this letter as I feel sure you will be glad of an opportunity to look through them and to assure yourself that the book contains no mis-statement of fact.

Yours truly,

STANLEY UNWIN

40 Museum Street, London W.C.1, 9 July 1951.

Dr. Watson to Sir Stanley Unwin

DEAR SIR, – I am greatly obliged to you for sending news of Mr. Brend's book together with proofs. It was quite like old times to receive such a package from a well-known publishing house.

My friend Mr. Sherlock Holmes has without doubt been a benefactor of the race, and I am glad to see that his genius is being increasingly recognised. I note, too, the various flattering references to myself, and, though I suppose I ought to have been rather nettled by the author's mention of Bachelor Watson, Widower Watson and so on, I begin to feel I am too old a campaigner to be easily put out by trifles of this kind.

When I saw your address on the letter, I confess I fell into a brown study. In the first place, I recalled that Holmes had rooms just round the corner in Montague Street before we went into partnership at 221b. In the second, I well remember passing your building one frosty night during the Christmas of '89 when he and I called at the Alpha Inn in that neighbourhood while in pursuit of the Blue Carbuncle.

In assuring you that the copy of Mr. Brend's book will be passed on to Mr. Holmes forthwith, I must add that I have taken the liberty of concealing our true addresses as, with advancing years, neither of us is able to cope with heavy correspondence as adequately as our numerous well-wishers might desire.

Yours very truly,

J. H. WATSON

London, 12 July 1951.

Dr. Watson to Sherlock Holmes

MY DEAR HOLMES, – But for the fact that my old wound is somewhat troublesome these days, I should have delivered the enclosed book in person. Instead, however, I must entrust it to Her Majesty's mail service – how I wish I could have sent it from the old Wigmore Street Post Office! I hope you will enjoy it, despite your well-known dislike of publicity. Personally I found it as gripping as one of Clark Russell's fine sea stories.

Not that I agree with everything the writer says. About one passage indeed – where he suggests that we were estranged during '96 – I found myself saying, "Good Heavens, Holmes, this is intolerable!" As if I should be likely to quarrel with one whom I have always regarded as the best and wisest man I have ever known! Little does our author realise that, with my old Service revolver in my pocket, I was constantly at your side during those months when you were engaged on the Protracted and Dangerous Affair of the . . . but why satisfy idle curiosity at this late date?

I am afraid that Mr. Brend also joins the ranks of those who find fault with my chronology. When in all modesty I first set down those early adventures everything seemed so simple – elementary, I think, was your word – but with all these new-fangled dates and data my poor head is in a whirl. Still, Mr. Brend does appear to be rather indulgent when he says, "We must not demand the same degree of precision that we might expect from some other writers." Do you think this is intended as a compliment to your old comrade?

Yours ever,

J. H. Watson

London, 12 July 1951.

Sherlock Holmes to Dr. Watson

MY DEAR WATSON, – Although, as you know, I am not one of those who rank modesty among the virtues, I confess that all this Festival Year notoriety might have proved a trifle embarrassing if we were still in our old quarters in Baker Street. In the circumstances, however, I am inclined to regard it somewhat impersonally as a belated tribute to one who made the air of London sweeter for his presence.

And now, Watson, to Mr. Brend's monograph. Overcoming the natural prejudice of my French descent against one who spells Montpelier with two "ls" on four different occasions, I found the fellow not without ingenuity and at times capable of a certain pawky humour somewhat akin to your own, as when he says: " 'The Veiled Lodger' mentioned a curious affair which involved a politician, a lighthouse and a trained cormorant. Apparently an attempt has been made to destroy Holmes's papers relating to this matter, but whether the aggressor was the politician, the lighthouse keeper or the trained cormorant is not known."

One of his most singular conclusions, however, is that during my absence abroad in the nineties poor Mycroft supplied you with code messages to incorporate in your always-rather-sensational chronicling of some of our earlier adventures. Now if I had published such a theory, I fear you would have pointed your egg-spoon at it and observed "Ineffable twaddle" as you did on another occasion!

I also wish to draw your attention to the curious incident of the illustration facing p. 48. Although the publisher has reproduced the admirable Paget drawing of the pair of us in Regent Street, the author has not perceived that it has been printed the wrong way round, just as it was in the original *Strand Magazine*. Yet an elementary application of my methods would have shown that your coat, my dear Watson, is buttoned right-over-left, that your stick is in your left hand, and that the traffic is on the wrong side of the road.

While for reasons such as these I might hesitate to describe the book as one of the most remarkable ever penned, it nevertheless has qualities which perhaps make it, like veteran police officials of our acquaintance, the best of a bad lot. Indeed the fact that Mr. Brend's meticulous researches sometimes come near to baffling *me* proves him to be a foeman worthy of our steel. It would of course be a capital mistake to reveal the whole mystery of those eventful years at 221b but I believe that our author does much to unravel the tangled skein. A seventy-seven per cent solution, shall we say?

Yours,
SHERLOCK HOLMES

Nr. Eastbourne, Sussex, 16 July 1951.

PUNCH

Double Bluff

Said Watson to Holmes," Is it wise –
Such false whiskers when hunting for spies?"
Said the sleuth, "I'm afraid
You're as dense as Lestrade:
I'm disguised as myself in disguise."

R. J. P. HEWISON
21 November 1951

Watson's War Wounds

To the Editor

DEAR SIR, – I was glad to see the picture I lent you came in useful for the interesting article about Mr. Holmes and the Dr. in your magazine last month. I can't say I understood it all properly but it seems to me that you were trying to work out whether the Dr. had been wounded in the leg or in the neck. This seems queer to me for the fact is I always understood from my Aunt that the Dr. had been wounded in both places. I often heard Aunt speak about the nasty scar at the root of his neck which she often saw in the mornings when she took up his tea in the nightshirts what gentlemen wore in those days.

About the one in the leg I remember my Aunt being cross with me when a little girl because I asked what made the gentleman walk funny and Aunt told me to hush because the Dr. was a very brave gentleman that had been wounded fighting for the Queen. Dear, oh dear, what a long time ago it seems now.

Well I hope this will give you a clue, as the saying goes.

Yours respectfully,
ELSIE HUDSON (MISS)
1b Victoria Mansions, Willoughby Crescent, Euston.

January 1952

THE SPECTATOR

The Death of Sherlock Holmes

The following announcement was recently accepted by the advertising department of *The Times* for insertion in the "Deaths" column:

HOLMES. On 9 June 1952, finally and peacefully, at his home in Sussex. Sherlock, brother of Mycroft.

The advertising department took out the word "finally", on the grounds that it was redundant, but the announcement (which had been paid for) would have appeared had it not been spotted by a member of the editorial staff. The reader who submitted it has now had a letter in which the Editor regrets his inability to publish the announcement and suggests that its originator may wish his cheque to be forwarded to a charity.

STRIX

20 June 1952

"Elementary, My Dear Watson!"

To the Editor

SIR, – I have recently re-read all the Sherlock Holmes literature only to find that the famous and oft-quoted remark: "Elementary, my dear Watson!" never occurs. In one short story Holmes refers to a problem as "elementary"; and in another he addresses his companion as "my dear Watson". But the two never appear together in the complete classical phrase. I wonder if any Holmes expert could throw any light on this matter. Has the original phrase missed my eye, or can it be true that it was in fact never spoken?

Yours faithfully,
MARTIN COOPER

St. George's Rectory, Tower Street, Birmingham

8 May 1953

THE TIMES

An Elementary Attribution

Some of the most famous and familiar sayings when run to earth in books of reference are found to bear the stigma of being "attributed". The Duke of Wellington's remark about the playing fields of Eton is, to say the least of it, suspect and there seems little doubt that he never said, "Up, Guards, and at 'em", although in his own words he "must have said and probably did say, 'Stand up, Guards'." Regarding a more peaceful battlefield another and a bitter blow has lately fallen; George Hirst has broken all our hearts by declaring that he did not say, "Wilfred, we'll get them by singles." He has pointed out that no batsman would thus deliberately deny himself the chance of a boundary, though we certainly have heard of Yorkshire doing so before lunch on the first day of the Lancashire match. Yet with all our cherished quotations being "debunked" one by one we had held fast to, "Elementary, my dear Watson." And now there comes along an iconoclastic and disenchanting gentleman (writing in the *Spectator* from the scene of "The Adventure of the Stockbroker's Clerk") who

233

roundly asserts that Sherlock Holmes never used those words. What is worse, a hurried and imperfect search seems to show that he is right. "My dear Watson" is easy; as the two men grew better acquainted it gradually superseded "My dear Doctor". The component parts of the desiderated phrase can nearly but, alas, not quite be found together in "The Crooked Man". " 'I have the advantage of knowing your habits, my dear Watson,' " said Holmes, and deduced that the practice justified a hansom. " 'Excellent!' I cried. 'Elementary,' said he."

This exclamation of "Excellent!" produced a particular reaction so nearly identical that students capable of a decent second class might well fall into error. In "The Reigate Squires", after a demonstration as to handwriting, " 'Excellent!' cried Mr. Acton. 'But very superficial,' said Holmes." Again, in *A Study in Scarlet*, the earliest of all the writings, is the passage: " 'Wonderful,' I ejaculated. 'Commonplace,' said Holmes." That is the best that can be made of a bad job on the spur of the moment. Heaven forbid that we should absolutely deny that those now almost sacred words can be discovered but they do not seem to be there. Holmes often used far more unkind expressions towards his friend, as when (in "The Sussex Vampire") he tartly observed in response to a suggestion, "We must not let him think this Agency is a home for the weak-minded." So too "Good old Watson" implied a certain derision not to be found in "My dear Watson". But that peculiarly galling epithet "elementary" appears to occur but once. It is a little sad; it would have been better, if the expression be permissible, to let sleeping attributions lie. And yet all but the most scholarly of us will soon get over the blow and will go on happily misquoting to the end of time.

(FOURTH LEADER)
12 May 1953

A Word to Watson

To the Editor

SIR, – While it is sad to discard the canonicity of "Elementary, my dear Watson", you are, perhaps, unduly pessimistic in regarding the use of "elementary" in "The Crooked Man" as a απαχ λεγσηενον. In "A Case of Identity" Holmes remarks: "All this is amusing, though rather elementary, but I must go back to business, Watson"; and in *The Hound of the Baskervilles* his first comment on Watson's reconstruction of James Mortimer is: "Interesting, though elementary."

Your obedient servant,
S. C. ROBERTS

The Lodge, Pembroke College, Cambridge.   *21 May 1953*

"Hand Me My Rattan, Watson!"

Mr. Martin Cooper's discovery, made public in a letter to THE SPECTA-TOR, that Sherlock Holmes never said, "Elementary, my dear Watson", produced a Fourth Leader in *The Times*, and that in its turn gave rise to some learned correspondence in that journal. So far no one has put forward what I feel sure is the true explanation of the phrase's wide-spread currency, which is that it was a line – possibly a curtain line – in one or other of the dramatisations, probably that made and acted in by William Gillette. I haven't been able to check this, but – to cite a roughly similar case – I was once told, and long believed, that the most dramatic line in English literature was, "Hand me my rattan, Watson!", uttered by Holmes when the snake in "The Speckled Band" began to descend the bell-rope. It was many years before I re-read the story, and found that the line does not occur in it. I bet it did occur in the play.

STRIX
22 May 1953

William Gillette as Sherlock Holmes

To the Editor

SIR, – I remember seeing William Gillette as Sherlock Holmes at the Lyceum Theatre just fifty years ago and I feel sure Strix is correct in saying that "Elementary, my dear Watson" was a line in the play. Gillette spoke in an eerie, sinister drawl, rather high-pitched, and, with his head thrown back and eyes half-closed, gave the impression that he was thinking of anything but the problem on hand. Only at the tense moments with Moriarty did he snap into life and become peremptory and incisive.

Yours faithfully,
AUBREY VINCENT

Whiteways, Canterbury

5 June 1953

The Exploits of Sherlock Holmes

To the Editor

SIR, – I regret to see that that fellow Holmes has reappeared. He may have survived the Reichenbach Falls, but I doubt whether he will survive the columns of your illustrious journal. However, should Holmes ever venture beyond the Iron Curtain, he will find me as ever a ready and powerful adversary.

Yours maliciously,
MORIARTY

A Club in London.

1 October 1953

Professor Moriarty and the Athenæum

To the Editor

SIR, – I am astonished that such a palpable forgery should have been published. If Professor Moriarty was a member of any club it would have been of this club. He would in that case have known better than sign a letter in the style of a peer.

D. W. BROGAN

The Athenæum, Pall Mall.

5 October 1953

The Adventure of the Black Baronet

To the Editor

SIR, – Much as I am intrigued with the new Sherlock Holmes narratives, I would remind the authors that they are somewhat incorrect in dating the Adventure of the Black Baronet as October 1889.

Both Mr. Sherlock Holmes and Dr. Watson were otherwise occupied during that period investigating the tragic death of my great-grandfather, Sir Charles Baskerville.

HUGO WILLOUGHBY BASKERVILLE

Baskerville Hall, Dartmoor.

5 October 1953

THE MANCHESTER GUARDIAN

The Sherlock Holmes Centenary

[News item: 6 January 1954 has now been agreed as the centenary of the
"birth" of "Sherlock Holmes".]

Sherlock! as members of that loyal band
Of readers who first met you in the *Strand*,
We pay our tribute now, great Master-sleuth,
On your centenary, Hero of our youth;
And greet, in turning each familiar page,
The good companion of advancing age.
To us, who knew the London of your prime,
You bring again the hansom cab bells' chime;
Your records echo with the beat of hooves –
Brisk rhythm to which the plot's swift action moves –
The years roll backwards as each case speeds on.
And you and Watson drive to Paddington
Or Charing Cross, on strange adventures bent,
Hot on some trail in Devonshire or Kent;
And we, set free from bounds of Time and Space,
Follow your cab, and join the immortal chase.

E. T.
6 January 1954

THE TIMES

An Old Friend's Birthday

To-night the B.B.C. celebrates the hundredth birthday of Mr. Sherlock
Holmes. Some successors of his, both imaginary and real, headed by
Lord Peter Wimsey, will pay tribute to his genius. We can only wish
that the shades of two of his mighty predecessors had been evoked to do
him similar honour, Inspector Bucket and Sergeant Cuff. That would
have been quite a party. Exactly how the date of his birth has been
arrived at we do not yet know. The chronology of the Holmes stories has
engaged some of the brightest intellects in this country. Their mental
gymnastics have sometimes been so brilliant as to seem almost exhaust-
ing. That at least is the view of many a common man who yields to none
in his adoration of the master. When all is said, most of us, devoted
though we be, are intellectually no better than good, honest, plodding

Watsons. There are about us unexpected possibilities of stupidity. In our humble, fundamentalist faith we take the sacred writings as we find them. We no more believe that, as hinted by perhaps the most sparkling of all the commentators, Mycroft Holmes was in league with Professor Moriarty than that Watson contracted a second marriage with Miss de Melville.

For such as us a simple clue or two will suffice. In "His Last Bow" Holmes, when in the guise of Altamont, is described as "a tall gaunt man of sixty". That adventure happened beyond question in 1914, on the eve of war, and so points to 1854 as the year of the birth. More complex and dubious evidence is derived from Holmes's career at Cambridge. Miss Dorothy Sayers, a great authority (though some respectfully think she went astray as to his college), believes that he was a third-year man in 1874. That too suggests 1854, the year favoured by a scholar of vast erudition, Mr. H. W. Bell; but it is fair to add that others have argued for 1853 or even 1852. However, as we have lately seen a mistake made as to an illustrious contemporary, Sir Herbert Tree, perhaps a single year does not matter.

This celebration of a famous character's birthday is not unique, for when Mr. Pickwick's centenary came around some years ago a large company drank his health at dinner to the strains of "He's a jolly good fellow". But Mr. Pickwick's sitting-room on the first floor front in Goswell Street has never been reconstructed for his admirers, whereas during the Festival of Britain many worshippers made pilgrimage to the model of 221b Baker Street, exactly as it had been in Mrs. Hudson's day. We have no positive information where Mr. Holmes will keep this anniversary, but there seems no reason to doubt that he still lives surrounded by his faithful bees on the South Downs. "Nothing of interest in the paper, Watson?" we can fancy him saying, harking back, as old men will, and then lighting with pleasure on his own name. If any listeners feel disposed to raise their glasses to him tonight, they must not fear lest his cold and reserved nature should disdain their homage. Let them remember how, in the little affair of the six Napoleons, he bowed to his audience when they broke into spontaneous clapping. "Thank you," he said, "thank you," and turned away to hide his emotion.

(FOURTH LEADER)
8 January 1954.

From the Casebook of Sherlock Holmes

Competition No. 202

In the opening paragraphs of several of the Sherlock Holmes stories reference is made to cases which the public never actually had a chance to read, e.g., the whole story concerning the politician, the lighthouse and the trained cormorant. Competitors were invited to submit the title and opening paragraph of an imaginary Sherlock Holmes story which was to include references to one or more further imaginary stories.

Report by J. P. W. Mallalieu

The title I chose as an example was fantastic; so I cannot complain if competitors offer me the affair of the "One-eyed Greek and the Disappearing Island", the adventure of the "Trapeze in the Abandoned Hansom", the case of the "Haberdasher and the Hairless Baboon" or the "Vicious Conduct of the Blind Televisionist".

But I prefer the simplicity of the case of the "Surrey Centaur", of the "Moneylender's Flute" or of "Dobwell, the Somerset Killer" – whose tidy mind led him to bury his victims in the local cemetery.

Even where their titles were promising, I barred facetious entries, e.g., Holmes, summoned to the Athenæum, says: "Come, Watson, better bring your revolver. We don't know whom we may meet there"; or "Are you ready for action, Watson? Is your revolver loaded? If so, leave it behind. It might go off", or even the case of the "Vegetarian League's Banquet", when the soup was flavoured with rabbit.

Glaring errors in the style of their opening paragraphs also barred a number of entries, e.g., "Pausing only to affix the Back-in-a-week notice to my surgery door" or allowing Watson to answer a question with the hockey-girl's "Ra-ther!"

The two entries which I have chosen to share the prize both have similar opening sentences and there is little to choose between the titles they invent or the genuineness of their style. I place Dr. Noel Hopkins, Provost of Wakefield, first because I feel that he has been getting inside information from his relative, the Inspector.

The Urbane Auctioneer

By Dr. Noel T. Hopkins

In looking over the notes of Holmes's Investigations for the year 189–, I have been impressed by their diversity, which made my choice difficult. I hesitated long over the macabre story under the innocent title of "The Downchester Chapter House", as well as the strange adventure of Matthew Norris, the Stepney taxidermist, which unearthed the sinister Tortoise Club, cost two lives, and nearly brought Holmes to his own death; while the activities of the California blackmailers, which took Holmes twice across the Atlantic, and brought him the life-long friendship of the American President, cannot yet be given to the world. In the end, for sheer criminal audacity, and as an example of Holmes's own versatile powers, which actually led him to assume in public the part of the very criminal he was pursuing, I have chosen the narrative of "The Urbane Auctioneer".

The Adventure of the Crying Mummy

By John Manning

Glancing over my records for the year 1887, I find selection difficult. There was the case, presenting certain bizarre features, of Miss Rose Madder-Browne, who vanished under grotesque and apparently inexplicable circumstances from a corridor coach in the Paddington express. And I cannot disclose, since one of the very important personages involved is still alive, the full story of Holmes's visit to the East, when he investigated the scandal in the Singapore Yacht Club and the subsequent exposure of Major Forbes-Mancrieffe with his Praying Mantis. In this period also I find my notes covering the tragic voyage of the *Clanwilliam Star* with its appalling cargo. I am now free, however, to make public the weird and terrible events leading up to the death of the Curator of the Lyme Regis Museum, since this case was, perhaps, most typical of my friend's wide and remarkable powers.

15 January 1954

THE EVENING STANDARD

[On 1 March 1954, among the "Situations Vacant" columns, there appeared a comic strip by Frank Giacoia and Edith Meiser. Mrs.

Hudson tells Dr. Watson that she is worried about Holmes: " 'E's in the doldrums again, if you'd get 'im to take a cup o' tea and a kipper! . . . 'E wouldn't even open the door so I could give him this letter!"]

A Letter from Professor Moriarty

To the Editor

SIR, – I rejoice to see the decline of that cursed, interfering fellow Holmes to a mere comic strip feature on a rather obscure page.

It is little wonder that he cannot be induced to leave his room, even for tea and a kipper.

Yours joyfully,
PROFESSOR MORIARTY

Valhalla.

4 March 1954

JOHN O' LONDON'S WEEKLY

Sherlock Holmes in Vienna

Sherlockians – and all who enjoyed our recent Sherlock Holmes Number – will be interested in a story I was told by a Viennese guide who claimed to know the whole of the canon. (Not being a Sherlockian, I could not test the extent of his knowledge.)

It seems that when the creator of Holmes came to Vienna in the 'nineties a hotel porter greeted him as "Mr. Doyle".

"But how do you know my name?" asked the astonished author. "I have never been in Vienna before."

The porter explained that he had read the name on the label and immediately connected it with the Sherlock Holmes stories, many of which he had read.

19 March 1954

The Living Image of Sherlock Holmes

To the Editor

SIR, – In 1908 I travelled down the rivers Volga and Kama into Kazan. I had a job as a tutor to the two sons of the Marshal of Nobility of that Province. I found all Russia crazy about Sherlock Holmes. Even the peasants (those who could read) had got hold of copies, cheaply printed and, no doubt, pirated. But evidently the Paget pictures had arrived,

241

too, and they knew what he looked like. This was evident when my two youngsters, seeing that I was tall, lean, clean-shaven and pipe-smoking, insisted that I was the living image of S.H. and begged that they might take me over to a nearby village and show me off as the genuine article! I have always regretted that I did not undertake the hoax.

GERALD HERRING

Parys Hotel, Parys, O.F.S., South Africa.

2 April 1954

X. SELECTED
CORRESPONDENCE
(1955–1978)

———————◆———————

Sherlock Holmes in Birmingham

To the Editor

SIR, – What on earth were Watson and friends thinking about when they went to New Street, Birmingham, from Paddington? If they were so wedded to that aristocrat of railways, the Great Western Railway of those days, why not the straightforward run Paddington to Snow Hill, Birmingham, competing with Euston to New Street?

I am, Sir, your obedient servant,

J. H. POWELL

Christ Church Vicarage, Nailsea, Nr. Bristol.

26 April 1955

The Timing of "The Stockbroker's Clerk"

To the Editor

SIR, – Your correspondent Mr. Powell asks why Holmes and Watson should be represented in your leading article (23 April) as travelling from Paddington to New Street (not to Snow Hill), Birmingham. He should have given more attention to the timing of "The Stockbroker's Clerk". Holmes called on Watson "one morning in June"; his client was waiting outside in a four-wheeler, and time pressed; "Whip your horse up, cabby, for we have only just time to catch our train." And it is not until seven in the evening that we find them walking up Corporation Street. Why this prodigious time-lag?

Holmes, as you saw, loved Paddington, though the Great Western was in those days much the longer route. Their train, therefore, was the 1.45; but Holmes had wasted time in making deductions about Watson's cold, and they threw themselves in at the last moment without tickets. Hall Pycroft was, however, in possession of a return half-ticket from Euston to New Street, and he persuaded his companions to change stations at Leamington; the 4.35 from Leamington Spa (Avenue) would get them into Birmingham with little more than half an hour's loss of time, and he would be fully armed with a ticket at the New Street barrier.

But this time their luck was out. They just missed the 4.35 and did not reach New Street till 6.49. At seven they were walking up Corporation Street; but already Arthur Pinner had received his early edition of the *Evening Standard*.

I am, sir, your obedient servant,

R. A. KNOX

Mells, Somerset.

29 April 1955

THE WAVE

A Naval Question

By G. Casey

Dr. Watson tells us in the "*Gloria Scott*" that the ship sank in N. Latitude 15° 20' and W. Longitude 15° 4'. He added that, at the time, Cape Verde was about 500 miles to the North and the African coast about 700 miles to the East. Would you imagine that Sherlock Holmes received this with his customary "Elementary, my dear Watson"?

By no means, for the first position lies in the heart of the Ferlo Desert in Senegal and the second does not exist.

Spring 1956

THE TIMES

The Author's Dilemma

The great Duke of Wellington complained that he was much exposed to authors. Authors in their turn are much exposed, if not to Dukes, though they must try to get them right, to persons having too accurate a technical knowledge. Thus we have recently been told how the late Mr.

Freeman Wills Crofts made £250,000 in single notes be carried in two suitcases, whereupon two arithmetically minded admirers pointed out that the notes would occupy ten cubic feet and weigh about two hundredweight.

Doubtless Mr. Crofts ought to have done the sum for himself but doubtless also very few of his many readers found him out, and anyhow there was nothing to be done about it. It is otherwise with pictures. It is recorded that a famous engineer bought a picture of Israelites in Egypt hauling along a Sphinx. He did the sum and found that there were not enough Israelites for the job. So he insisted on some more being painted in, to which the artist agreed with perfect docility. In literature the difficulty is that facts sometimes disagree with plots.

Sir Arthur Conan Doyle unquestionably took liberties. Even those of us who care nothing for racing always found it odd that the best known horse in England should appear in disguise with face and leg painted and from a training stable other than his own and win the race unchallenged. Yet we continue to read "Silver Blaze" with undiminished pleasure. Again there are some who have pernickety minds on social precedence and manners of address. They are perpetually if mildly annoyed with Sherlock Holmes for being palpably shaky on such matters. "Lord Robert St. Simon," announced the page boy. "Good day Lord St. Simon," said Holmes. "Pray take the basket chair." The same remark applies to the confusion between a court and a quadrangle at St. Luke's College. Holmes, who was unquestionably at one of the two Universities, probably Cambridge, must have known better, though his creator – or was it Watson? – did not. Here we may blame the author, since the plot would have been in no way affected, whereas Silver Blaze had to win that race in disguise.

The law insists on accuracy though it does not always get it. We know that Stevenson, most scrupulous of artists, was much exercised in his mind and sought legal advice as to how Lord Hermiston could try his own son. Clearly he would not have done so and yet the scene cried out for him. Since the great book remained unfinished we do not know how he would have solved the problem. Sometimes the law can be overridden. Dickens as palpably "knew his stuff" in law as he did not in cricket. He knew that Serjeant Snubbin would never have allowed his inexperienced junior, Mr. Phunky, to cross-examine Mr. Winkle, but the thing had to be. If there is a moral it is that the author should get his technicalities right before he constructs his plot; but if the plot is good enough the devil may fly away with the technicalities. A great plot quits all scores.

(FOURTH LEADER)
13 May 1957

245

The Bonds of Fact

To the Editor

SIR, – Apart from an arbitrary, parenthetical, and unsupported reference to the identity of Holmes's University, your leading article today [13 May] pleasantly recalls a remark of the late W. E. Heitland that certain stories deserve to be emancipated from the bonds of fact.

Yours faithfully,
S. C. ROBERTS

The Master's Lodge, Pembroke College, Cambridge.

14 May 1957

THE GLASGOW DAILY RECORD

Sherlock Holmes and the Treble Chance

I stepped straight into Sherlock Holmes's Victorian sitting-room yesterday in a new pub named after him in Northumberland Street just off Trafalgar Square, London. It's a long way from Baker Street's No. 221b – reputedly the great detective's address – but the room is a replica of that described by Sir Arthur Conan Doyle.

Oddly enough among the deer-stalker hat, pipe, magnifying glass, and other Holmesian bric-à-brac I noticed a letter addressed: "S. Holmes, Esq., 221b Baker Street, London." Inside was a request from a football pool company to join their happy ranks. I couldn't help wondering whether Sherlock could have worked out the treble chance.

PETER LYALL
13 December 1957

THE DAILY EXPRESS

The Adventures of Henry Baskerville

A British company remaking *The Hound of the Baskervilles* will not mention Sherlock Holmes in the advertising. The reason: "Teenagers think of him as the fuddy-duddy hero who appealed to their great-grandparents."

11 September 1958

246

A Protest by Professor Moriarty

To the Editor

SIR, – I cannot say how grieved I am at the insult paid to Mr. Sherlock Holmes by the uncouth persons who consider him to be old-fashioned and worthy of no respect.

Sir, the memory of a desperate struggle on the edge of "a ghastly abyss", and of many other valiant ventures, has convinced me that Holmes, Englishman though he may be, is no fuddy-duddy.

PROFESSOR MORIARTY

c/o Charles Milverton, Rosslyn Hill, Hampstead, London, N.W.

15 September 1958

THE WORLD VETERAN

Sherlock Holmes on the Conan Doyle Centenary

To the Editor

SIR, – You have assuredly noticed, as I have, the near-servility with which the world press has been celebrating this year the centenary of a certain well-known author. I have no ill-will, on my word, against the competent chronicler in question; but I cannot but be struck by the contrast between the fuss made over *his* centenary and the utter indifference displayed some years ago over *mine*. One had modestly supposed that one had played some small role oneself in the adventures recorded by Dr. Watson under the pen-name of Sir Arthur Conan Doyle.

You may wonder, sir, why I choose to address my protest to your publication rather than to *The Times* or the *Telegraph* which, in a more active period of my career, were my preferred journals. The fact is, that in pleasing distinction to their fulsome celebration of Sir Arthur's centenary, you have chosen to ignore the occasion altogether. It is to your credit, sir. Moreover, I have always taken an interest, as must any inquiring and developed mind, in veterans' affairs. A glance at *Who's Who* will show you that I did not myself ever have the honour of bearing arms in Her Majesty's service; but my work on the case of the Second Stain, my recovery of the Bruce-Partington Plans, and a variety of similar performances entitle me, I feel, to consider myself in some sense a soldier. I trust I am not guilty of excessive vanity when I say that the First World War might have taken a very different course had not Herr

247

Von Bork had the misfortune to come up against me. Looking back, indeed, my services to my country doubly underline the curiously gross ingratitude of the press in ignoring my centenary. But I shall not labour the point.

There is another reason, too, for the interest I have always taken in your publication. You will recall, I am sure, that my good friend Watson was very much of a veteran, having served with distinction in the Afghan War. Had your Federation existed in his day, so badly-wounded a man would surely have been adequately looked after instead of wandering pointlessly around London watching his tiny savings dwindle away. I need not remind you that pension laws were rather inconsistent in those days.

I might further add that your Federation's work in the field of rehabilitation might have permitted Dr. Watson to decide once and for all whether that Jezail bullet "struck his shoulder, shattered the bone and grazed the subclavian artery" (as he asserts in *A Study in Scarlet*) or whether it struck his leg so that "it ached wearily at every change of the weather" (as he tells us was the case in *The Sign of Four*).

And, while on these medical topics, I wonder if any of your experts have yet triumphed over those exotic diseases which I mentioned in the tale called "The Dying Detective"? I refer, of course, to Tapanuli fever and the black Formosa corruption. I have seen no reference in your pages which would indicate that research on these scourges was even under way. Yet they may conceivably one day interfere very seriously with your land settlement projects.

Let me end on a note of self-doubt. You will doubtless recall how astonished was my poor Watson when I promptly identified a passing civilian as a "retired sergeant of Marines". The deduction was, of course, simplicity itself.

But, in the present epoch, I wonder if even I – even my brother Mycroft – could undertake to pick out members of the multitudinous branches of the armed services. Could I identify a frogman in civilian attire? Or a man who "counts down" rockets? Or a radar operator? It is doubtless due to increasing age, but I doubt it.

Thank you, sir, for extending to me the courtesy of your columns and permit me to wish you all good luck in your estimable work.

Your obedient servant,
SHERLOCK HOLMES

221b Baker Street, London, N.W.1.

July 1959

Mementoes of the Silver Blaze Case

To Major Simon Whitbread, J. P., South Hill Park, Bedfordshire

DEAR MAJOR WHITBREAD, – A friend of mine, Sir Danvers Osborn, suggested that I should write to you about an interesting find among some old things of my mother's. He felt that possibly what I am sending you might be acceptable for the Sherlock Holmes Museum in London.

I am enclosing a letter which is self-explanatory, which was evidently written by Col. Ross to my grandfather, who must have been staying in Devon at the time of the Silver Blaze Case. This I found in an old box at home, together with the plate to which it refers, which I now send you.

I feel sure that they will both be of interest.

Yours sincerely,
G. HOWARD HEATON

The Tee, Martley, Nr. Worcester

17 May 1961

The Letter from Colonel Ross

MY DEAR ASTON, – It is some months since you were here, but I have been much occupied with the horses, and choosing a new man, and that is why I have not written to you before this.

Silver Blaze had a fair season only, after that remarkable day at Winchester, but the Wessex Cup is on the sideboard in the dining-room to remind me of that extraordinary turn of events. I want you to have a memento of that epic occasion, so I am sending you one of the plates which he wore and in which he ran in the famous race. Please accept it with my grateful thanks for your patient hearing of my troubles and the encouragement you gave me when things looked so bad.

Ever your sincere friend,
JAMESON ROSS

King's Pyland, Nr. Tavistock, Devon,   29 September 1895.

Sherlock Holmes on the Radio

To the Editor

SIR, – I am concerned about the representation of Sherlock Holmes's voice. I remember that his had the thinner, almost reedy, quality, as of a celibate scientist, or of a judge, and not the full-blooded, well-wined, *bon-viveur* character of recent broadcasting. If anything, this latter was the voice of my dear, rather silly old grandfather.

Would any of your readers who might have known the great man better than I confirm or deny this?

S. HOLMES WATSON, M.D.

London, W.1

28 December 1961

A Letter from Mycroft Holmes

To the Editor

SIR, – A friend of mine has drawn my attention to a letter by Dr. Watson in THE RADIO TIMES regarding the representation of my brother's voice on the wireless.

As so often happens, Dr. Watson is inaccurate, and I must confirm that Mr. Carleton Hobbs's portrayal of my brother is excellent.

MYCROFT HOLMES

Pall Mall, S.W.1.

18 January 1962

The Astringent Voice of Mr. Carleton Hobbs

To the Editor

SIR, – My dear, rather silly old grandfather always used to recall meeting Holmes in his prime year of 1895, and being addressed by him thus: "Woodman's Lee, cabby, as quick as you can go!"

The tones in which this thrilling command was uttered he always described as "high and somewhat strident", the very term used by Watson of his friend's voice in "The Stockbroker's Clerk".

Highly strident leading players are little favoured by modern audiences. What might be termed "astringency" of voice is a good microphone substitute; and if ever there was an astringent voice it is surely that of Carleton Hobbs, whose portrayals, according to numerous listeners, epitomise the Sherlock Holmes of their imagination.

MICHAEL HARDWICK

London, W.1.

18 January 1962

THE SUNDAY TIMES

From the Personal Columns

HOLMES, arrived Syon Lodge, Isleworth, Middlesex. Signs of recent struggles. Thousands of antiques in mansion and grounds but can detect nothing spurious. Mr. Crowther opens seven days a week; states struggles all occasioned by clients fighting impulses to purchase. Returning tomorrow! Please accept delivery at Baker Street of Chippendale chimneypiece on my behalf. WATSON.

16 April 1967

THE TIMES

From the Personal Columns

SHERLOCK HOLMES, late of 221b Baker Street. Writer anxious to contact anybody personally acquainted with, or possessing authentic documents or effects. Please write Box 0668 H. THE TIMES.

27 April 1968

From the "In Memoriam" Columns

HOLMES, – In affectionate memory, on his birthday, of "S.H.", beloved by countless friends in Cambridge, in England, and in the United States.

20 May 1968

THE OXFORD MAIL

Sherlock Holmes on the Destruction of Dogs

To the Editor

SIR, – My attention has been drawn to my friend Watson's admirable proposals on dog-shooting ("Letters", 13 February 1976). He has

251

always been keen on this. See, for example, his account of my case entitled "The Copper Beeches", where he disposed expeditiously of Carlo the mastiff: "There was the huge famished brute, its black muzzle buried in Rucastle's throat, while he writhed and screamed on the ground. Running up, I blew its brains out, and it fell over with its keen white teeth still meeting in the great creases of his neck."

In his account of *The Hound of the Baskervilles*, Watson wrote: "But the next instant Holmes had emptied five barrels of his revolver into the creature's flank. With a last howl of agony and a vicious snap in the air, it rolled upon its back, four feet pawing furiously, and then fell limp upon its side." He concludes with the following lines of verse (unintentionally, I trust): "I stooped, panting, and pressed my pistol / To the dreadful shimmering head, / But it was useless to press the trigger. / The giant hound was dead."

You will note that whereas it took me five shots to kill the Hound, it took Watson only one to kill the mastiff. He must have had some good practice with his service revolver, shooting pariah dogs in India.

SHERLOCK HOLMES

221b Baker Street, London.

20 February 1976

A Letter from Sherlock Holmes's Brother

To the Editor

SIR, – Concerning the shooting of dogs, I have to hand the letter ascribed to Sherlock Holmes and I must say I view it with some scepticism. Indeed, I find it difficult to believe that the text emanates entirely from the hand of my compassionate, revered brother.

Naturally, neither Sherlock nor Watson would hesitate to dispatch an enraged animal intent on the butchery of human life, especially when circumstance admitted no alternative; but that is quite different from the calculated destruction of the average obedient dog.

To add credence to this argument I quote just three passages from Watson's chronicles which indicate my brother's considerable sympathy, regard, and affection for the *canis domesticus* (the narrative is pure Watson, the dialogue his vivid recollection of Sherlock's own words, and the italics are mine):

(1) The professor . . . began to provoke it in every possible way . . . And then in a moment it happened! . . . The savage creature had him fairly by the throat, its fangs had bitten deep, and he was senseless before we could reach them and drag the two apart. *It might have been a*

252

dangerous task for us, but Bennett's voice and presence brought the great wolf-hound instantly to reason. ("The Creeping Man")

(2) 'Well, Watson, that's done it. . . . He thought it was his mistress and he found it was a stranger. *Dogs don't make mistakes."* . . . (3) "By the way, that was a most beautiful spaniel that was whining in the hall. . . . *I am a dog-fancier myself.*" ("Shoscombe Old Place")

Now I greatly respect Watson's prowess as a raconteur and readily affirm what I have said before: I hear of Sherlock everywhere since Watson became his chronicler. But it seems to me that the competent narrator has somehow taken to reconstructing even the great detective's letters to the Press!

And can it be that Mr. Stuart Palmer's mildly misleading treatise entitled "Notes on Certain Evidence of Caniphobia in Mr. Sherlock Holmes and his Associates" has had a somewhat exaggerated influence?

MYCROFT HOLMES

c/o The Diogenes Club, London

23 February 1976

WORLD MEDICINE

The Red-Headed League

One of the odder little jobs which Jekyll does from time to time involves assessing the efficiency of the various medical classified columns, by seeing how fast they print adverts which I send in to them. This is quite an enjoyable task, since like many doctors I often want to buy or sell something. But this year I decided to celebrate 1 April by sending in an advert that wasn't *entirely genuine*. I don't know if you noticed it, but it appeared in the classifieds like this:

RED-HEADED LEAGUE. On account of the bequest of the late Ezekiah Hopkins, of Lebanon, Penn., U.S.A. there is now another vacancy open which entitles the chosen Dr. to four pounds a week.

Well now, readers who know their Sherlock Holmes are perhaps not entirely unfamiliar with *that* particular advertisement. It occurs in a celebrated story in which the sleuth of Baker Street foils the villainous Mr. Clay in his fiendish plot to rob the City & Suburban Bank of its shekels – and I didn't expect anybody to take it very seriously.

Much to my surprise, over the last few weeks I've received a steady stream of letters from doctors who want to join the Red-Headed League and collect the four quid a week. I haven't the nerve to write back to any

253

of them, so perhaps I could just take this opportunity of apologising to them all – especially the chap who sent a very nice letter asking for the four pounds for a red-headed missionary friend of his.

I should also record that I received one note from Yorkshire very properly written on a Mogadon scribble pad – which read:

> DEAR DOCTOR (or is it JOHN CLAY?), – You are a scoundrel, Sir! I would have thought you had learnt your lesson last time! I have informed Mr. Merryweather of the City & Suburban of your dastardly intentions – and very shortly my cocaine-imbibing colleague (and Mr. Jones of Scotland Yard) will be calling to arrest you. As for myself, I have a case to attend to.
>
> Yours sincerely,
WATSON

Jekyll has been unable to deduce the identity of "Dr. Watson" with absolute certainty, but he appears to practice at 222 Kingston Road, Willerby, Hull. If he will let me have his real name, I think the least I can do is to let him have the four quid.

DOCTOR JEKYLL
31 May 1978

NOTES TO
THE INTRODUCTION

———————◆———————

1 "Books of the Quarter (*The Complete Sherlock Holmes Short Stories, The Leavenworth Case*)", T. S. Eliot, *Criterion*, April 1929, Vol. VIII, pp. 552–6.
2 "Sir Arthur Conan Doyle", E. T. Raymond, *Outlook*, 29 November 1919, Vol. XLIV, p. 564.
3 "Moulders of Public Opinion. VII – Sir Arthur Conan Doyle", E. T. Raymond, *Everyman*, 15 February 1919, Vol. XIII, pp. 428–30; collected in *All & Sundry*, T. Fisher Unwin, 1919, pp. 194–200.
4 "Sherlock Holmes (*The Sherlock Holmes Long Stories*)", Hesketh Pearson, *G.K.'s Weekly*, 5 October 1929, Vol. X, p. 59
5 "Readers' Reports. The Advantages of Sherlock Holmes" Desmond MacCarthy, *Life and Letters*, August 1930, Vol. V, pp. 123–7.
6 "Mr. Holmes, They Were the Footprints of a Gigantic Hound", Edmund Wilson, *New Yorker*, 17 February 1945, Vol. XXI, pp. 73–8; collected (with the two other articles attacking detective fiction) in *Classics and Commercials*, Farrar, Strauss, N.Y., 1950 (W. H. Allen, 1951), pp. 266–74.
7 "Sherlock Holmes, Detective. As seen by Scotland Yard", Sir Robert Anderson, K.C.B., *T.P.'s Weekly*, 2 October 1903, Vol. II, pp. 557–8.
8 "The Unromantic Detective", George Edgar, *Outlook*, 3 December 1910, Vol. XXIV, pp. 788–9.
9 "The Evolution of Sherlock Holmes. A Comparison of the Detective Stories of Conan Doyle with those of Edgar Allan Poe and Emile Gaboriau", Robert Blatchford, *Clarion*, 24 July 1897, p. 234.
10 Publishers' announcement for *Beeton's Christmas Annual, Publishers' Circular*, 1 November 1887, Vol. 50, p. 1303.
11 "Literature, Christmas Numbers, &c.", *Lloyd's Weekly (London) Newspaper*, 11 December; "Reviews of Books, Magazines, &c.", *Weekly Times and Echo*, 11 December 1887; "Our Library Table. Christmas Annuals – IV", *Bristol Mercury*, 21 December 1887.
12 A. Conan Doyle, A.L.S., Southsea, 3 September 1889, to (Joseph Marshall) Stoddart; Redmond A. Burke Collection, Wisconsin, Letter No. 4.
13 A. Conan Doyle, A.L.S., Southsea, 17 March 1890, to (Joseph Marshall) Stoddart; *loc. cit.* 12 (Letter No. 4).
14 "An Adventure of Sheer Lecoqmes", *Privateer* (a journal for the students of

University College and Hospital), 16 June 1892, Vol. 1, pp. 3–4; this may be tentatively ascribed to E. V. Lucas, who was President of the University College Literary Society at the time.

15 *The Uncollected Sherlock Holmes*, Sir Arthur Conan Doyle, Penguin Books, 1983, "The True Story of Sherlock Holmes", pp. 345–51 (from *Tit-Bits*, 15 December 1900).

16 A. Conan Doyle, A.L.S., South Norwood, n.d. (June 1893) to Mrs. (Charles) Charrington; Ergo Books, London.

17 "Monody on the Death of Sherlock Holmes", "K" (E. E. Kellett); collected in *Jetsam. Occasional Verses*, E. Johnson, Cambridge, 1897, p. 76.

18 *Op. cit.* 15, "The Last of Sherlock Holmes", pp. 353–5 (from the *Daily Mail*, 8 October 1904).

19 *Over the Plum-Pudding*, John Kendrick Bangs, Harper & Brothers (Harper's Portrait Collection of Short Stories, Volume VI), N.Y., 1901, pp. 3–19.

20 "On the Threshold of the Chamber of Horrors", Montgomery Carmichael, *Illustrated Sporting and Dramatic News*, 27 October 1894, Vol. XLII, p. 259; collected in *Sketches and Stories. Grave and Gay*, Archibald Constable, 1896, pp. 97–107.

21 "A Student of Sherlock Holmes", William Raynor, *Tit-Bits*, 29 December 1894, Vol. XXVII, pp. 227–8.

22 "Sherlock Holmes and the Missing Box" (advt.: Beecham's Pills), *Family Doctor*, 18 November 1893, Vol. XVIII, p. 192.

23 *A Double Barrelled Detective Story*, Mark Twain, Harper & Brothers, N.Y. (Chatto & Windus), 1902, p. 109.

24 "Literary Chat. Sherlock Redivivus. Dr. Conan Doyle brings his useful friend, Detective Holmes, to life again", *Munsey's Magazine*, N.Y., December 1901, Vol. XXVI, p. 447.

25 "Chronicle and Comment", *Bookman*, N.Y., December 1899, Vol. X, p. 299.

26 "Chronicle and Comment. Lecocq [*sic*] and Sherlock Holmes", *Bookman*, N.Y., October 1900, Vol. XII, p. 107.

27 "Chronicle and Comment. The Gruesome in Conan Doyle", *Bookman*, N.Y., December 1900, Vol. XII, pp. 330–1.

28 *Op. cit.* 15.

29 "Chronicle and Comment. The Genesis of Shelock Holmes", *Bookman*, N.Y., February 1901, Vol. XII, pp. 550–3.

30 "Seven Novels of Some Importance. I. Conan Doyle's *The Hound of the Baskervilles*", Arthur Bartlett Maurice, *Bookman*, N.Y., May 1902, Vol. XV, pp. 252–5.

31 "Sherlock Holmes Again (*The Hound of the Baskervilles*)", *New York Sun*, 19 April 1902.

32 *The Hound of the Baskervilles* (advt.: McClure, Phillips), *New York Sun*, 23 April 1902.

33 "Chronicle and Comment. A Sherlock Holmes Understudy", *Bookman*, N.Y., March 1907, Vol. XXV, pp. 6–7.

34 A. Conan Doyle, A.L.S., Hindhead, 24 January 1895, to his mother (Mary Doyle); Arthur Conan Doyle Archives (London).

35 "Chronicle and Comment. The Novels of 1902", *Bookman*, N.Y., January 1903, Vol. XVI, p. 437.

36 "Chronicle and Comment. Some Assassins of Fiction", *Bookman*, N.Y., April 1903, Vol. XVII, p. 124.

37 "Chronicle and Comment. The Impressions of the Junior Editor", *Bookman*, N.Y., July 1903, Vol. XVII, p. 447.

38 "Chronicle and Comment. The Return of Sherlock Holmes", *Bookman*, August 1903, Vol. XVII, p. 551.

39 "Chronicle and Comment. Raffles", *Bookman*, N.Y., January 1904, Vol. XVIII, pp. 466–8.

40 "A Ballade of Detection", Carolyn Wells, *Bookman*, N.Y., May 1902, Vol. XV, p. 231.

41 "How It All Began (2)", Sir Gerald Kelly, P.R.A., *Sherlock Holmes Journal*, July 1954 (Centenary Number), Vol. 2, pp. 4–5.

42 *Eton and King's, Recollections, Mostly Trivial, 1875–1925*, M. R. James, Williams & Norgate, 1926, pp. 176–7.

43 *Out and About. Random Reminiscences*, Archibald Marshall, John Murray, 1933, p. 5.

44 "Sherlock Holmes in Russia. The Story of a Skat Scoring Book", Maurice Baring; collected in *Russian Essays and Stories*, Methuen, 1908, pp. 264–95.

45 "From the Diary of Sherlock Holmes", Maurice Baring, *Eye-Witness*, 23 November 1911, Vol. XXIII, pp. 717–18; collected in *Lost Diaries*, Duckworth, 1913, pp. 74–84.

46 *Charles Dickens*, G. K. Chesterton, Methuen, 1906, p. 102.

47 "At the St. James's Theatre", Max Beerbohm, *Saturday Review*, 6 May 1905, Vol. IC, pp. 589–90; collected in *Around Theatres*, William Heinemann, 1924, Vol. 2, pp. 133–9.

48 "Authors I Have Known. Thumbnail Sketches. A. C. Swinburne", H. Greenhough Smith, *John O' London's Weekly*, 3 May 1919, Vol. I, p. 98; collected in *Odd Moments*, George Newnes (John O' London's Little Books, No. 3), 1925, pp. 179–81.

49 *The Secret Kingdom*, Frank Richardson, Duckworth, 1905, pp. 81, 85, 93.

50 "Sherlock Holmes", Harry Graham; collected in *More Misrepresentative Men*, Fox, Duffield, N.Y., 1905, pp. 98–108.

51 *The Great Skene Mystery*, Bernard Capes, Methuen, 1907, pp. 290, 292, 295.

52 *Carrington's Cases*, J. Storer Clouston, William Blackwood, Edinburgh, 1920, pp. 147–60.

53 ("Lost Opportunities"), *Punch*, 24 February 1904, Vol. CXXVI, p. 134.

54 "How Holmes Tried Politics (By His Friend Watson)", *Border Advertiser*, Galashiels, 1 November 1904.

55 "The Mystery of the Three Grey Pellets", Laurence Kirk, *Billiard Monthly*, March 1913, No. 29, pp. 2–3.

56 *Decorations and Absurdities*, Bohun Lynch and Reginald Berkeley, W. Collins, 1923, pp. 77–80.

57 "Sherlock Holmes and Certain Critics", Ellis G. Roberts, *Light*, 2, 9, 16 November 1918, Vol. XXXVIII, pp. 349, 354, 362–3.

58 *Rather Like . . .*, Jules Castier, Herbert Jenkins, 1920, pp. 91–104.

59 *Jugged Journalism*, A. B. Cox, Herbert Jenkins, 1925, pp. 258–63.

60 Op. cit. 18.

61 G. Cullis, A.L.S., Bournemouth, 12 June 1951, to the Borough Librarian, St. Marylebone; St. Marylebone Collection.

62 W. R. Robertson (Public Relations Officer, London Transport Executive), T.L.S., London, 31 August 1951, to G. Stephens (Borough Librarian); *loc. cit.* 61.

63   A. Conan Doyle, A.L.S., Crowborough, 28 July 1928, to George H. Doran; Pepper & Stern, Santa Barbara.

64   *The Chronicles of Barabbas 1884–1934*, George H. Doran, Harcourt, Brace, N.Y., 1935 (Methuen, 1935), pp. 245–6.

65   "Studies in the Literature of Sherlock Holmes", Ronald Knox, *Blue Book*, Oxford, July 1912, Vol. I, pp. 111–32; *Blackfriar's*, Oxford, June 1920, Vol. I, pp. 154–72; collected in *Essays in Satire*, Sheed & Ward, 1928, pp. 145–75.

66   "A Note on the Watson Problem", S.C.R. (S. C. Roberts), *Cambridge Review*, 25 January 1929, Vol. L. pp. 216–17; privately printed (100 copies), Cambridge University Press, 1929.

67   "Miscellany. The Truth about Professor Moriarty", A. G. Macdonell, *New Statesman*, 5 October 1929, Vol. XXXIII, pp. 776–8. A revised version, called "Mr. Moriarty", was written for *Baker Street Studies* (1934) and was later collected in *The Spanish Pistol*.

68   "Miniature Biographies. III – Dr. Watson", Desmond MacCarthy, *Listener*, 11 December 1929, Vol. II, pp. 775–7; collected in *Memories*, MacGibbon & Kee, 1953, pp. 165–71.

69   *Adventures with Authors*, (The Late) S. C. Roberts, Cambridge University Press, 1966, p. 228.

70   "The Mathematics of Mrs. Watson", Ronald A. Knox, *New Statesman & Nation* (Literary Supplement), 12 November 1932, Vol. IV, pp. 588, 590.

71   *Unpopular Opinions*, Dorothy L. Sayers, Victor Gollancz, 1946, p. 7. "Dates in 'The Red-Headed League' " was first published in the *Colophon* (January 1934), and "Dr. Watson's Christian Name" in *Queen Mary's Book for India* (1943).

72   "The World of Books. Baker Street Studies. The Diversions of Scholarship", Desmond MacCarthy, *Sunday Times*, 26 August 1934.

73   "Mother Watson (*The Private Life of Sherlock Holmes*)", Cyril Connolly, *New Statesman & Nation*, 21 July 1934, Vol. VIII, pp. 95–6.

74   "Sherlock Holmes The God", G. K. Chesteron, *G.K.'s Weekly*, 25 February 1935, pp. 403–4.

75   "Sherlock Holmes and Dr. Watson", a clinical lecture given at Guy's Hospital (5 October 1934), and a Paper read to the Abernethian Society at St. Bartholomew's Hospital (1 November 1934), *Guy's Hospital Gazette*, 22 December 1934, Vol. XLVIII, pp. 524–30; 5. 19 January 1935, Vol. XLIX, pp. 2–7, 17–33; Ash & Co., 1935; revised edition, 1951.

76   "The Private Life of Sherlock Holmes", Vincent Starrett, *Bookman*, N.Y., December 1932, Vol. LXXV, p. 818; collected in *The Private Life of Sherlock Holmes*, Macmillan, N.Y., 1933, p. 93; Ivor Nicholson & Watson, 1934, p. 87.

77   "221B", Vincent Starrett, Privately Printed, Edwin B. Hill, 1942; collected in *Autolycus in Limbo*, E. P. Dutton, N.Y., 1943, No. 32.

78   "Sherlock Holmes among the Illustrators", Edmund Pearson, *Bookman*, N.Y., August 1932, Vol. LXXV, pp. 354–9.

79   *Those Days*, E. C. Bentley, Constable, 1940, p. 250.

80   "Shouts and Murmurs. The Baker Street Irregulars", Alexander Woollcott, *New Yorker*, 29 December 1934, Vol. X, p. 64; collected in *Long, Long Ago*, Viking Press, N.Y., 1943 (Cassell, 1945), pp. 172–5.

81   "Life Goes On. Holmes for Heroes?", Lionel Hale, *New Chronicle*, 24 January 1940.

82   *The Case of the Baker Street Irregulars*, Anthony Boucher, Simon & Schuster (An Inner Sanctum Mystery), N.Y., 1940, p. (v).

83 "Watson was a Woman", H. Allen Smith, *World-Telegram*, N.Y., 1 February 1941. Rex Stout's speech was published in the *Saturday Review of Literature*, 1 March 1941, Vol. XXIII, pp. 3–4, 16.

84 "Film Notes. 'You know their methods, Watson.' Hollywood's Sherlock Holmes", Dilys Powell, *Sunday Times*, 9 July 1939.

85 "Films in Glasgow. Sherlock Holmes and the Hound. Mr. Holmes Reports", *Glasgow Herald*, 24 October 1939.

86 Borough of St. Marylebone, *Report of Public Libraries Committee*, 3 October 1950, p. 220, paragraph 2b.

87 "Moriarty is on top in Marylebone", *Daily Graphic*, 27 October 1950.

88 "Baker St. Blues", *Evening Standard*, 28 October 1950.

89 "Alas, Poor Holmes", *Evening News*, 28 October 1950.

90 "Irregular", *News Chronicle*, 28 October 1950.

91 Hugh B.C. Pollard, A.L.S., Savile Club, n.d. (April 1951), to the Librarian, St. Marylebone; *loc. cit.* 61.

92 Will Nickless, A.L.S., St. John's Wood, 9 April 1951, to the Librarian, St. Marylebone; *loc. cit. supra.*

93 "The Baker Street Exhibition", *Truth*, 13 April 1951, Vol. CXLIX, p. 370.

94 "Sherlock Holmes . . . puts on a show", *Perth Daily News*, Western Australia, 23 May 1951. The London Correspondent, John Broderick, had stated that Holmes's old lodgings, "complete to the familiar seventeen steps up which he walked", were now open to the public. (A somewhat similar error may be found in the *Saturday Review of Literature*, 1 March 1941, where a photograph of William Gillette holding a large patent cigarette lighter has the caption: "Mr. Holmes and His Gasogene"!)

95 Mrs. R. Patricia Wynne-Jones, A.L.S., Crouch End, N.8, 24 August 1951, to C. T. Thorne; *loc. cit.* 61.

96 "Some Observations on Sherlock Holmes and Dr. Watson at Bart's", Adrian Griffith, *Saint Bartholomew's Hospital Journal*, December 1951, Vol. LV, pp. 270–5.

97 "The Air-Gun, Colonel Moran", J.B. Boothroyd, *Punch*, 3 February 1954, Vol. CCXXVI, pp. 173–4.

98 *Letters from England*, Karel Capek, Geoffrey Bles, 1925, p. 25.

99 *Crowded Nights – and Days*, Arthur Croxton, Sampson Low, Marston, 1931, p. 50.

100 "The Londoner's Diary. Pilgrims of Baker Street", *Evening Standard*, 16 February 1933.

101 Dr. Gray Chandler Briggs, A.L.S., St. Louis, 30 October 1921, to Frederic Dorr Steele; Philip S. Hench Collection, University of Minnesota.

102 "Sherlock Holmes in Pictures", Frederic Dorr Steele, *New Yorker*, 22 May 1937, Vol. XIII, pp. 35–8, 40, 42.

103 *Sherlock Holmes and Dr. Watson: The Chronology of Their Adventures*, H. W. Bell, Constable, 1932, pp. 75–8.

104 *Sherlock Holmes: Fact or Fiction?*, T. S. Blakeney, John Murray, 1932, pp. 49–50 (footnote).

105 *My Dear Holmes. A Study in Sherlock*, Gavin Brend, George Allen & Unwin, 1951, pp. 46–53.

106 *Sherlock Holmes and Dr. Watson: A Medical Digression*, Maurice Campbell, 1935 (*op. cit.* 75), pp. 45–8.

107 "The Master adds a Postscript", James T. Hyslop, *Baker Street Journal*, 1947, Vol. II, No. 2, pp. 113–18.

108 "The Back Yards of Baker Street", Bernard Davies, *Sherlock Holmes Journal*, Winter 1959, Vol. IV, pp. 83–8.
109 *Back View*, Sir Harold Morris, Q.C., Peter Davies, 1960, pp. 46–56.

ORIGINAL HEADINGS

———————— ◆ ————————

Only titles that differ from those used are given here. In the list that follows, an asterisk denotes that the article or letter has been shortened; dates are given where the item has been arranged out of sequence.

Page 63 "The writer . . . ": "Literary Notices".

Page 64 "Buttons wishes to know . . . ": "Answers to Correspondents".

Page 64 "Dr. Conan Doyle commands . . . ": "Personal Tit-Bits"*.

Page 66 "Next week we shall . . . " and "It is perfectly correct . . . ": "Answers to Correspondents".

Page 66 "Those people who admire . . . ": "Are English Detectives Less Clever than Foreign?"*.

Page 66 "Whenever I get . . . ": "Should Detectives be Specially Educated?".

Page 68 "I believe that . . . ": "Is Our Police System the Best?".

Page 69 "A.C.L. sends us . . . " to page 70 "We are going to have . . . ": "Answers to Correspondents".

Page 71 "The Prize of Five Guineas . . . ": "Sherlock Holmes Examination Paper", "Answers to Correspondents".

Page 75 "We have had . . . ": "The Literary World".

Page 77 "The news of the death . . . ": "Answers to Correspondents".

Page 79 "Many tears . . . ": "What Does Sherlock Holmes Teach?".

Page 80 "You are not the only . . . " to page 84 "It is not true . . . "; page 85 "some fifteen months ago . . . " to page 87 "S.P., in reading . . . ": "Answers to Correspondents".

Page 87 "Dr. Conan Doyle . . . ": "Novelists Caught Napping"*.

Page 88 "Three Castles comes . . . ": "Answers to Correspondents".

Page 88 "In the February *Bookman* . . . ": "The Bookman's Letter-Box".

Page 89 "L.E.B. has recently . . . " to page 90 "We have very great pleasure . . . ": "Answers to Correspondents".

Page 91 "Dealing with the *Strand* . . . ": "George Newnes, Limited, Annual Meeting"*.

Page 104 "Your speculations . . . " and page 105 "I have very much . . . ": The two letters are untitled.

Page 106 "Observe the Messenger Boy . . . " to page 108 "Behold the man . . . ": Untitled.

261

ACKNOWLEDGEMENTS

———◈———

The editor wishes to thank all those whose work is reprinted here (or their heirs and executors) and also those who have helped in other ways. These include, in alphabetical order: Dr. Edward V. Bevan, Barbara Brend, Blythe Morley Brennan, Catherine Cooke (Librarian at the Marylebone Public Library), Patsy Dalton, Dr. David Delvin ('Dr. Jekyll'). Maureen, Marchioness of Donegall, F. Stanbury Flood (the author of Mycroft Holmes's letter to the *Oxford Mail* in 1976), Michael Hardwick, Howard Haycraft, The late James Edward Holroyd, Ian M. Leslie (author of the Dr. Watson letters to *The Times* in 1950), Stanley MacKenzie, Captain W.R. Michell, Michael Murphy (Literary Executor, Vincent Starrett), The Earl of Oxford and Asquith (Literary Executor Ronald A. Knox), Colin Prestige (the author of Mrs. Hudson's letter to *The Times* in 1950), Edgar P. Smith, C.T. Thorne, Nicholas Utechin (Editor of the *Sherlock Holmes Journal*), Dr. W.T. Williams, and Sir Hugh Wontner.

Special thanks are also due to the Marylebone Public Library, the Abbey National Building Society, and the House of Whitbread; to William Collins, I.P.C. (George Newnes), and Methuen; to Messrs. A.P. Watt and Son; and to the editors of the following magazines and newpapers: the *British Medical Journal*, *Country Life*, the *Daily Mail*, the *Daily Telegraph* (incorporating the *Morning Post*), the *Glasgow Herald*, the *Guardian* (formerly the *Manchester Guardian*), London Express News and Feature Services (for the *Daily Express*), the *Observer*, *Punch*, the *Radio Times*, *Saint Bartholomew's Hospital Journal*, the *Spectator*, the *Southern Daily Echo*, the *Standard* (incorporating the *Evening News*), the *New Statesman*, the *Scottish Daily Record*, Times Newspapers Limited (for *The Times*, the *Sunday Times*, and their supplements), the *World Veteran*, and the *Yorkshire Evening Post*.